D1016883

© Heidi Burke

MONTE BURKE is a contributing editor at *Forbes* magazine and has also written for the *New York Times, Outside, Men's Journal, Town & Country,* and *Garden & Gun,* among many other publications. He is the author of the books *4th & Goal* and *Sowbelly* and is a recipient of Barnes & Noble's Discover Great New Writers Award. He grew up in New Hampshire, Vermont, North Carolina, and Alabama, and now lives in Brooklyn with his wife and three daughters.

SABAN

THE MAKING OF A COACH

MONTE BURKE

SIMON & SCHUSTER PAPERBACKS

New York London Toronto Sydney New Delhi

Simon & Schuster Paperbacks
An Imprint of Simon & Schuster, Inc.
1230 Avenue of the Americas
New York, NY 10020

First Simon & Schuster trade paperback edition August 2016

SIMON & SCHUSTER PAPERBACKS and colophon are registered trademarks of Simon & Schuster, Inc.

For information about special discounts for bulk purchases, please contact Simon & Schuster Special Sales at 1-866-506-1949 or business@simonandschuster.com.

The Simon & Schuster Speakers Bureau can bring authors to your live event. For more information or to book an event, contact the Simon & Schuster Speakers Bureau at 1-866-248-3049 or visit our website at www.simonspeakers.com.

Manufactured in the United States of America

1 3 5 7 9 10 8 6 4 2

The Library of Congress has catalogued the hardcover edition as follows:

Burke, Monte.
Saban : the making of a coach / Monte Burke.
pages   cm
Includes bibliographical references.
1. Saban, Nick.   2. Football coaches—United States—Biography.
3. University of Alabama—Football—History.   I. Title.
GV939.S35B87   2015
796.332092—dc23   2015018182

ISBN 978-1-4767-8993-4
ISBN 978-1-4767-8994-1 (pbk)
ISBN 978-1-4767-8995-8 (ebook)

To Lucia Shook

"Football is not *Hamlet*. It's not tragedy. It should be fun."

—Nick Saban

"What a piece of work is a man!"

—William Shakespeare, *Hamlet*

CONTENTS

SABAN

INTRODUCTION

On the first morning of 2007, as sleet fell from a dull sky, Mal Moore, the athletic director at the University of Alabama, hustled onto the tarmac at Tuscaloosa Regional Airport. With one last glance over his shoulder, he ducked his head and boarded an airplane bound for South Florida. The plane was not owned by the university—it had been loaned to him by an Alabama booster and Huntsville defense contractor named Farid Rafiee. Moore was going to great lengths to keep this trip a secret. A little more than a month earlier he had fired Mike Shula, the son of a coaching legend, and the University of Alabama's fourth football coach in seven very mediocre years. Thanks to flight trackers on the Internet, Moore's every move had been followed ever since as he searched—in vain, to that point—for a new head coach.

This trip *had* to remain clandestine. Moore was after the biggest prize in the game. A man named Nick Saban. News of a meeting with him would cause, as Moore put it, "quite a ruckus." The main reason for that: Saban, who was then the head coach of the National Football League's Miami Dolphins, had publicly denied any interest in the Alabama job, over and over and over.

Moore was flying somewhat blind. He did not have an appointment set up with Saban. The Dolphins coach had refused to take his calls.

Mal Moore had a down-home manner about him. He mumbled a bit when he talked, and had the lumbering body of an ex-football

1

player. He'd been the backup quarterback on Alabama's national championship team in 1961 under Paul "Bear" Bryant, one of the most successful coaches in the history of football and a man who had attained divine status within the state long before his death in 1983. Moore had parlayed that brush with Bryant's robe into his current job, one that he now was in jeopardy of losing.

Moore became Alabama's athletic director in 1999. The first football coach during his tenure was Mike DuBose, who was also a former Alabama player. During his time at Alabama, Dubose posted a 24-23 record, was accused of sexually harassing a secretary, and his program underwent a recruiting scandal that led to crippling NCAA sanctions. DuBose's successor, hired by Moore, was a promising coach named Dennis Franchione. He led the Crimson Tide to two consecutive winning seasons but bolted with a ten-year, $15 million contract on the table because he felt hamstrung by the NCAA sanctions. Moore replaced him with a man named Mike Price, who was fired before even coaching a single game because of a rowdy trip to a strip club, after which he may or may not have spent the night with a stripper named Destiny. Then came Shula, who had the right pedigree—he'd been an Alabama quarterback and had that football-famous last name. But Shula never came close to living up to his father, Don's, legacy, and he appeared overwhelmed as the head coach, running the football program in a sloppy manner.

In those seven years, the Alabama football team—winner of twelve national titles at the time and, formerly, a perennial contender for said titles, and the source of much pride and meaning in the football-mad state—had spiraled downward into, at best, irrelevancy on the national stage. At worst, it had become college football's horror show.

For years, Moore had relied on Alabama's name and past glory to acquire head coaches. After firing Shula, though, he found himself in a bind. The shine had worn off. Suddenly, the Alabama job was one that no coach of any real stature seemed to want to touch. Moore had been turned down by Steve Spurrier, the cheeky head coach at South Carolina, a football program that didn't come close to Alabama in terms of pedigree. Moore had offered the job to Rich

Rodriguez, a young, up-and-coming coach at West Virginia, and believed that he had accepted it. As Moore was working out the final details of the contract, he was blindsided by Rodriguez, who suddenly changed his mind and announced that he was staying at West Virginia. In the end, Moore appeared to have been merely played by the West Virginia coach for a raise and an extension.

The bungled coach search had earned Moore a new nickname within Alabama football circles. They called him "Malfunction Moore."

Now Moore was attempting to woo the fifty-five-year-old Saban, who had been a master as a college head coach, reviving three different programs and winning the 2003 national title at his last stop on that level, with Louisiana State University. Saban had left the college game after the 2004 season to take his first head-coaching job in the NFL. In two seasons with the Dolphins, he'd posted a less-than-mediocre 15-17 record. But his reputation as a college coach still burned brightly, and his name came up anytime a major college program needed a new head coach.

Saban, though, appeared to be staying put. The Miami media horde had persistently asked him about the coaching vacancy at Alabama. Saban had begun to get testy. At a press conference just ten days before Moore arrived in Miami, he'd declared, rather definitively: "I guess I have to say it. I'm not going to be the Alabama coach."

At this point, Moore had no other viable options left. His trip to South Florida was all-or-nothing. He knew that his job was on the line. "I told the pilots when they dropped me off in Miami that if I didn't come back to this plane with Nick Saban, they should go on and take me to Cuba," he said.

Moore, however, had reason to feel a sliver of optimism. By coincidence his nephew, Chuck Moore, a home builder, had remodeled Saban's lake house in Georgia during Saban's years at LSU. Saban, of course, knew who Chuck's uncle was. During the last few weeks of the 2006 Dolphins season, despite his public denials, Saban had called Chuck a few times to tell him that he was possibly interested in the Alabama job, knowing full well whom Chuck would call the minute they hung up the phone.

Moore had also been in contact with Saban's agent, Jimmy Sexton. Six days after Shula was dismissed, Moore and Sexton had secretly met in New York during the National Football Foundation awards dinner. Sexton had told Moore then that if Saban were to leave the NFL, Alabama would be at the top of his list.

Though Saban continued to rebuff Moore, the Alabama athletic director knew that at the very least, the coach's interest was piqued. What Moore didn't know at the time was that a far more important ally was waiting for him in Miami.

On the evening of January 1, 2007—after trying, in vain, to reach Saban all day while hunkered down in a hotel room—Moore finally made contact. During a brief phone conversation, Saban made it very clear that he wanted to talk to Wayne Huizenga, the Dolphins' billionaire owner, before he did anything else. He ended the call with a promise to contact Moore the following day around lunchtime.

The next day, Moore waited. The call never came. Moore contacted two of the most important Alabama trustees: Angus Cooper II, a shipping magnate from Mobile, and Paul Bryant Jr., the son of Alabama's most famous coach. (The trustee duo had passed some of their own nervous hours by going quail hunting.) Moore told them that Saban hadn't yet called him back and still refused to meet with him. "We thought we'd lost Nick then," says Cooper. "We knew Huizenga was trying to keep him, and we thought that meant he'd pay him a lot more money."

After waiting by the phone a bit longer, Moore finally gave up. He checked out of his hotel and had his driver—Francisco Rengifo, whom he called "Frankie"—take him to the airport. As they drove, Moore—on a whim—decided to make a last-ditch detour. He asked Frankie to drive him to Saban's neighborhood in Fort Lauderdale.

They parked a few blocks away, which gave him a view of the comings and goings of the Saban house. Moore sat there, staring out of the car window like a papal supplicant waiting for the white smoke. He later described his first day and a half in Miami as "excruciating."

It wasn't exactly pleasant for Saban, either. He paced the floors of his spacious house. He called former colleagues and old friends for advice. He talked to Sexton. He endlessly ran through everything with his greatest confidante: his wife, Terry, whom he'd married during his junior year in college. Saban knew how it would look if he left the Dolphins, after just two seasons and in the wake of his litany of flat-out denials of any interest in the Alabama job. He would be called a liar, a failure, and a quitter.

Most of the dread he felt, though, came from the fact that he already knew what he wanted to do. The NFL was not for him.

Saban had been an assistant coach in the NFL in the 1980s and '90s, but the game had changed significantly since then. Free agency had blossomed, turning some of the best players into prima donnas who often placed the desires of their agents and themselves over those of their coaches and their teams. The NFL had become more of a socialist enterprise than the meritocracy that Saban preferred. "In the NFL you were penalized for success," Saban says. A good season meant a more difficult schedule in the following one. It also meant a lower position in the subsequent NFL Draft. This left Saban feeling constricted. "In the NFL you only get one first-round draft pick, and that's if it hadn't already been traded away," he says. "You couldn't really outwork anybody. In college, I could recruit ten players with first-round talent every year." In the college game, he had more control.

He knew that Alabama wasn't a turnkey program. Hell, it was practically in ruins. It would take some time to streamline everything, to get everyone on the same page, and to restore the Alabama football name to recruits and to the nation. The potential was there, however, and Saban knew that the university was desperate enough

to return to football glory that they were willing to give him everything he needed. Moore wouldn't have been in South Florida now
if that weren't the case.

Still, Saban felt a strong sense of loyalty to Huizenga, a man he
very much admired. He'd made a pledge to the Dolphins owner, on
many different occasions, to turn around the franchise. Huizenga
also had demonstrated complete faith in Saban: He'd never said no
to one of his coach's requests—for more control, for more money
to spend on assistant coaches, for newer, better facilities. If it were
totally up to Saban, he would stay with the Dolphins and give Huizenga what he believed he owed him.

But the decision wasn't his alone.

After sitting in the car for some time, Moore finally talked to Sexton, who called Terry and asked her to invite Moore in. She did.
Saban wasn't home—he was at the Dolphins' complex, where he
had a meeting with Huizenga. Terry and Moore hit it off right away,
sensing a mutual interest. She served him lunch while the two talked
about her husband. She made it clear to Moore that Saban was miserable in the NFL and dearly missed coaching in college. She also
made it clear that she wanted out. In the NFL, the coach's wife had
no real role in the community. On a college campus—particularly at
a place like Alabama—the coach's wife was a figure of prominence,
a queen bee. Terry also believed that a college town was a much
healthier place to raise their two children. After lunch, she invited
Moore to come back for dinner that night.

Sometime after Moore left, Saban called home and told Terry
that he had made up his mind: He was staying with the Dolphins
and he didn't want to meet with Moore. Terry then informed him
that Moore was actually coming over for dinner that night.

Over dinner, Moore pitched Saban on the merits of the job.
Saban would get an unprecedented amount of power and control
of the football program. He would also be paid a blockbuster eight-
year, $32 million salary, the highest ever in college football. Saban

remained palpably reticent throughout the evening. As Moore was leaving, Terry pulled him aside and told him that they had to find a way to get her husband on the plane to Tuscaloosa the next day. As heartened as he was by Terry's words, Moore still had no idea what Saban was going to ultimately decide.

Saban spent another night agonizing over the decision. Terry knew it would be better for him—for them—back in college, and she spent the evening trying to convince him that it was okay to leave the Dolphins, to think of his own—and his family's—well-being and happiness. The next morning, Saban had one more conversation with Huizenga. The Dolphins' owner realized by then that he had lost his coach. He eased Saban's agony a bit by telling him to do what was in his heart.

Finally, Saban called Moore and accepted the Alabama job.

Moore and Frankie rushed over to the Saban house. By this time, the media had caught the scent that something was in the offing. Press helicopters hovered over the Sabans' house as Frankie backed his white Mercedes sedan into the garage. Saban, Terry, their daughter, Kristen, and a school friend of hers entered the garage through the house, carrying a few hastily packed suitcases. The three women sat in the backseat, their luggage in their laps. Saban sat shotgun. Moore squeezed himself in between Saban and Frankie, sitting on the console. Helicopters chased them all the way to the airport.

On the plane, Moore and Saban sat across from each other, with Moore facing the cockpit and Saban facing the rear of the plane. As the plane took off, with its nose pointed toward the sky, Moore found himself looking up at his new coach. He would never forget this moment, and would tell the story frequently to his closest friends, in various versions.

"Mal, let me ask you something," Saban said over the roar of the plane's engines, gazing down at Moore. Saban's leg had started to bounce. At this point, adrenaline was staving off exhaustion. Any pretense he might have felt had been completely stripped away. "Do you think you've hired the best coach in the country?"

Moore was a bit taken aback by the question, not exactly sure where it was heading. He still didn't know Saban well, still found him hard to read. Moore rubbed his big hands together and cleared his throat. "Why, Nick, of course I do," he said, while thinking to himself: *For four million dollars a year, I sure as hell hope so.*

"Well, you didn't. I'm nothing without my players," Saban said, locking eyes with Moore. "But you did just hire a helluva recruiter."

With that, Moore exhaled audibly.

PART I

1

The Diamond

NICK SABAN started recruiting in 1962. He was ten years old.

He was acting on behalf of his father, "Big" Nick Saban, who was the founder, general manager, head coach, and director of transportation of the Idamay Black Diamonds, a Pop Warner football team in West Virginia.* The father-son duo canvassed the elementary and middle schools that served Monongah (where the Sabans lived), Idamay, Farmington, Carolina, Worthington, and Hutchinson—the tiny coal-mining satellite towns surrounding the "big city" of Fairmont, which was the area's commercial hub. Big Nick's recruiting pitch to the ten- to fifteen-year-old boys was straightforward: *I'm forming a Pop Warner football team. I can teach you to play the game of football and get you prepared for your high school team.* Saban, working his way through the schools grade by grade, appealed more to the hearts and minds of his peers: *We've got football, cheerleaders, and ice cream.* Both approaches worked.

In the next decade, hundreds of boys would play for the Black Diamonds and the team's exceedingly demanding and intense coach. Those boys would earn countless victories but draw very little praise for those achievements.

---

* Pop Warner is a youth football, cheerleading, and dance organization that was founded in 1929.

Even years later, opinions about Big Nick are complicated and varied. "He was, frankly, a total dick," says one former Black Diamond. Others, like Kerry Marbury, who played for Big Nick in the mid-1960s, view him differently. "It was just tough love. We always knew he cared for us."

Regardless of how they felt about him, Big Nick's former players all agree on one thing: The man played an unusually significant role in their young lives.

His biggest impact, though, would be on his only son.

Nick Saban's hometown is located right on top of a band of coal-rich earth that extends from Pennsylvania to Alabama. By the late nineteenth century, with the steel industry, steamships, and electrical grids in cities all needing coal for fuel—and with newly laid railroad tracks enabling coal producers to meet that demand—this small nook in West Virginia became one of the country's top coal producers. It also became the site of a tragedy.

At 10:20 a.m. on December 6, 1907—the Catholic calendar's Feast of St. Nicholas—two massive explosions destroyed the Fairmont Coal Company's Nos. 6 and 8 mines in Monongah. Officially, 362 men were killed, though the number was likely higher since many of the bodies within the mines were never recovered. The blasts are believed to have been set off by a string of coal cars that broke loose and rolled back into the mouth of the No. 6 mine. The Monongah Mining Disaster, as it became known, remains one of the biggest industrial accidents in American history.

Accidents—and there were many—were merely an unfortunate part of coal-mining life. Most of the miners in the early twentieth century were recent immigrants or sons of immigrants who had come primarily from eastern and central Europe. They absorbed these tragedies, dusted themselves off (literally), and moved on. They had no other choice. There was little—if any—socioeconomic mobility for these miners at that time. Daily wages were counted in pennies. Unions were only in an infancy stage. The mining companies "owned your soul," as the old coal miner saying went. They built—and owned—the towns, houses, stores, and baseball fields that surrounded the mines.

Thirteen years after the Monongah Disaster, Nick Saban's paternal grandfather, Stanko Saban, a Croat, immigrated to the United States from what would later become known as Yugoslavia. Stanko (who would change his name to the more Anglican "Stanley") first moved to Oregon, but came back east to the Fairmont area. He worked in a coal mine in Carolina, a town located between Idamay and Monongah. He married a woman named Anna. They had four children, one of whom was Big Nick, who was born on June 11, 1927.

Big Nick was a deeply serious boy who decided early on that his primary goal was to stay out of the mines. He was darkly handsome, with thick hair he always kept neatly trimmed. In high school, the 5'11", 200-pounder became a standout athlete in football and baseball, and later played some minor-league baseball. He enlisted in the navy after graduating from high school but decided against a career in the military and returned home, where he devised his strategy to stay aboveground: He started his own business.

Saban's Service Station was located at the intersection of Route 218, which led to Idamay, and U.S. 19, the main road to Fairmont. Big Nick, with the help of some neighbors, built a small, redbrick, split-level house behind his filling station, right next to a stream named Helen's Run, which emptied into the sluggish West Fork River, a tributary of the Monongahela River. He later opened another business in a building across the street, trying his hand at running first a restaurant and then a Dairy Queen.

Big Nick married a woman named Mary Conaway, who was from nearby Farmington. Her father, "Pap," was a coal miner. Big Nick and Mary had a daughter, Dianna (who sometimes goes by "Dene"), in 1950. When Mary became pregnant again soon afterward, the family was convinced she was carrying a boy. Dianna took to calling the unborn baby "Brother." Nicholas Lou Saban Jr. was born on Halloween in 1951. To this day his childhood friends still refer to him by the nickname his sister gave him.

"When you grew up here, you expected that you would work in the mines, own a four-wheel-drive truck, get married, and have kids," says Donnie Evans, a childhood friend and former high school football teammate of Nick Saban.

Big Nick succeeded in carving out a different life for himself. He ran two full-time businesses, an adult baseball team, and, eventually, the Black Diamonds. He was constantly in motion because he had to be. Life in the mines was only one business mistake away. The Sabans weren't as poor as a few of their neighbors, some of whom survived on welfare, but they had to work nearly constantly to stay above that line—the station was open from 7 a.m. until midnight six days a week, manned by Big Nick, his son, and one or two local boys who were paid $1.25 an hour. Mary and Dianna worked at the Dairy Queen (Mary also worked for a time at a bank). Margins were hair-thin, and there was no safety net in place. When the Saban home flooded—which happened with some frequency in the spring when the snowmelt-swollen West Fork would back up Helen's Run—they didn't wait around for insurance. The family simply went to work and cleaned out the silt and garbage, then went on with life.

As determined as he was about his own life, Big Nick wanted even more for his children and, in particular, his son. And that came with a price.

Big Nick, to some, might fit neatly into the stereotype of the stern, no-nonsense, tough-love father of the 1950s and '60s, a male-dominated era of true patriarchy that has been in a long, slow fade ever since. But to those who knew him, he surpassed that stereotype in spades. His temper was enormous and easy to arouse. He didn't hesitate to make a move for his belt. Things went the way he wanted in his house, and that was that.

He also either lacked the time or the desire to engage in some of the simplest of human pleasantries. When the Sabans had guests over, they usually gathered in the living room and talked over glasses of wine. Everyone, that is, except for Big Nick, who would hole up alone in another room and watch television. On the street or at home, he frequently walked by people without saying hello or even looking at them. His lack of social grace was magnified by his physical presence. "He was a big man," says Evans. "When he walked, there was this *boom, boom, boom.* You were afraid to be in his way."

The women who knew him have resorted to comparative math to describe his personality. Dianna once told a reporter that her brother wasn't "50-percent as intense as Daddy was." Saban's wife, Terry, once told a Miami newspaper: "People think Nick is so tough, even to the point that they think he doesn't have social skills and can't tell a joke. Well, multiply that by 100, and you'll understand his dad." Big Nick sometimes wouldn't even acknowledge Terry's presence after she and his son started dating in high school.

Though Big Nick desired a better life for his children, they had to earn it. Saban started working at the filling station as soon as he was old enough to handle a gas pump. It was a true full-service station—he also wiped windshields, changed oil, rotated tires, and washed cars. "I can still see Brother walking out of the gas station with a blue towel in his back pocket as a car pulled up," says Evans, who worked part-time at the station. "He'd say, 'Fill her up? How's that oil doing?' The thing is, it was never menial to Brother. It was important to do it right."

The reason for that was Big Nick and his demands. Saban often tells the story about washing cars at the station, that if he left so much as a tiny spot on a car, his father would make him rewash it entirely. (Saban hated dark-colored cars for that reason.) Occasionally, when he was dissatisfied with his son's work or effort, Big Nick would fire Saban for a few days and suspend his pay. Evans remembers a cold, rainy day when Big Nick asked him, Saban, and another boy to clean out a drain that was down a hole by the station. There wasn't much debris in the drain, and the water was getting through it just fine, but Big Nick wanted it cleared anyway. After just a few minutes, the boys had pretty much removed anything that could have possibly blocked the drain. But Saban stayed down in the hole. "He wouldn't quit until it was absolutely spotless," says Evans. "We were telling him, 'Come on, man. It's fine. Let's go. It's cold.' But Brother said, 'We're going to do it right. I don't want to listen to it later on.'"

What "it" was remained unclear to the boys because, though it was obvious to Evans and Saban's other childhood friends that his father was particularly harsh on him, Saban never talked about it, never mentioned any types of punishments or discipline in specific. But what was clear to everyone who knew them was that Saban was intent on trying to please his father, to truly strive for the impossible perfection that was demanded. To make that quest possible—even survivable—Saban adapted his own behavior. He learned to derive pleasure and satisfaction in the very act of doing. Put another way, Saban, at a very young age, learned to embrace and love the process of doing.

It turned out that the place that put that adaptation to its biggest test—the place where his father rode him the hardest—was the football field.

Big Nick got the idea for a Pop Warner football team after meeting some men who worked for the *Philadelphia Inquirer* and were visiting the Fairmont area to meet with deliverymen. The *Inquirer* men told him about the Pop Warner teams they had back in Pennsylvania. Big Nick liked the idea of providing the boys in these small towns with an activity, something that would keep them busy and build character. He enlisted his friend Willie Criado, the local postmaster, to help him start the team.

Criado still lives in the house in which he grew up, right across the street from the football field in Idamay. The well-kept, balding, eighty-eight-year-old holds Big Nick in nearly worshipful regard. It's with pride that he points out that the two men were born on the same day. Criado says he followed Big Nick—or tried to—everywhere he went. When Big Nick played baseball, the less athletic Criado did, too. When Big Nick joined the navy, Criado tried to enlist as well, but didn't pass the physical exam. Criado helped his friend in any way he could. "I did taxes for [Big] Nick because he really didn't like to do them," he says. Big Nick returned the devotion by occasionally treating Criado to a Pirates game in Pittsburgh. Criado says he thinks he knows why Big Nick liked him: Criado served as a reality check. "With him, it was his way or the highway," says Criado. "I was one of the few people who could talk to him."

Big Nick and Criado approached the Pop Warner league in Fairmont to see if they could join it with a team made up of kids from some of its surrounding towns. The leaders of the league were initially opposed. "If we got in, they would have had a five-team league, which would have meant too many bye weeks," says Criado.

Shortly thereafter, though, one of the Fairmont teams dissolved. Big Nick and Criado got the old uniforms—orange tops and black pants. They decided to name the team the Idamay Black Diamonds. The nickname came from anthracite, the most coveted type of coal—lustrous, carbon packed, and clean burning.

The original idea was for Big Nick to be the commissioner of the team, with Criado as his secretary. They found a field: an unleveled patch of grass and dirt (the back of the south end zone veered sharply up a big hill) right next to the Bethlehem No. 44 mine, where some of the players' fathers and grandfathers worked. They found three football players from nearby Fairmont State College to volunteer for coaching duties. By midsummer in 1962, after he and his son had done their recruiting, Big Nick believed they had enough boys to form a team. Sign-up and practice would start on August 1, 1962.

That day, Big Nick and Criado were at the service station when they decided to head up to the field to see how many players were coming out. They found a gathering of anxious boys, all holding their birth certificates, but no coaches. The three players from Fairmont State had failed to show. "[Big] Nick turned to me and said, 'You sign them up, and I'll take them to the field and make it seem like we're doing something,'" says Criado. The three coaches were no-shows again the next day, so Big Nick started to run an actual practice, seeing who could throw, who could catch, and who could hit. "Each day, he just got more and more into it," says Criado. "When the coaches finally showed up a few days later, he just told them to leave." The Black Diamonds were Big Nick's team now. He discovered, by accident, that he loved coaching and was good at it and that, in the end, he couldn't live without it.

Then came the bus. Big Nick didn't want his players walking or hitchhiking to and from practices and games—some lived as far as five miles away and the roads were hilly, winding, and treacherous—and he believed that providing transportation would act as an incentive for more boys to come out for the team. The bus also happened to provide him with a good deal of control over the team: Being in charge of transportation meant he could determine when practices were held, and he could keep the boys on the field for as long as he thought was needed. Big Nick didn't allow the kids' parents on the practice field.

The bus was an old twenty-seater, retired from school duty. Big Nick painted it orange with black trim. Mary decorated the interior with motivational sayings and aphorisms, written in Magic Marker, ranging from the clichéd "When the going gets tough, the tough get going" to the less prosaic "Be nice to people on the way up because you'll see them on the way down" and "Practice makes players." Big Nick was a fan of such maxims and frequently spat them out during practices. The kids could be forgiven if two of his favorites seemed to convey a mixed message. "Be like grass—the more manure they throw on you, the stronger you get" was one. "The grass is always greener on top of the septic tank" was the other.

From August through November, Big Nick drove the bus through the hollows on practice days to centralized locations in the towns—a post office, a store, a barbershop—to pick up the kids, then reversed the route after practice. Each trip took up to forty minutes.

The bus had its troubles. "We had to get out and push it a few times," says Tom Hulderman, a former player. Occasionally, the brakes would give out and Big Nick was forced to use the hand-brake while trundling down a hill, which made an awful noise and filled the bus with pungent plumes of smoke.

Saban was the first Black Diamond, of course, but at age ten, he didn't see the field much in that first year. It was just as well. The Black Diamonds were beaten 48–6 in their first game and recorded only one win in that season. They improved very quickly, though. The next year, the team went 5-5. "Then, this little team from the sticks started kicking ass," says Nick Demus, one of the local adults who helped with organizing and fund-raising for the team.

In year three, the Black Diamonds started a run that attained legendary status and continued until the death of the team's founder, becoming so dominant that they came to the attention of a young football coach at West Virginia named Bobby Bowden. When he was in the Fairmont area, Bowden would stop by to see Big Nick to chat about former Black Diamonds that he was recruiting.

All Big Nick needed was time—to get the right boys and turn them into a football team.

One of the key players early on was an African American boy named Kerry Marbury. Marbury lived in Carolina, West Virginia, and was the fourth of seven children raised by a single mother on welfare. Though Carolina was a segregated mining town, Marbury says he didn't ever feel any racism while growing up. "I didn't really know what that was until I got to college," he says. "We all—black and white—played together, ate together. There was no name-calling. You didn't know you were any different."

Marbury was one of the Black Diamonds' easiest recruits. He first met Saban at age five (Saban is a year older), and they immediately became best friends. Saban's paternal grandparents lived in Carolina, a block or so from the African American part of town, and he spent parts of his summers there. He and Marbury met on a nearby field, where kids from both sides of the line met to play ball.

Soon Marbury was hanging out at the station and having meals with the Sabans.

Marbury played running back and defensive back for the Black Diamonds, and was particularly lethal when returning kicks. Joining Marbury were Charlie Miller and Nate Stephens, who would later be drafted by NFL teams. Perhaps the most athletically gifted player on those early teams was Tom Hulderman, who lived steps from the field in Idamay. He could do it all—run, catch, pass, and kick (his specialty was his uncannily accurate drop kick). Hulderman probably would have been the team's quarterback if it weren't for a slight stutter that seemed to flare up at unfortunate times, like in the huddle or at the line of scrimmage. So the starting quarterback job ended up going to the coach's son. Saban was not particularly tall. (As an adult, various reports have listed him between 5'8"and 5'11". He is closer to the former.) He wasn't fast, either, and he did not possess a strong arm, but he was smart and driven. "He studied hard and learned the game and knew it inside and out," says Criado. "He knew exactly what to do in different situations, given the down and distance."

Big Nick was tough on everyone. "We feared him. We were scared to death," says Mark Manchin, who played with Saban for Big Nick for three years. "You'd be in the huddle just waiting for the kick in the butt or for the clipboard to come flying at you."

Criado remembers a practice when he was coaching the defense, and Saban took a shot at a kid who was smaller than he was. "I gathered the defense and told them, 'Let's get him. Let's get him back for that.'" But the players didn't do anything. Whether that was because they feared Big Nick or pitied Saban remains unanswered.

They had plenty of reason to feel the latter. No one begrudged the coach's son for being the starting quarterback because no one on the team had it worse than Saban. "[Big] Nick was always tougher on Brother," says Hulderman. "Always." Marbury says he "felt sorry for Brother. His father was so much more demanding of him than he was of the rest of us. We all noticed it."

Saban never talked about it. He felt it, though, at least according to another teammate. "Brother might have a different recollection, but I don't remember him ever finishing an entire practice without crying. His father just drove him unmercifully," says Manchin. "I always thought Brother had two options growing up: to become a great success or go crazy."

Practices, as one of the sayings in the bus declared, were what made a team, according to Big Nick. His were legendary for their physicality and duration. The kids hit hard. They often stayed out until after dark, using car headlights to illuminate the field. "I worked harder in Pop Warner than I ever did in high school, college, or the pros," says Marbury, who would later play at West Virginia and in the Canadian Football League.

Big Nick particularly stressed conditioning. On the south end of the field was a fifty-foot hill, terraced and steeply inclined. Big Nick sent the boys up and down the hill for what seemed like hours. "You were crab-crawling by the end," says Marbury. When it got too dark to tell if the players were actually running to the top of the hill, Big Nick demanded they bring down a leaf from one of the trees on the ridgeline as proof.

Football was not supposed to be fun to Big Nick. It was a teaching tool, a way of starting the process of turning these boys into disciplined men. This was Big Nick's team, molded in his image. "Our practices were no-nonsense," says Manchin. "No laughter, total commitment, and constant teaching." The only bit of frivolity came at the end of practice when, traditionally, Big Nick—perhaps sensing that the kids needed to blow off some steam—would take a snap from center and let the kids gang-tackle him. More than one kid saved their biggest hits of the day for that moment.

In the third year of their existence—when Saban was in seventh grade—the Black Diamonds went undefeated and un-scored-upon, part of what would end up being a thirty-nine-game winning streak. The following year, in a game against a team from Shinnston, Saban didn't "make weight" (Pop Warner has strict weight restrictions), so another kid filled in at the quarterback position. Early in the game, Big Nick decided to go for it on a fourth down, deep in his own territory. The Black Diamonds were stopped and turned the ball over on downs. Shinnston then scored a touchdown on a passing play. It ended the Black Diamonds' season-and-a-half-long scoreless streak, though they still won the game handily. "I think [Big] Nick was relieved that we finally got scored on," says Criado. "The streak was putting an awful lot of pressure on the kids."

If he was relieved, he certainly didn't show it to the team. On the bus ride home after the game, a few of the boys started goofing off and laughing. Big Nick immediately stopped the bus and got up and walked back to his players. "I don't want to hear another sound!" he yelled. "Do you boys realize what just happened to you?"

The Black Diamonds were primarily a running team, so Saban didn't get a chance to pass the ball often. When he did, he was usually accurate with his throws. His father, though, always found fault in his play, no matter how sound. Even after a touchdown pass, Saban would get an earful on the sidelines—about a missed read, poor throwing form, or a loose spiral. To Big Nick, it wasn't about the result, it was about perfect execution. And the execution was never perfect. "He drove us really hard, but Nick Senior was a great coach. I cannot say anything clearer," says Manchin. "With his attention to detail and knowledge of the game, I think he could have been a college coach."

Big Nick also occasionally doled out little acts of kindness that Criado says no one else knew about, helping out his players and never calling attention to the charity. Criado remembers one kid who showed up with huge rips in his tennis shoes. "[Big] Nick asked the kid when he was going to get new shoes," says Criado. "The kid said, 'On my dad's payday.' So Nick let him borrow a pair of shoes, and he never asked for them back."

Some rewards were more publicly given, but only if properly earned. Big Nick treated the boys to ice cream at his Dairy Queen

after some wins, but not all of them. "When he wasn't satisfied with
the way they won the game, they didn't get ice cream," says Criado,
which happened more often than not.

At the Dairy Queen, the players were graced with the welcome presence of Mary, who greeted each of them with a huge smile. She was
"a beautiful, beautiful woman," says Evans, with long light hair
that curled at its ends. She always dressed nicely, and took great
pains to present herself well in public, never venturing from her
room with curlers in her hair or without makeup. She gave off an
air of composure and class. She, too, was athletic, a good golfer
who was a cheerleader in high school when she met Big Nick. Her
work ethic rivaled that of her husband's.

Yet Mary Saban stood in stark contrast to her husband. She was
warmhearted, nonconfrontational, and rarely raised her voice. She
enjoyed social occasions and parties and rousing games of bridge.
She was the soft, extroverted presence that smoothed the roughest
edges of her husband. Big Nick was the stern, Old Testament–like
father who demanded obedience and demonstrated his love through
discipline and sacrifice. Mary was the forgiving mother figure who
doled out soul-soothing scoops of ice cream.

Whenever Big Nick went off on one of his tirades, or pulled off
his belt for a whipping, it was Mary who picked up the pieces, hud-
dling the rest of the family together as if waiting out a hurricane.
She showed her emotions openly, not afraid of shedding tears in
the aftermath of a Big Nick blowup. That was her sole defiance.
Saban turned to his mother whenever the pressure from his father
became too overbearing. He could relax a bit with her, something
that should not be discounted in its importance. Saban would later
tell a reporter that his mother instilled confidence within him. That
confidence enabled him to not only survive but even thrive as a
child. It made it so the pressure from his father formed him instead
of breaking him.

As a child, and as he is now, Saban was shy and introverted. During the winter of eighth grade, he refused to stand up and sing in front of the other students in a music class run by a teacher named Ms. Helminski. So she gave him a D. Big Nick was furious, and his reaction was both swift and dramatic. He first forced his sports-mad son to turn in his basketball uniform, and made him quit all sports until his grades were better. He then drove Saban to the Bethlehem No. 44 mine, right near the Black Diamonds' field, and, with the help of some miner friends, took his son down into the mine, 550 feet underground. "If you don't do better in school, if you don't get a college education, this is where you will end up," he told Saban. "Is this what you want? Do you want to end up down here for the rest of your life?" Saban started to sing in music class.

In the summer of that same year, Saban attended a 4-H science camp near Fairmont, and first met the girl who would one day become his wife. Saban and Terry Constable, who lived in East Fairmont, hit it off immediately. At least that's what she thought. She invited him to come bird-watching with her at five o'clock one morning. Saban said yes on the spot. He later realized that he had a softball game that same morning, so he stood her up. (This would be Terry's first lesson in being a coach's wife.) Saban would get a shot at redemption a few years later, and he wouldn't make the same mistake twice.

By all accounts, Saban was an unusually serious child. "Brother was mature beyond his years," says Evans. Manchin recalls that it went beyond maturity. "Brother was never a kid. He was an adult when we were ten. I don't remember him ever laughing or smiling. I don't remember him being happy. I swear I don't. He was always so serious and disciplined. I'd spend the night at his house and he'd go to bed at ten o'clock. I'd stay up and watch TV all by myself." Saban, of course, had to be ready to work the next morning.

Roman Prezioso, another former teammate of Saban, recalls that whenever he went by the filling station, "if Nick wasn't pumping gas, he and Hulderman were throwing the football to each other over the gas pumps. There was no wasted time. He grew up in that culture of no wasted time, of a serious work ethic. It was almost like behavior modification."

Football became a respite of sorts for Saban, despite his father's unrelenting demands. He had fun playing it, and soon became obsessed with the game. "We'd sit at the Dairy Queen and talk football," says Evans. "It was always on his mind, and he always seemed happy when we were talking about it."

In the ninth grade, with some of his teammates moving on to their high school teams, Saban decided to stay and play one more year for the Black Diamonds. Doing so ensured playing time (it was unusual back then for freshmen to play much for their varsity high school teams). There was likely another reason for his decision. Though Big Nick never let Saban relax during practices and games, off the field the game became a safe harbor for the father and son, a space separate from the rest of their lives where Big Nick sometimes loosened up, if only a bit. Big Nick occasionally took Saban to West Virginia practices and games, and the two would endlessly go over different plays and formations, and talk football strategy at the dinner table. Marbury says he used to stay at the Sabans' and that after dinner, Saban and his father would head into the TV room to watch 8 mm films of games. "They'd ask me if I wanted to join them," says Marbury. "I'd say 'no thanks.' The two of them would sit there and watch for hours and love it."

Big Nick continued to coach after Saban left the Black Diamonds to play high school football. The team remained a superpower in the region, twice beating a formidable Pop Warner team from Monongahela, Pennsylvania, which was quarterbacked by a talented boy named Joe Montana.

The beneficiary of Big Nick's great recruiting and coaching with the Black Diamonds was a man named Earl Keener, the head coach of the Monongah High School football team. Many of the best Black Diamonds—Marbury, Hulderman, Saban—went to Monongah High, a three-hundred-student school. Keener was a local boy, born in Carolina, who enlisted in the navy and fought in the Pacific Theater in Word War II, then was drafted by the Los Angeles Rams (though he never played in the NFL). He was known as a vocal, inspiring coach. His assistant, Joe Ross, was deeper into the X's and O's.

Saban made the Monongah High team as a sophomore. Keener initially believed that Saban was too short to play quarterback for the Lions, and started another boy at the position in 1966. "That pissed [Big] Nick off," says Demus.

Keener's stance changed after the first game of the season, after the Lions "got our heads handed to us by East Fairmont," says Prezioso, who was a halfback and senior captain on that team. Prezioso, along with his two fellow captains, approached Keener after the game. "We knew we had this young kid who had come through a very successful Pop Warner team with his dad, that he was smart and a quick learner," he says. They told Keener they wanted a change.

Keener listened and installed Saban as the starting quarterback. Saban, who also played defensive back, turned out to be as described by his teammates. "He was calm, cool, and collected, and understood the game," says Prezioso. The Lions didn't lose another game that season, finishing 8-1-1.

Saban grew into a position of leadership, leading by example. On defense, he hit as hard as he could, flinging himself at the ballcarrier with little regard for his own well-being. As a quarterback, he specialized in making tough one- or two-yard runs for first downs, absorbing hits from defensive linemen twice his size. In the huddle, after barking out the play call, Saban would pause and look at his teammates in the eyes and say: "Let's beat them on this play."

Saban still wasn't fast or big and he lacked arm strength, but he succeeded in spite of those deficiencies. "It was all heart and brains," says Marbury. The Lions ran a quick and deceptive offense. Saban didn't throw a lot, but could do so proficiently when needed, especially when opposing defenses would stack eight players near the line of scrimmage to try to stop Marbury. Saban always received a general game plan from Keener and Ross, but once the game started, he called all of his own plays. Behind it all, though, one voice remained the most significant. "I always had the feeling that his father really was his coach, not Keener, that when he was calling his own plays, he was listening to his father," says Demus.

Any coaching by Big Nick wasn't necessarily evident to the naked eye. "Senior would come watch the high school games but he wasn't one of those parents who yelled from the sidelines," says Evans, who was a lineman for the Lions. "He just sat and watched him play. But you could tell he was paying very close attention and was making mental notes, particularly about mistakes." After the games, and whenever they could squeeze it in around work, school, and practices, Big Nick and Saban talked football and watched film together. "I remember stopping by the station during the season and seeing those two watching film," says Prezioso. "We didn't have film in high school. I remember thinking, *This is unbelievable*. But Nick [Jr.] was so far ahead of the other players on the team in terms of understanding the game, and that was all due to his father, who was always teaching him."

By Saban's junior season, the Lions had begun to take on his persona. As they won more and more games, he seemed to get more and more intense. "When you messed up, he wasn't running up and screaming at you. He could just look at you with a look that said, 'What are you doing? You missed that block. We can't win games doing that,'" says Evans. "When we scored a touchdown or won a game, he wasn't jumping up and down, high-fiving or hugging people. He was no-nonsense, sort of like 'we have a job to do, let's go do it.'"

The players who surrounded him made that job easier. Hulderman was a three-time all-state player at split end. In the backfield, "no one could stop Kerry [Marbury]," says Evans. One of the only real concerns Saban had as a quarterback who called the plays was figuring out how to spread the ball around evenly so everyone remained happy. Evans gives Saban credit for getting the best out of the other players on the team. "I mean, Kerry was great, but Brother is the one who helped him perform at that level. He got the best out of him. It was the strangest thing. Here's this five-eight or five-nine kid, and all you wanted was his approval. You wanted him to come up to you and say 'good job' and pat you on the back. I feel like that was because Brother was always pushing himself, always seeking some sort of approval himself."

In Saban's junior year, Monongah made the Class AA state championship game, but lost badly to Ceredo-Kenova. The next year, Saban, Marbury, and Hulderman lead the Lions to the Class A state championship, a 21–12 victory over Paden City. Saban, who made the all-state team, played in that game despite a broken ankle. Later that year, he would also be named all-state in both basketball, as a point guard, and baseball, where he batted .465 as a shortstop.

In the classroom, Saban worked hard on his grades. He loved studying history and was particularly good in Ms. Turkovich's demanding math class. He graduated as a member of the National Honor Society. "He was different from the rest of us," says Evans. "I think Brother was already thinking about his future then. He was making good grades in high school while the rest of us were fooling around. He wanted to get out."

None of his childhood friends remember him ever joining the other boys to drink beer. "He didn't think you were cool if you drank," says Evans. "He didn't approve of it, but he didn't say anything. He figured you were a big boy and could make your own decisions. That's what he did: make his own decisions."

Saban had another thing on his mind, too. Though he and Terry had run into each other a few times during high school, it wasn't until his senior year when he finally took real notice. She caught his eye at a football game against East Fairmont, where Terry was a "Honey Bee," which was a dancer for the team. (Terry would later become the "Queen Bee," which is the on-the-field leader of the dancers and band.) "She had eye-popping attributes," says Earl McConnell Jr., the current director of the Honey Bees and son of the founders. "She had personality like crazy, she worked very hard, had a good head on her shoulders, and was a beautiful young lady."

Terry, the oldest of four girls, was a year younger than Saban. Her father was a miner; her mother, a teacher's aide. After the game, Saban approached her. She apparently forgave him for standing her up four years earlier. After the football season, during the Thanksgiving break, the couple went on their first formal date, catching *Gone with the Wind* at a theater in Fairmont. Saban hitchhiked the nine miles from his house to visit Terry in East Fairmont throughout his senior year. He says he always considered her a city girl who took in a country boy. They've been together ever since.

Even though Saban's father had avoided a life in the coal mines, it was impossible for anyone living in the Fairmont area at that time to fully escape the reach of the region's main economic engine. Mines and miners were a central feature of Saban's young life. He saw miners every day at the station, clean if they arrived before a shift, sometimes dusted with coal ash if they came by after. Reminders of the hardships and tragedies faced by these men and their families—and, really, the entire community—were everywhere. Saban's high school building was perched on a bluff just across the West Fork River from the old Fairmont Coal Company's Nos. 6 and 8 portals, the site of the 1907 disaster. His childhood home is located two miles down the road from the explosion site.

The tragedies never ceased. Just before Thanksgiving during Saban's senior year in high school—right before his first date with Terry—the Consol No. 9 coal mine exploded near Farmington. (It was the same mine where Saban's maternal grandfather once worked.) The blast was felt miles away. After fighting the mine fire for ten days, officials decided they couldn't stop the blaze and made the almost unspeakable decision to seal the mine and trap the seventy-eight bodies within. These horrors and others like them were the sources of nightmares and the subjects of late-night, real-life ghost stories for the children of the area.

The football played by these boys, in some significant way, mimicked life as a coal miner. There were no real divisions according to race and class. The work was physically miserable, and the teamwork absolutely essential: If one person screwed up, everyone paid the price. "[Big] Nick always made it a point to tell us that what one person on the football team did affected everyone," says Hulderman. At Monongah High, the team practiced on a dirt field across the street from the school. After practices, if there had been no recent rains, the boys appeared as dusty as some of their fathers did leaving the mines.

For much of the first two-thirds of the twentieth century, this broader area of West Virginia, Ohio, and Pennsylvania—coal-mining and steel-producing country—was football's breadbasket. Paul Brown, Chuck Noll, and Don Shula all came from the area. Saban's own tiny Marion County produced, along with him, former NFL players Sam Huff and Frank Gatski, and coaches Fielding Yost (an early-twentieth-century Michigan coach who won six national titles) and Rich Rodriguez. Jimbo Fisher, who was an assistant coach for Saban at LSU and later became a national-title-winning head coach at Florida State, is from Clarksburg, just twenty miles away from Monongah. Football for these children of miners and millworkers was "the first step in the Americanization process," as David Halberstam once wrote, and one of the first, clear-cut ways for a younger generation of boys to avoid the same working fates as their fathers.

Football was Saban's ticket out of a place that profoundly affected the person he is today. As much as he took away from Monongah, though, Saban's story is also seen in relief, in what he left behind.

In late 2004, Saban and Terry returned to Monongah for the funeral of his grandfather, Pap Conaway. One day, they took a drive. Monongah and its surrounding area are hauntingly beautiful, full of hollows and clear, cool streams and narrow roads that twist their way through shadowy hills that close in the area and give it an isolated feel. Most of the old mines are now sealed, leaving only faint scars on the face of the landscape. The clusters of houses built and once owned by the mining companies remain.

The Black Diamonds' field in Idamay is now named "Nick Saban Memorial Field" (after Big Nick), and it's one of the better-kept places in town (thanks in part to Saban's annual five-thousand-dollar donation to the team). Saban's high school no longer exists—

with a lack of new students from the area, it was consolidated in 1979. His old house still stands, behind the service station, but it is easy to miss, just another run-down domicile in an area where the economic lifeblood was drained decades ago. The service station no longer pumps gas. The Dairy Queen is now Fly's Bar & Grill, a joint favored by area bikers. Saban told the *South Florida Sun-Sentinel* that at one point during that drive through Monongah, he turned to Terry and asked: "How in the hell did we ever get out of here?"

Many of his former teammates remain. Kerry Marbury now lives near his old home in Carolina. Marbury went to West Virginia on a football scholarship after high school. He played there for Bobby Bowden for two years and, on more than one occasion, flashed his incredible talent. In one game he rushed for 291 yards in just three quarters. But he never got along with Bowden, and left school early, making unfulfilling stops in the Canadian Football League and the World Football League. "I was a lot happier when I was playing football for ice cream," he says. He and Saban remained close, and served as the best men in each other's weddings.

After his football career, though, Marbury found trouble. He drifted away from his wife and family, then ended up in prison on drug-related charges. It was Saban who helped him get back on his feet. "He was the first person to call me when I got out. I was feeling so helpless. It was vital," says Marbury. He eventually finished his undergraduate degree and earned a master's.

Four years ago, Marbury was diagnosed with a terminal form of prostate cancer. Saban found out, and flew him down to Birmingham for a second opinion. "They treated me like a god down there," says Marbury. "They were like 'that's coach's friend.' " Ultimately, the Alabama doctor confirmed the initial diagnosis. "But it was good to get that second opinion. Once I got it, I decided I wanted to live," he says.

In the late spring of 2014, Marbury sat at his desk at Fairmont State, where he spent twenty-one years as a teacher and safety co-ordinator (he retired later that year). Though the cancer was eating him from the inside, he appeared physically healthy, bald and trim, resembling a young Samuel L. Jackson. A sign on his desk read: "Silence is better than bullshit," a saltier version of some of Big Nick's old sayings. "I don't know where I'd be without Nick," Marbury says. "I still call him my best friend, though I don't talk to him that much. I don't know where I'd be without his father, either. I didn't have a father of my own. He was stability in my life. He sacrificed a lot for us." Marbury repaid that sacrifice in part by coaching the Black Diamonds for a few years.

Tom Hulderman lives in the house in which he grew up, a short walk from both the old Bethlehem mine and the Black Diamonds' field. Out of high school, Hulderman was drafted by the Chicago Cubs and played minor-league baseball for a handful of games before he injured his wrist. He ended up in the mines. His body is broken down. He has a full set of false teeth.

He laughed about those baseball days with the phlegmy croak of a heavy smoker. Those laughs quickly became sobs, though, when the talk turned to Big Nick. "He beat us up with love," he says. Hulderman puts flowers on Big Nick's grave twice a year. A Christmas card from Saban and Terry adorned with a big Crimson *A* and a handwritten note inside sits on the mantel above his television in the basement of his house.

At 11 a.m., Hulderman sat at the bar at Prunty's Pub in Monongah with one other patron, nursing a drink and watching *The Price Is Right*. From behind the bar he pulled down a picture of the old scoreboard from Monongah High. It read:

Monongah: 50
Alabama: 0

A few years ago Hulderman says he had climbed a ladder to rearrange the scoreboard. "I sent it to Nick," he says with a grin.

In the bar there were helmets from the Lions and an Alabama jersey signed by Saban. There was also a framed newspaper article about the Lions, accompanied by photos. One was of a young

Saban in his No. 12 Monongah jersey, posing as if about to pass. Next to him was Hulderman, also in uniform, strapping, blond-haired, and handsome, smiling from joy and not sentimentality. Hulderman touched the frame and mentioned Big Nick. Then his ice-blue eyes filled with tears, perhaps not just for the loss of his former coach.

When Saban graduated from Monongah High in the spring of 1969, he received a nomination from West Virginia senator Robert Byrd for the U.S. Naval Academy. He passed all the tests and physicals, but at the last moment he withdrew his application. "I wasn't crazy about going there and then going into the military for five years afterwards," he says. The ongoing war in Vietnam certainly played a role in that thinking. Lyndon Johnson had been escalating the war effort for years by then, and though first-year president Richard Nixon would eventually start withdrawing troops, there appeared no end in sight for what was becoming a grim and unpopular war.

Saban also wanted to play football in college. His dream was to play at West Virginia. "But I wasn't good enough," he says. Too short, too light, and too slow.

By the summer of 1969, his options seemed to be drying up. A July 20, 1969, article in the *Beckley Post-Herald* called Saban a "fading star in desperate search of a galaxy" who had "yet to accept a college scholarship" and whose future "looked dimmer all the while." Keener seemed angry at the insinuation that his former quarterback couldn't play football in college. "Some big school is really missing out if they don't give Nick a chance," he told the paper. "That kid has more heart than anyone I've ever seen in 20 years of coaching. All he knows how to do is beat you."

Saban did have some options, but they didn't include any big-time programs. Ohio University, Miami of Ohio, and Kent State all offered him scholarships. Though Kent State had the worst football program of the three, Saban felt the most comfortable there. To that point in his life, he'd never spent much time out of West Virginia, and he had an uncle who lived in Canton, Ohio, just thirty miles away from campus. (Uncle Sid has been attending his games ever since.) Saban accepted the scholarship to play for the Golden Flashes, who had gone 1-9 in 1968 under new coach David Puddington. Saban was determined to try out for quarterback, though he realized he'd likely end up in the secondary. His only misgiving was that he was leaving Terry behind. She had one more year of high school left.

One morning in the summer of 1969, Saban and Donnie Evans loaded into Big Nick's Dodge and headed north on Interstate 79 to Kent, Ohio. Evans volunteered to make the three-hour drive to drop off Saban at school, then drive back to Monongah.

Evans would stay close to home after graduating from Monongah High. He fooled around with college at Fairmont State for a few years, bought a four-wheel-drive truck, got married, had kids, and spent thirty years in the mines. He eventually put all three of his kids through college. "That's my claim to fame," he says.

Unbeknownst to either of the boys on that drive to Kent that day, Saban was just beginning an odyssey that would lead him to the peak of a profession that he had no intention of ever entering.

Saban didn't talk much during the drive. "He seemed like his thoughts were somewhere else," says Evans. When they pulled up to the campus, Saban stepped out of the car, grabbed his bags, and said to his friend since grade school, simply, "See you later, buddy. Thanks." Then he walked away. "That was it," says Evans. "It was like 'I've got things to do.'"

2

How Many More?

ON MAY 4, 1970, in the final weeks of his freshman year at Kent State, Nick Saban attended an 11 a.m. class in a building near a patch of open acreage on the campus known as the Commons. Though it was a beautiful, bright, and breezy spring day, the campus had an edgy feel to it. For the previous four days, students had been protesting Nixon's invasion of Cambodia, an act that appeared to contradict the president's pledge to end U.S. involvement in the Vietnam War. A copy of the U.S. Constitution had been buried in protest. Parts of the city of Kent were vandalized. The university's Army Reserve Officer Training Corps (ROTC) building was set on fire.

Everything that had happened to that point, though, was merely a lead-in to the main event: a huge rally planned for that day at noon. The Ohio National Guard had already been called in to keep the peace.

Kent State's head football coach, David Puddington, gathered his team together before the planned protest. "I told them not to go to the rally and to stay away from big groups in general," says Puddington, who now lives in a retirement home in upstate New York.

He had every reason to believe they would heed his wishes. The football players at Kent State were anachronisms, in sharp contrast to many of their classmates who were caught up in the increasing liberalism of the late 1960s and early '70s, flush with feelings of newfound individualism. Many of the football players still kept

35

their hair clipped martially short. They respected authority and the chain of command because, well, they had to if they wanted to see the field. They even lived in isolation, sequestered in Harbourt Hall, a dorm on the outskirts of the Kent State campus.

For the most part, the members of the Golden Flashes football team indeed did stay away from what would become a horrific and historic scene on the campus of Kent State that day. But two players nearly let their curiosity get the better of them.

After his class, Saban met up with his good friend and teammate Phil Witherspoon, an African American who played tailback. Witherspoon wanted to go to Blanket Hill, where the students had begun to gather, and check out the scene. Saban suggested they first go to the cafeteria for lunch.

At noon, with the sounding of the Victory Bell (which usually rang for football victories), the protest began on the Commons. The Ohio National Guard, with fixed bayonets, showed up and unsuccessfully tried to disperse the crowd with tear gas, which was blown away harmlessly by the breeze. They marched up and down a steep hill (Blanket Hill) and through the crowd to, of all places, the football practice field, which was surrounded on three sides by a chain-link fence. The guardsmen were immediately flustered, finding themselves stuck between the field and the protestors, who had begun to hurl rocks at them. The guardsmen turned and began to march back up Blanket Hill. Suddenly, there was gunfire, a thirteen-second barrage. It was 12:24. Four students lay dying. Two of them hadn't even been involved in the protest. Nine other students were wounded.

Saban and Witherspoon walked out toward Blanket Hill about five minutes later and came upon a chaotic and surreal scene. Some people were running and screaming at the top of their lungs. Others were merely standing completely still in disbelief. Helicopters hovered, and the sound of sirens gathered in the near distance. Years later Saban would tell the journalist Terry Frei that what he most remembered from that day was seeing the "large pools of blood" from the dead and wounded. One of the students killed was Allison Krause, a pretty nineteen-year-old honors student who was in Saban's English class. An ambulance later drove around campus and, through a loudspeaker, instructed all students to pack their belongings and go home. Kent State was closed immediately. Students finished out the rest of the year by correspondence.

Many of the football players wondered openly if the team would even play the following season. Puddington says, in the context of the tragedy, football didn't matter all that much. He did have a practical concern to deal with, though: On the morning of the shootings, he had mailed out national letters of intent to the team's recruits, offering them scholarships. Puddington and his staff eventually got together and called each one of them. "They all ended up coming," he says. One of those recruits was a high school quarterback from Ohio who wanted to play linebacker but had been shunned by the big schools because of his relatively diminutive size. His name was Jack Lambert.

Saban had tried to avoid the Vietnam War when he decided not to attend the Naval Academy, but the war had found him anyway. The young man from an isolated small town in West Virginia had borne witness to an international incident. In 2010, on the fortieth anniversary of the shootings, Saban told *USA Today*: "There's not a May 4th that goes by that I don't think about it. Really think about it."

When he went home that spring, the eighteen-year-old was in a state of shock, but he dealt with it the way he dealt with everything else: He dove into working for his father, got into great shape for the upcoming football season, and spent every spare moment he could with Terry.

In his first year at Kent State, Saban played on the freshman squad (freshmen back then weren't allowed to play on the varsity), competing for a spot at quarterback. His size and lack of speed and arm strength were magnified at the collegiate level, so he started the transition to becoming a full-time player on the defense, as a safety. There his smarts and toughness made up for any physical limitations.

The football players were among the first students back on campus after the shootings, reporting in the late summer for training camp. The hope was that the team could become a rallying point for the entire school. That hope didn't seem too misplaced: Puddington's team finished 5-5 the previous year, rebounding from a 1-9 record in his first season. The players wore T-shirts that read: "Kent State, Stay United." The president of the university addressed the players, stressing their role as leaders on campus. "We all grew up a lot then," says Steve Broderick, Saban's roommate and a quarterback on the team. "Healing was a big deal to the administrators and to us."

The football players remained the "squares" on campus, and Saban was perhaps the squarest of them all. While he hung out with his dorm mates—Broderick, Witherspoon, and Ted Bowersox, another quarterback—on weekdays and weekends at Harbourt Hall, he was never one to party or even stay up late at night talking with his friends. "Nick was a very serious person," says Broderick. "He was a good student. That was very important to him, and he worked hard at it. Most days, he'd go to class, practice football, go to the gym and shoot hoops, then study. And when it came to smoking dope in college in 1970, the question was 'Who *didn't* do it?' The answer was 'Nick Saban.'" Bowersox remembers that, "even at age nineteen and twenty, Nick wasn't joking, laughing, or goofing around at all."

Saban had his college life refined down to his studies, his sports (which would later include baseball), and Terry. He wrote letters to her almost daily, and was constantly on the phone with her. "I could be wrong, but I think he rang up a two-hundred-dollar phone bill one month, which in those days was a lot," says Broderick. Though Saban was not very social, Broderick says there was one thing about him that stood out in social contexts: He was one of the few players on the team who was at ease with both blacks and whites. "Nick was really blind to color, and this was during a time of some real racial unrest in the country. I always noticed that there seemed to be no difference for him," he says. Witherspoon, an African American, was perhaps his best friend in college, just as Marbury had been back at home.

In his sophomore season, Saban played strong safety and acquitted himself well. "He was really quiet and never said much, but he was smart about football and was always in the right spot on the field," says Puddington. The team, however, was terrible. After splitting their first four games, the Golden Flashes lost five games in a row and finished the season 3-7. Puddington resigned, citing as one major reason the "prevailing contagious negativism on campus and in the community" as a result of the shootings the previous spring.

Kent State's next hire was a man who would change Saban's life.

Like Saban, Don James played both quarterback and defensive back during his football career. The difference between the two is that James played quarterback in college and excelled at it, setting school passing records during his career at the University of Miami in the early 1950s. He was born and raised in Massillon, Ohio, a steel mill town, and, after college, did a two-year stint in the army. James's coaching career began in 1956 as a graduate assistant at Kansas, then weaved through defensive assistant and coordinator stops at Florida State, Michigan, and Colorado. He perfectly fit the profile of a Mid-American Conference (MAC) coach, then and now: a promising, yet unproven young coach on whom a school was willing to roll the dice. James turned out to be a good bet.

James immediately brought organization and discipline to the program. "We had a plan for everything," says Skip Hall, who came to Kent State with James as an offensive assistant. "Everything was written up, and everyone knew what was expected of them." James implemented a rigorous off-season conditioning program and a new set of academic standards for the players. His practices were notorious for their almost neurotic precision. "Everything we did in practice was down to the second," says Ken Dooner, a wide receiver and tight end. "One drill would end at exactly four minutes and seven seconds. The horn would sound and we'd move on to the next drill, which would run exactly four minutes and thirteen seconds."

After Puddington's less rigid tenure, and the chaos of the spring of 1970, James was a shock to the system. "Half of the players were afraid of him and the other half were afraid to let him down," says Hall. (Saban, then a junior, was in the latter group.) "Don wasn't Mr. Warm and Bubbly," says Bob Stull, James's offensive line coach. "He didn't compliment the staff or players much. He just expected you to do your job."

James's first season got off to a rousing start. The Golden Flashes upset North Carolina State 23–21 in Raleigh. Then the old habits started to kick in. The team finished 3-8, last in the MAC. "Some of the holdovers on the team didn't want to pay the price," says Hall.

A month after the team's last game, a 41–6 loss at Toledo, Saban went home for Christmas break and married Terry. They moved back to Kent State together and Terry enrolled. "We didn't see him around much after that," says Broderick.

In Saban's senior season in 1972, the Kent State Golden Flashes had some talent and reason for optimism. Jack Lambert, a junior, was firmly established in the middle linebacker position after the player ahead of him on the depth chart had given up football to become a weight lifter. The team featured Gary Pinkel at tight end (now the head coach at Missouri), an all-conference player who would lead the team in receptions. Gerald Tinker, a wide receiver, would go on to win a gold medal in the 1972 Olympics as a member of the U.S. 4x100-meter relay team.

Then there was Saban. He was still undersized but, as in high school, he was also a true student of the game. "Some guys, they want to learn their position and forget about the rest," James recalled in an interview years later. "But you could tell he was smart and interested in knowing the whole concept of defense. He was a competitor . . . a tough, tough kid."

Saban studied film obsessively, to get an edge at his position and to help him organize the linemen and linebackers in front of him on the field. He was also fearless. "He would figure out where the ball was and he'd arrive in a bad mood, just like Lambert," says Hall. Greg Kokal, who quarterbacked the 1972 team, says: "Lambert had better skills, but Nick was tougher."

Saban was also a leader, something the Golden Flashes desperately needed that year. The team started the season 1-3-1. Kokal says that during a particularly painful loss against San Diego State, he threw an interception, and Saban came over and picked him up off the field. "He told me, 'Get off your ass and quit feeling sorry for yourself,'" says Kokal. "You remember things like that."

On October 28, the Golden Flashes traveled to play at Northern Illinois. The school was one of the first in the area to install Astro-turf in their stadium. Kokal remembers that the turf was a complete unknown and very unpopular with the players. "They even had a shoe bank there because the turf was so different," he says. During the game—a 28–7 loss—Saban broke his ankle, possibly because of the turf. He awkwardly hopped off the field on his own, using his hands and his one good foot.

Kent State won its next three games to earn the MAC title for the only time in school history, gaining a berth in the Tangerine Bowl against the University of Tampa, an 8-2 team that featured running backs Freddie Solomon and Paul Orndorff (who went on to become professional wrestling's "Mr. Wonderful"), and the defensive lineman John Matuszak. The team was led by Earle Bruce, in his first head-coaching job.

The Golden Flashes were intimidated before the game even started. During the week of the game, the two teams went out one night to the same movie theater. Kokal remembers that Matuszak—perhaps on purpose—arrived after the lights had gone down. "He walked in front of the projector and the entire room went black," he says. "He was the biggest, baddest man I've ever seen in my life."

Kent State fell behind 21–0 in the first half. It fought back in the second half, scoring three touchdowns. But the Golden Flashes failed to convert any extra points, and lost 21–18. Saban, who had been furiously rehabbing his ankle for two months in the hopes of playing, dressed for the game but never made it onto the field.

Though he had the baseball season in the spring to look forward to, at that point Saban believed that his life in football was over. After he graduated, his goal was to one day run a car dealership. "I thought it was better to sell cars than fix them up," he says.

Any postgraduate plans had to be put on hold, though, because Terry had one more year of classes needed for her degree. Saban had to hang around the Kent area and find something to do. James found it for him.

After the 1972 season, James hired a new coach for his secondary. He believed that the new coach needed help getting acquainted with the schemes, so he asked Saban if he would help with the defensive backs as a graduate assistant (GA). Saban accepted the offer, forgoing his last season of baseball and entering into a master's program for sports administration. (He had graduated with a BA in business.) To make money, Saban loaded trucks at Roadway at night during the season, and drove a truck for Coca-Cola in the summer. Terry worked in the registrar's office.

Saban became a jack-of-all-trades for the football team. He helped out with the secondary and was the defensive coordinator of the freshman team. He did on-campus recruiting (as a GA, he was prohibited from recruiting off-campus) and assisted with evaluating recruits on film. He was also in charge of getting film developed, which meant driving an hour and forty minutes one way to the headquarters of the Pittsburgh Steelers, a team then in the nascent period of its dynasty years under head coach Chuck Noll. Saban took full advantage of those trips, and got to know the coaches, including defensive line coach George Perles. "He'd just hang around the team and watch film and watch practice and talk to the coaches," says Perles. "I have no idea how he got in, but he was there a lot, just soaking it all in. We'd have a beer sometimes after practice and he'd just pick my brain about football. I liked him." (By this time, Saban had eschewed the life of a teetotaler and had adopted some of the habits of his coaching brethren.)

As a GA, the already-intense Saban took it up a notch. "He knew the guys on the freshman team well and coached them hard, from one whistle to the next," says Skip Hall, who coordinated the freshman offense. "He stayed on top of them constantly. He was very competitive. I can remember during the freshman games, he would yell at them, 'Do the right thing and do it right now!' He made the transition to an authority figure and was all business."

That transition caught some of his former teammates by surprise. "When Nick became a GA, he made it a point to let me know I had to be in for curfews," says Kokal. "I said, 'Nick, what happened? A year ago you and Terry and I were going out on double dates.' I missed having him out on those dates. He was a handsome guy, and having him out helped with the girls. But he wouldn't go anymore. He told me, 'Greg, the game has changed.' "

The 1973 Kent State team started off the year with an impressive win over Louisville. It was Saban's first game in a coaching role. That night, he excitedly called Big Nick. "I said, 'We won. We beat Louisville,' and I told him that I figured that this was something I wanted to do," he says.

It turned out to be the last conversation he would ever have with his father.

Broderick, Saban's roommate during his early years at Kent State, says Saban would occasionally talk to him about Big Nick. "You could tell he had total respect for him, that if his dad told him to do something, he did it," says Broderick. After one holiday break, Broderick says, Saban returned to school with a story. "I guess his dad thought that Nick was getting a little too big for his britches. So his dad cleared out a bedroom and tossed Nick some boxing gloves. Nick told me, 'I thought he was screwing around, but the next thing you know, I was defending myself. I couldn't hit my dad. I couldn't swing at him.' Nick was in great shape at the time. He would have whooped his dad. But he didn't touch him, and Nick said his dad beat him to a pulp."

What Saban didn't know at the time was that his father's heart had begun to fail. "I knew [Big] Nick had a heart problem, but he didn't want me to know too much because he was afraid I'd tell Mary," says Willie Criado. After a Black Diamonds practice in 1972, Big Nick told Criado that he was getting pains up and down his arms. One of his players told Criado that Big Nick had passed out at a practice when Criado wasn't there. At a baseball game in 1972, Big Nick told his team that he wouldn't be managing them the next year. "I think he knew then that things weren't looking too good," says Criado.

In the summer of 1973, Big Nick went to a heart doctor, who told him that he had serious heart trouble. Big Nick told the doctor that he was still going to coach football. "The doctor said, 'You can't do that. You get too mad out there.' And [Big] Nick said, 'I don't get mad,'" says Criado. "I told him, 'Nick, that doctor told you that you're putting your life on one side of the scale and the Black Diamonds on the other.' He said, 'I don't care. I'm going to coach.'"

To stay in shape, Big Nick and Mary often jogged on the Idamay field. On September 22, 1973, Big Nick felt like he hadn't gotten enough exercise after a run and asked Mary to drop him off on the side of Route 218, paralleling the small creek—Helen's Run—that flowed from Idamay to the Saban house. He wanted to jog home.

Mary arrived back home and waited for him. When he didn't show up after a while, she became worried and started calling her neighbors. Nick Demus and Criado and a few others went out to look for him.

At some point during his run, Big Nick had suffered a massive heart attack and pitched over into a hedge near the stream. By the time Criado arrived, Big Nick was lying on the ground and a man he didn't know was administering CPR. "I reached into his pocket and found a nitroglycerin pill and put it in his mouth," says Criado. An ambulance eventually came, and he and Mary followed it to a hospital in Fairmont. In the waiting room, a nurse came and told Mary she had a phone call. "It was Brother," says Criado. Mary left to take the call. The nurse then told Criado that Big Nick was dead. He was forty-six.

Saban decided after his father's death that he would quit his position as a GA at Kent State and move home to run the service station. His mother, though devastated, was against the idea. When Bobby Bowden, the head coach at West Virginia, heard that Big Nick had died, he called and offered Saban a position on his staff as a GA. "I didn't know him at all, but I knew his dad, and that was good enough for me," says Bowden. Saban politely refused the offer. He conferred with James and Hall. "We didn't really try to talk him out of leaving the program, but we did let him know that his father would have probably wanted him to continue with his future and his goals," says Hall. In the end, Saban decided to return to Kent State.

Big Nick's funeral was attended by many of his former players. Kerry Marbury, playing in the CFL, told his team that his Pop Warner coach had died and he needed to go to the funeral. The team refused his request. Marbury went anyway, and he was cut. "It didn't faze me," he says.

Big Nick was buried at Mount Carmel Cemetery in Fairmont, on the side of a hill nearly as steep as the one on the Idamay Black Diamonds' field. Under his name, his tombstone reads: "No man stands as tall as when he stoops to help a child."

There is an old African tale about fathers and sons. In the story, a father and son go hunting together. Early on, the father kills a small rat and gives it to the son. The son believes the rat is worthless, so he throws it away. No more game is found that day, and as the father and son sit around the campfire, the father asks the son for the rat so they can cook and eat it. "I threw it into the bush," the son says. With that, the father "took up an axe, and hit his son, who was knocked unconscious; and the father then left the boy lying where he was."

The point of the story, according to the poet Robert Bly, in his book *Iron John: A Book About Men,* is that all of us sons, at one point or another, throw away the rat and feel the subsequent blow. "Almost every man remembers that blow coming in," Bly writes.

"So this event seems to be part of the father-son material: the father gives the blow, the son gets it. And it's a wound the boy remembers for years."

Saban was the exception. He was not that boy. He wasn't the feckless and careless son. When Big Nick handed him the rat, he held on to it. He did the right thing—he studied, he worked hard, he obeyed his father. Yet, he still received the blow. Over and over.

In the simplest terms, the primary motivating factor in Saban's life is this dynamic of the impossible-to-please father pushing his son for an impossible-to-achieve perfection. It is the reason that, years later, Saban's assistants and players will marvel at the fact that he does not seem happy in the moments after winning national titles, that he instead seems stuck on some tiny miscue that happened during the game, or weighted down with thoughts of how he is going to motivate an overly satisfied bunch the following year. The result isn't the point to Saban, even if that result is a national title. Nothing is perfect. There will always be a spot left on the car.

Big Nick never saw his son coach a game, never saw him eventually reach the pinnacle of his profession, again and again and again. Saban felt he never fully pleased his father, never fully gained his approval and, once Big Nick died, the chance to do so disappeared forever. However, he's never stopped trying, and it's perhaps the fundamental reason that he's pushed himself so relentlessly, that he's switched jobs so often in his career, that he derives pleasure from the act of doing and not achieving, and that he never seems satisfied, with himself or others.

At one point in the 1973 season, Saban's first as a GA, the Golden Flashes were ranked as high as nineteenth in the country. They finished 9-2, second in the MAC. The next year the team had another winning record, at 7-4, but after that season James was poached by the University of Washington (this seems to happen to all rising star coaches in the MAC). James would go on to coach the Huskies for eighteen years and win a national championship.

The influence that James had on Saban as a coach cannot be

underestimated. Saban was a firsthand witness to James's remarkable turnaround of the Kent State program. It's a skill that Saban, too, would eventually come to develop and master. Saban still uses a version of James's exhaustive recruiting evaluations that covered physical, mental, emotional, and academic attributes. James was a defense-oriented coach who was an absolute stickler for details. Through the years, Saban has often mentioned James as a coaching role model. When James died in late 2013 of pancreatic cancer at age eighty, Saban told a newspaper: "He was systematic about everything he did and defined what the expectations he had for everything in the organization were," which is a pretty fair description of what Saban does today with his program.

When James left, Saban decided to stay at Kent State.* The new coach, Dennis Fitzgerald, hired Saban to coach the linebackers for eight thousand dollars a year. Saban worked for Fitzgerald for two seasons. In the process, he discovered, like his father had before him, that he loved this profession that he'd fallen into, and that he was damn good at it.

---

* James took another GA named Dom Capers with him to Washington.

3

Wanderlust

AT THE end of the 1976 Kent State season, Saban first developed what the journalist Jack Ebling has described as "the itch." Simply put, it is the itch of ambition, of wanting something more—a job at a bigger school, a bigger paycheck, and deeper, more convincing demonstrations of devotion and approval. That itch propelled Saban through six different assistant coaching jobs in the following thirteen years—all requiring long days and nights and little pay. He would average a stay of just more than two years at each stop. The itch provided him with his first taste of true big-time college football and of the NFL. It also would, at various different places, piss off a boss who questioned his loyalty, get him fired, and lead to fistfights with some of the players he coached.

Above all, though, that itch exposed Saban to both the successes and failures: of football programs, his fellow coaches, and his players. He would eventually put that knowledge and experience to very good use.

In early 1977, Saban, looking for a job, called Lee Corso, the head coach at Indiana, but Corso had no openings on his staff. Saban also tried Frank Cignetti Sr. at West Virginia to no avail. Somewhere along the line, he heard that Syracuse was looking for a linebacker coach. So he contacted Frank Maloney, and then had Don James follow up to vouch for him.

Maloney was entering his fourth year at Syracuse and was in the unenviable position of having followed up a legend: Ben Schwartz-walder had coached the Orange from 1949 until 1973, and had won a national championship. In his first three seasons, Maloney had compiled an 11-22 record. He was under intense pressure to deliver a winning season in his fourth.

Maloney was an emotional man. He would throw a fit—tossing trash cans and uniforms around the locker room—then break down in tears and hug his players close to him, all in the same meeting. He was a disciple of Bo Schembechler, the legendary Michigan coach, oriented toward defense and, as it turned out, more adept at attracting excellent young assistants than he was at winning games.

Syracuse had some talented players on the roster that year, in-cluding the Hall of Fame wide receiver Art Monk (though he played running back then) and Craig Wolfley, an offensive lineman, who went on to play eleven years in the NFL. In retrospect, the most impressive thing about the 1977 Syracuse team was the group of coaches who roamed the sidelines. Jerry Angelo, who would later become the general manager of the Chicago Bears, coached the de-fensive line. Tom Coughlin, who has won two Super Bowls as the coach of the New York Giants, was in charge of the offensive backs. And then there was Saban, who was hired by Maloney to coach the outside linebackers and defensive ends for $14,500 a year.

Of those three coaches, Angelo was the one most loved by the players. "He was a wild man who could relate to the kids," says Tim Ahern, a back on the team. "He wasn't as buttoned-up and straight-laced as the other two." Coughlin, even at age thirty-one, was ex-tremely old-school in his approach, very demanding and somewhat impersonal. Saban, though six years younger than Coughlin, was in that mold, too. He was serious and stern, projecting an air of authority that exceeded his experience. "Saban wasn't out there to make friends," says Dennis Hartman, a fullback. "He was feisty and pretty tough on his players." Bob Avery, another running back, believes that Saban was caught somewhat between two worlds: He couldn't go out and have a beer with his players, and he hadn't yet earned the total respect given to the older coaches. Avery says Saban handled his nebulous standing with his players "by taking little sarcastic shots at you, all with a smirk and a gleam in his eye. It wasn't ever really nasty, but it was barbed."

Some of the more established players—only a few years younger than Saban—occasionally fired back. "I'd walk by him and say, 'Hey, Nick, you look like you're sucking on a lemon,'" says Wolfley.

Though Angelo and Saban would remain lifelong friends, the Syracuse assistant who had the biggest impact on Saban's life was Dennis Fryzel, the team's defensive coordinator, who helped talk Maloney into hiring the young coach. Fryzel, as a coach, was everything Saban was not. He was a gregarious and funny extrovert who reached his players in a rather zany fashion. "[Fryzel] demonstrated tackling techniques even though he wasn't wearing pads," the *Tampa Bay Times* wrote about his coaching style. "He head-butted players even though he wasn't wearing a helmet. In the pregame frenzy he might do something wild, like remove his false teeth. Getting jacked up was, of course, how Mr. Fryzel lost his teeth in the first place. But that only helped his cred with the players."

Maloney's job was in some serious jeopardy after Syracuse won only two of their first seven games. A four-game winning streak to end the season provided him with a bit of a reprieve. Saban, though, was unnerved by his boss's job insecurity during the season. It didn't help that the winter of 1977 in upstate New York was particularly harsh, something neither he nor Terry enjoyed very much. (Saban had been stranded on icy roads a few times while recruiting.) More important, Terry—alone for all but a few hours a day in a town where she knew few people—was beginning to feel homesick.

After the 1977 season, Saban got a call from Frank Cignetti at West Virginia. He needed a new secondary coach. Though Saban preferred coaching that unit on the defense, he didn't pay much mind to the first call, figuring he'd stick it out at Syracuse despite the challenges. But Cignetti kept calling. Finally, Saban gave in and took a job at the university. He found out later that Terry had been secretly talking to Cignetti and had urged him to stay after her husband. It was the first but certainly not the last time that she played a major role in one of her husband's job changes.

Maloney was angry that Saban left so soon, a feeling that he seems to have hung on to for some time. Speaking to the *Chicago Tribune* in 2008, Maloney, who left football for good after being fired by Syracuse after the 1980 season, was critical of the many times Saban has moved in his career. Asked specifically about the 1977 year, Maloney said: "You could tell he was going to be very good. But you could also tell he was always looking to go somewhere else."

That somewhere else was his home state's team, the one for whom he had dreamed of playing as a child. Cignetti had been Bobby Bowden's offensive coordinator from 1970 to 1975, then took over the Mountaineers when Bowden left to coach Florida State after the 1975 season. Cignetti knew a little bit about Saban already: He had recruited Kerry Marbury at West Virginia, so he'd seen his new secondary coach in action a few times as a high school player at Monongah High.

Cignetti's first two seasons at West Virginia had ended in identical 5-6 records. Though he was not in as much peril as Maloney had been at Syracuse, the Mountaineer alumni and administration were anxious about the 1978 season, Saban's first with the team.

The West Virginia job appeared to be a perfect fit for the Sabans. Terry was happy to be so close to her family and friends— Morgantown was a mere twenty miles from Fairmont. Saban was coaching his favorite position, the one he knew best, and he now had a few years of coaching under his belt. He felt more confident, and demonstrated that confidence on the field. "He was intense and he got after it," says Oliver Luck, an executive with the NCAA who was a quarterback at West Virginia at the time. "But what really made him stand out was his exuberance."

Like Fryzel, Saban actually went through the various practice drills with his players. He didn't do it for show, though. "He was big on technique and hitting and being physical," says Everett Pettaway, one of his cornerbacks at West Virginia. "And he got right out there with us, punching through the tackling dummies, showing us the correct footwork." Saban also began to assert himself more as a leader of his unit. He made it a point to bond with his players in the secondary, frequently dropping by the dorm to check on them, and once a week, taking them to his house to visit Terry and the couple's Doberman pinscher. "Terry would cook for us," says Fulton Walker, a defensive back. "And, boy, she could really cook." Walker says Saban even let him borrow a car on the weekends for dates.

Yet, he demanded much of his players on the field—above all, obedience. Along with Walker, Jerry Holmes, a free safety, was the most talented player Saban had in his secondary (both would play in the NFL). Holmes at times would challenge Saban. After one incident, when Holmes ran off the field after practice before Saban could address his players, Cignetti called Holmes into his office. "He told me to always do what Saban wanted me to do," says Holmes. "He respected him, too." Walker says the discipline made Holmes a better player, "and that trickled down to us, too."

The 1978 season turned out to be a horrid one, both on and off the field. The Mountaineers went 2-9, beating only Richmond in the opener (by two points) and Virginia in the ninth game of the season (by three points). West Virginia was outscored 364–157 that season, giving up an average of thirty-three points per game on defense, which made them, statistically, the fifth-worst defense in Division I football that year. Though the problem was mainly with the run defense (which gave up an average of 255 yards a game) and not in the secondary, the defensive failures didn't look good for anyone involved.

It turned out that there was a bigger reason for the team's poor play. During the season, Cignetti fell ill. He would later be diagnosed with cancer. He went into the hospital after the season, then had a relapse and went in again the summer before the 1979 season. Twice he was read his last rites. He survived, but the team suffered without its leader. "I lay a lot of the blame for what happened on me," says Cignetti. "For those two years [1978 and 1979], my energy level just wasn't there."

Saban, Cignetti says, was one of his assistants who picked up the slack. "During practices, he was disciplined and organized and a great teacher," he says. Where Saban helped the most was off the field in recruiting. "He really did such a great job, spending the time and effort, establishing a person-to-person relationship with the kids and parents," says Cignetti. Saban's blindness to color became an asset on the recruiting trail. Pettaway says he initially had some concerns about West Virginia and possible racism. "My high school coach told me I'd be going to a school with a bunch of hillbillies who might not be used to blacks," he says. Pettaway strongly considered an offer to go to Alabama, until Saban came after him hard. "He spent a lot of time with me and made me feel very comfortable," he says. "After that I had no worries about race or whether he or anyone else there favored players based on color."

In recruiting, Saban was in charge of northeastern Ohio, a very competitive area, especially for a school like West Virginia. The area was mainly Ohio State's turf, and it had been dominant there for decades. Despite the competition, back in those days there was a bit more of a collegial atmosphere to recruiting. "We'd all battle each other during the day, and then go have dinner or beers at night," says Glen Mason, an assistant for Ohio State who also recruited the area. Mason says he was impressed with Saban as a recruiter. "He was a young guy and he gave us a run for our money there," he says. "He shouldn't even have been in our league. It was pretty impressive."

Though Saban couldn't beat Mason when it came to getting the best high school players in Ohio, he did have a little fun at Mason's expense. After the 1978 season, Saban, Mason, and a coach from Purdue named Randy Hart (who is now at Stanford) were all recruiting in the Youngstown area. One morning they all met for breakfast. Mason planned on heading back to Columbus for an Ohio State bowl practice afterward. "During breakfast, Nick starts talking about this prospect, this offensive lineman who could really play—six-foot-four, two-eighty. He talked him up big-time, then turned to Hart, who nodded and said, 'Yeah, he's really good,'" says Mason. Saban asked Mason what he thought of the kid. "I'd never heard of him, but I didn't tell them that," says Mason. "So I settled up and told them I was driving back to Columbus. But I drove straight to this little school in the sticks. I found the coach and was all fired up and said, 'I gotta see this kid.' The coach said, 'You do?' Then the kid comes out. He's scrawny, five-foot-ten, two-fifteen. And I thought, 'Those sons of bitches.'"

The impromptu stop caused Mason to be late for Ohio State's practice and he subsequently was chewed out by Buckeye head coach Earle Bruce. "After practice I called Nick and he answered the phone and just started laughing. He knew exactly why I was calling," says Mason.

Despite Saban's recruiting efforts during the off-season, the 1979 version of the Mountaineers started the season with three straight losses. "We were a really young team," says Gary Tranquill, who was West Virginia's defensive coordinator. "We had to take chances to force the action all the time." In one game, a critical midseason contest against Boston College, Tranquill and Saban ran safety blitzes with Jerry Holmes all game. Late in the fourth quarter, West Virginia had a two-point lead, and Boston College had a third-and-twelve near midfield. "On the headset, I said, 'Nick, let's do it again,'" says Tranquill. "All I heard was silence. Then I heard this faint 'okay.' It was our thirteenth safety blitz of the game." Holmes hit the quarterback, whose pass fell harmlessly to the ground, and West Virginia held on for the win.

The Mountaineers were 5-4 heading into their last two games. The defense had improved markedly, thanks in part to the emergence of a linebacker named Darryl Talley. A bowl game invite was in reach. But West Virginia lost those two games, Cignetti was fired, and Saban's coaching career was tossed into uncertainty.

Though the incoming West Virginia coach, Don Nehlen, wanted to hang on to him, by this time Saban had received a better offer: Earl Bruce at Ohio State needed a new secondary coach. Both Dennis Fryzel, by then the Buckeyes' defensive coordinator, and Mason, the offensive coordinator, lobbied hard for Saban. Bruce hired him in December 1979.

Right around the time of Saban's hiring at Ohio State, a revolution had begun to take root in college football. It started in the Big Ten, which was on the vanguard of the college football scene. The revolution was the modern passing attack. For decades, the leading college football programs—like Ohio State and Michigan— had relied on relatively simple offensive schemes, running out of an I-formation that focused on a strong running attack complemented by play-action passes that usually occurred in long-yardage situations. Defenses around the country were built to blunt that type of attack, playing safeties who excelled at stopping a running back if and when he broke through the line of scrimmage and scooted past the linebackers. By the late 1970s and early 1980s, though, some of the lesser-regarded Big Ten schools, like Purdue and Illinois, were beginning to move away from those traditional offenses.

Bruce was an old-school coach, firm in his belief that what had made Ohio State successful in the past would continue to work in the present and future. Nick Saban, twenty-eight years old when hired, was of a newer generation who saw the writing on the wall. He believed that defenses, particularly at the safety position, would have to adjust to the modern passing attack or they'd become hopelessly vulnerable. This belief—really, a generational rift—would be one of the primary reasons that Saban would last for only two years under Bruce.

Bruce says that Saban impressed him during his interview as a "very knowledgeable young coach." After Saban was hired, but before he started working, Bruce took him along with the team to the Rose Bowl at the end of the 1979 season, to get accustomed to the program. The Buckeyes were 11-0 and ranked number one in the nation. A win over USC would have almost guaranteed a national title. It was Saban's first up-close exposure to a game of this magnitude. Just eight years into his career, Saban realized he'd arrived in the big leagues and would soon be coaching for one of the game's all-time great programs. He watched as the Buckeyes lost a gut-wrenching game by one point, and finished fourth in the year-end rankings.*

Aside from Fryzel and Mason, no one on the Ohio State coaching staff knew much about Saban coming into the 1980 season. "Earle just told us, 'Here's our guy, make it happen and mesh,'" says Fred Zechman, who was the team's quarterback coach. The secondary coach Saban had replaced—Pete Carroll—was effervescent and a total players' coach. "Pete was more laissez-faire," says Zechman. "He would go out and play basketball with his players, go do a five-mile run with them. He got really close to his players. Nick was just the opposite. He was a hard-ass."

Saban's most readily apparent strength was in recruiting. "He worked really hard at it," says Bruce. "He was a good evaluator of talent and a good listener. And he was observant. When he discovered something about a kid that he thought would be a good lead, he went after it."

Representing the powerhouse Ohio State program helped boost his recruiting skills. Anthony Griggs, a defensive back, was going into his senior year at Villanova when the school (temporarily, it turned out) dropped its football program. "Someone tapped me on the shoulder one day and said, 'There's a school here that wants to see you,'" says Griggs. "I went into an office and there was Nick Saban. He was very confident, very sure of himself. He told me, 'We're Ohio State and we're interested in you,' in a monotone voice. The entire time as he talked he was twirling an Ohio State ring on his finger." Griggs enrolled right away.

Saban also went after another Villanova defensive back named Tom Anthony. "He walked me through my career path, step by step," says Anthony. "He told me how great the school was and what it was like to step on the field at Ohio State. Whenever I had

---

* The national title that year went to Alabama, coached by Paul "Bear" Bryant. It was his fifth national title. The offensive coordinator for the Crimson Tide that year was none other than Mal Moore.

an objection, he had it covered. He was like a psychologist." One of Saban's biggest recruits at Ohio State was a cornerback named Shaun Gayle, who would go on to play twelve seasons in the NFL and win a Super Bowl as a member of the 1985 Chicago Bears. Gayle says he didn't much like the way Ohio State recruited him and was seriously considering his other options . . . until Saban came in. "I immediately liked him. My family really liked him. He is the reason I went to Ohio State," says Gayle.

Ohio State entered the 1980 season ranked number one in the polls, but an upset loss at home to UCLA in the fourth game of the season, coupled with an excruciating loss to rival Michigan, took the team out of title contention. After losing to Penn State in the Fiesta Bowl, the Buckeyes finished the season ranked fifteenth.

That season put Bruce under some pressure. He had succeeded the infamous Woody Hayes at Ohio State, the coach who had won five national championships but was most well known for getting fired after punching an opposing player in the throat. Hayes had established a precedent for Ohio State football: Anything less than true contention for a national title was deemed unacceptable. Three-loss seasons were huge disappointments. (Saban would find himself in this exact situation later on down the road at LSU and Alabama.)

Ohio State held a preseason ranking of number eleven going into the 1981 season. The team's main concern was with its young and inexperienced defense. Saban felt that the team had been issued a loud and clear warning sign in the previous year that they were not ready for the new-school passing attacks fashioned by a few teams in the Big Ten. In 1980, a mediocre 3-5-1 Illinois team had come to Columbus late in the season and pushed around the defense and, in particular, Saban's unit. Dave Wilson, the Illini quarterback, threw for a record 621 yards in the game, which the Buckeyes still somehow managed to win, 49–42. By 1981, Saban wanted to change the way his secondary worked to combat these pass-heavy attacks. Bruce did not, which led to confrontation.

On the field, Saban "wanted to do things in coverage that were a bit more sophisticated, looking for a better way," says Steve Szabo, the defensive line coach. Gayle remembers that Saban was "really an independent thinker" and was constantly pushing to try new things in the secondary. Saban also wanted to start recruiting a new breed of safety. "Earle was sort of back in the 1970s," says Szabo. "He felt like a strong safety should be a guy like Jack Tatum, a big guy. But Nick believed the safeties had to be multitalented guys, had to be able to play the pass in a zone or even man-to-man coverage."

Saban, entering his tenth year as a coach, now had his own firm beliefs about how the game should be played in the secondary. He was not shy about voicing those opinions, even if they contradicted those held by his head coach. Off the field, things between Earle and Saban began to get a little tense. "Nick made some statements a couple of times during staff meetings that were really offensive to Earle," says Szabo. "When he said them, you could hear a pin drop in the room."

In the 1981 season, Saban's fears about his secondary were realized. After winning their first three games, the Buckeyes lost two in a row to unranked opponents (Florida State and Wisconsin). Even subsequent wins exposed the team's flaws. In a 45–33 victory over Purdue, Saban's secondary gave up 516 passing yards to Boilermaker quarterback Scott Campbell. The lone bright spot of the season for the defense came against archrival Michigan, when Saban was allowed to craft a game plan for his secondary designed to stop Michigan's receiving star, Anthony Carter. "Nick did a great job neutralizing Carter," says Szabo. The receiver was limited to fifty-two yards in four catches and the Buckeyes intercepted three passes in a 14–9 upset of the seventh-ranked Wolverines.

Though Ohio State had managed a share of the Big Ten Championship, the season had been a disaster for its defense, which had long been the strength of the team under Hayes. The 1981 squad gave up 253 points and a whopping 3,278 passing yards, which made them the worst passing defense in Division I. "Everybody was all over our pass defense," Fryzel would tell Louisiana's *Shreveport Times* years later. "And that was Nick's. The fingers were pointed at him. The media and the fans were murdering him."

Despite the pressures on and off the field that season, Saban stayed tight with his players, just as he had done at West Virginia. "He seemed to genuinely care about us," says Anthony.* Terry cooked them meals. Saban helped his players find housing and summer jobs. "He taught us about more than just football," says Gayle.

Saban also found time to hang out with his fellow assistants. He went out for beers with them and frequently played golf with Fryzel, Zechman, and Mason. "He was a good golfer and pretty intense out there," says Zechman.

Mason fondly recalls the Nick Saban of those days. "Nick always worked really hard and was good at what he did, but he wasn't uptight back then. He smiled and joked around, and actually seemed like a happy-go-lucky guy. But all that's changed. He's different. He's all business now and very intense. I saw him a few years ago at a conference and I said, 'Nick, you used to laugh and have a beer and relax a bit.' He looked at me and said, 'You know, I just don't have time for that anymore.' "

What happened next at Ohio State had a lot to do with that change.

Despite the upset of Michigan in Ohio State's last regular season game, the 8-3 Buckeyes were relegated to the Liberty Bowl in Memphis against an unranked Navy team. It was a serious letdown for the team. "It felt like a dump bowl to the coaches and the players," says Zechman. Bruce—agitated, but wanting to keep any and all ill feelings in-house—had barred his assistants from talking to the media. "I told them I wanted them to keep their mouths shut," he says. He wanted to be the team's sole voice.

Navy was not a good team. They'd lost to Yale earlier in the year and had tied an awful Army team. Ohio State, though, barely avoided what would have been a devastating upset, winning 31–28, by overcoming a career day by Navy's unheralded quarterback,

---

* Anthony and a teammate once met with Saban to talk to him about possibly getting into coaching after college. "Saban told us, 'Don't do it, fellas. There's no money in it,' " says Anthony.

who threw for nearly double his per-game average. Bruce was livid. And what happened after the game put him over the top.

As Earle walked from the field to the locker room, he saw Fryzel standing in front of some reporters, holding court. "There he was, laying it all out for them," says Bruce. Bob Tucker, the linebacker coach, was walking with Bruce at the time. "I just remember him saying, 'That's it. That's it. It's over,'" says Tucker.

After the team flew home, Bruce says, he couldn't sleep, so he walked the streets of Columbus for four hours, thinking about what he had to do. He called a staff meeting for the next morning at eleven. Zechman remembers that Earle addressed Fryzel, listed some of the problems he had with his coaching, and told him he was fired. "Then Nick says, 'Coach, it wasn't all Denny's fault.' In the heat of the moment, Earle says, 'You're out, too,'" says Zechman.

Bruce remembers the meeting differently. He says on his walk through the streets the night before, he'd come to the conclusion that he had to fire Fryzel, Szabo, Tucker, and Saban. (Tucker was eventually hired back.) Bruce admits that there was some friction between him and Saban over defensive philosophies and some tense moments during some staff meetings, but says, "that didn't seal his fate. It was really nothing Nick did. It was just that he'd gotten really close to Fryzel."

So, at 11:10 a.m. on December 31, 1981, Saban was fired for the first and only time in his career, in what later became known as the "New Year's Eve Massacre."*

According to the other assistant coaches, Fryzel was already on thin ice before he held his impromptu press conference after the Liberty Bowl. "Denny was off the wall," says Szabo. "He was a gambler. He called a game by picking plays out of a hat. Nothing about him was structured." He was also extremely outgoing, sometimes to a fault. "Denny loved to be a big-timer. He was out

---

* Saban was replaced by Dom Capers, which meant that in the span of three years, Bruce had the remarkable succession of Pete Carroll, Saban, and Capers coach his secondary. Carroll won the 2013 season Super Bowl with the Seattle Seahawks; Capers won a Super Bowl as the defensive coordinator of the Green Bay Packers; Saban has won five national titles in college.

there rubbing elbows with the money people and the boosters at the school, trying to be in the same social circles as Earle. I think that rubbed Earle the wrong way," says Szabo.

Still, Bruce says firing Fryzel was the hardest decision he ever made as a coach. "Fryzel was my best friend in coaching," says Bruce, who first hired him in 1972 at the University of Tampa. "We went to the track together. Our families were close. Do you hear me? But I thought it was time I moved on. I told him, 'You can get a new job and take that guy [Saban] with you because he's attached to your hip.' "

According to the *Shreveport Times*, in his exit interview after being fired, Fryzel told Bruce: "I'll take the hit for the defense, but the best football coach on this whole staff is Nick Saban. He's the best recruiter. I'll take the shot, but don't fire Nick." Fryzel said Earle just sat there with his hands on his desk, without speaking a word, "just shaking his head 'no.' "

Fryzel would never coach football again. He continued to play a significant role in Saban's life, though. The man who had helped Saban land two assistant jobs at two different universities became one of the closest friends Saban would ever have, despite the wild contrast in their personalities. In the ensuing years, Fryzel would become a frequent presence on the sidelines with Saban, bearing witness to some of his friend's biggest victories. Later, he would help prod Saban into leaving the Miami Dolphins to take the Alabama job, then zealously defend that move. When Fryzel fell ill with renal cancer, the Sabans loaned him their Georgia lake house for a few weeks. In the summer of 2009, Saban visited Fryzel the day before he died and, according to the *Tampa Tribune*, looked his old friend in the face and said, "Thank you, buddy, for everything."

The day after he was fired, Saban met with the media. "I can hold my head high. . . . I can walk tall. I'm not ashamed," he said. "I did as good a job as I could do. And the kids were great."

In 1981, Saban had been forced to start three sophomores and one freshman in his secondary. Though they had been burned most of the season, they had improved, something they'd demonstrated in the Michigan game. His players appreciated his dedication and loyalty. After Saban was fired, they showed up at his house and presented him with a plaque that read: "Thanks for the confidence this season and we'll miss you as a coach and a friend—1981 Defensive Secondary."

Though they put on a brave face, privately both Saban and Terry were crushed. Saban, at age thirty, was facing his first real career crisis. He would admit years later in his book, *How Good Do You Want to Be?*, that the firing made him totally reassess his career in coaching and wonder whether it was all worth it. He wrote that he "questioned not only my career choice but my abilities as well. I had failed. I was devastated and humiliated."

He was also prepared. Even early on during his Ohio State stay, Saban was already eyeing the future. "Nick stayed connected by talking on the phone to a lot of other coaches, building a network," says Tucker. Szabo says that Saban was "a rather private guy, and I always felt that if it was just he and I in a conversation, I was always mindful of what I said to him because I felt like he had another agenda. Even at Ohio State he was already working on the next job, wherever that may be. It's not necessarily a fault, but he was an extremely ambitious guy."

That preparation came in handy. After they were fired, Saban and Szabo attended a national coaching convention together. "You felt like an outcast," says Szabo. "Regardless of the reasons for the firing, it's a firing, it's a slap in the face. But I thought Nick was in a much better frame of mind than I was." *

Saban found a new job thanks to an old friend. Gary Tranquill, the defensive coordinator during Saban's last year at West Virginia, became the head coach at Navy in 1982, taking over for George Welsh, who had left for Virginia. Tranquill asked Saban to join his

---

* Szabo would go on to a long career as a defensive assistant in college and the NFL.

staff and, in January 1982, Saban accepted a job with the program that had contributed to his dismissal a few weeks earlier. Tranquill hired Saban to coach his secondary, but "Nick kind of ran the defense. I didn't have a defensive coordinator in name, really," he says.

While the hiring was a coup for Tranquill, taking a job at the Naval Academy was a step down for Saban, in the prestige of the program and in the quality of the players. Navy's glory years as a football program were a distant memory, and the player pool from which they could recruit was much shallower than most other Division I programs. The rigidity of the school in general was a turn-off to many big-time recruits and the postgraduation commitment to enlisting made playing in the NFL more difficult. Publicly, Saban stood tall. When asked if he was disappointed about the job, he told the *Bryan (Ohio) Times*: "I have no qualms about going to the Naval Academy. It's another type of challenge, with the type of people I'll meet and the type of recruiting."

He didn't have many other options at the time, anyway, and it was fairly clear to those around him that Navy was just another rung in the ladder. "The rumor we all heard when he came in is that he wanted to be the youngest defensive coordinator in the country," says Mark Brodowicz, a defensive back on the Navy team.

Tranquill and Saban had some serious work to do. Welsh had taken most of his staff with him to Virginia, and the 1982 team had no returning starters. Navy had two promising running backs— Napoleon McCallum and Ronald McDonald—but they were young and raw. The situation in the secondary was particularly grim. Graduation, injuries, and academic problems left Saban with only a few guys who had ever played the position before. Saban realized the trouble he was in after spring practice, so he cut a deal with Tranquill that would allow him to poach players from other positions to fill out the secondary.

One of those players was a backup quarterback and wide receiver named Eric Wallace. "When Saban told me I was going to be playing cornerback, I laughed out loud," says Wallace. "I hadn't tackled anybody in years." (Saban has always liked having former quarterbacks in his secondary—they naturally pick up reads and the tendencies of opposing quarterbacks.) Wallace had one summer to prepare. "I was on the other end of a fire hose. But Nick spent a fair amount of time with me, convincing me that I was going to be All-American," he says. Saban basically started at square one with Wallace and the other defensive backs. "He taught us how to notice things," says Wallace. "He taught us to play through the offensive tackle, to watch his first step, which meant you had to keep your eyes on the player you were defending and the tackle. It was hard to do those two things at once, but he drilled it into us, and eventually I could tell if the offense was going to run or pass."

Saban also got his team immersed in film study, to unearth the tendencies of opposing players. "He did things like show us that one guy would get lower in his stance if it was a run play or wiggle his fingers if it was a pass play. He picked up all that stuff," says Wallace.*

Saban's attention to detail extended off the field as well. Back then, the Navy players and coaches would have meetings at lunch. Brodowicz remembers one of the early meetings, when the players had no idea who Saban was. "Saban walks in there wearing a suit and carrying a briefcase," he says. "All the other coaches, even Tranquill, wore khakis and golf shirts. But here comes this guy. He set his briefcase down in front of him, then took off his jacket and methodically put it on the back of his chair so it wouldn't wrinkle, then opened up the briefcase and started handing us stuff. I remember calling my brother afterwards and telling him, 'This guy is so methodical and sophisticated. He wants to be a great coach.'"

Saban also had his secondary sit in their meetings exactly how they lined up on the field. "The safeties sat in the middle and were flanked by the cornerbacks," says Kurt Dixon, a safety on the team.

---

* In 2010, Saban, by then at Alabama, was at the home of a friend of Wallace while recruiting a player named Jabriel Washington. Wallace says he hadn't seen Saban since 1982. Wallace happened to have sent this friend a Christmas card that year, and it was tacked on to his refrigerator. Saban spotted the card and asked the man how he knew Eric Wallace. "My friend called me and said, 'I have someone who wants to talk to you,'" says Wallace. "Then I hear Nick Saban say, 'Hello, Eric.' I couldn't believe he remembered me." Washington ended up enrolling at Alabama.

"That way, when I wanted to talk to the cornerback, I had to look to my left, just as I did on the field. It was unbelievable."

Saban's intensity caught some of his players off guard. Chuck Bresnahan, who would later coach under Saban at the Cleveland Browns, was a linebacker on that 1982 Navy team, his second year in the program. "At Navy, football was traditionally seen as a break from the military part of the school," he says. "But that wasn't the case when Nick came. He was just so demanding."

Navy started the season with a home game against their ex-coach, Welsh, and his new Virginia team. "Nick told me the entire training camp that Welsh was going to come after me, because he knew me as a quarterback," says Wallace. They did come after him, but Wallace played well, and Navy won the game. The season was bookended with a big win over rival Army, but a 6-5 record meant no bowl game. As many had suspected, Saban wasn't sticking around much longer, anyway. He had bigger things on his mind.

Saban left Navy after just one season. The story goes that when he resigned, a member of the Navy athletic department said: "Nick Saban left without ever saying good-bye." To which Navy basketball coach Paul Evans supposedly replied: "That's all right. He never said 'hello.'" The Navy year was a significant one for Saban, career-wise, though, because it's where he first got to know a man who would become a friend, boss, and mentor: a young NFL assistant named Bill Belichick.

According to Belichick, the two first met when Saban was at Ohio State and Belichick, who was the linebacker and special teams coach for the New York Giants, was preparing for the NFL Draft. It was later at Navy, however, where their relationship began to blossom. Belichick's father, Steve, was a longtime scout and assistant coach at Navy. In a 2005 article in the *Palm Beach Post,* Steve Belichick recalled that the Saban he knew at Navy was "very intense. He was very nervous. He couldn't sit down to take a phone call. I remember saying he'd tear up ten miles of carpet in a three-minute phone call. He'd bite his fingernails."

His son and Saban, similar in ambition and age (Saban is six months older), bonded over their shared passion for the game of football. "Bill would come home from the Giants in the summer, and we would talk ball," Saban says. The two budding football savants sat for hours on the front porch of Steve Belichick's house and went over linebacker strategies, exotic blitzes, pass coverage concepts, and even offensive schemes. "Nick is a great defensive coach, but he understands everything about offensive football and how to attack and defend the offensive schemes used on the other side of the ball," says Bill Belichick, who adds that one of Saban's other important attributes is that he is also "ultracompetitive."

Those initial front porch sessions led to the two men, both of Croatian descent, being linked from then on. Belichick says that even today, "Nick and I communicate with each other on a regular basis, several times a year."

Saban has often given credit to Belichick for showing him how to run a football program from top to bottom. The popular conception of the duo is that they are a lot alike. But they would discover in the mid-1990s that they weren't quite as similar as they initially believed.

It would take Saban three more career stops to get to that point, though.

4

The Making of a Head Coach

IN **THE** living room of his East Lansing, Michigan, house—right next to a golf course he can no longer play—the eighty-year-old George Perles sat in a La-Z-Boy. When he talked, his voice occasionally rose in volume and his jowls reddened, as if he were back stalking the sidelines of a football field, or holding court in a locker room. He draped his big hands over the chair's arms. On one finger: a 1980 Pittsburgh Steelers Super Bowl ring. A walker was within arm's reach, a visual reminder of the price he's paid for his thirty-eight years in football, as a player and a coach. From 1983 to 1994, Perles was the head coach of the Michigan State Spartans. For his first five years there, he employed Nick Saban as an assistant coach.

Perles, of course, had known Saban for a decade before he hired him, from when the young graduate assistant from Kent State visited the headquarters of the Steelers, where Perles was the defensive line coach and, later, the defensive coordinator. "We were just putting in the four-three stunt defense then," says Perles. "Nick was always picking my brain about it." It was a defense that would later become known as "the Steel Curtain," a key part of the Steelers' dynasty in the 1970s.*

Perles says that though he did see some special spark in Saban

---

* In the most basic terms, a 4-3 defense means there are four defensive linemen and three linebackers. A 3-4 defense has three defensive linemen and four linebackers, though one or more of those linebackers sometimes set up on the line of scrimmage before the snap.

back then, his hiring of Saban in 1983 was in large part out of necessity. "I didn't hire him because of his past record. He'd been fired at Ohio State, but that didn't bother me," he says. "I needed a secondary coach at the time and he came to mind. He was a friend, socially. I didn't have much money to pay my guys. I paid all of my assistants thirty thousand dollars a year. I couldn't just go out and get anyone I wanted." Saban was easily the least well known of the assistants Perles hired in 1983.

Perles liked working with Saban right away. "Nick doesn't get weakened by sentimentality or emotional things," he says. "He's not worried about what you feel about his decisions, he doesn't care who likes it. He makes every decision based on winning football games. He was unusual like that."

During their time together in East Lansing, the two continued to hang out socially. They were partners in paddleball. "Nick was a good smoker and beer drinker back then, too," says Perles. "I admired the way he could get along with the people he needed to and wanted to."

According to Perles, Saban had one clear ambition: "He valued our relationship in part because of my connection with the pros, because I had been with the Steelers. I think he thought that maybe he'd meet people through me. He wanted to get into pro football. He wanted pro football bad."

When asked what might have motivated Saban, why he worked as hard as he did and why he continually networked, Perles stared straight ahead. Then he raised his right hand and rubbed his index and middle fingers against his thumb. "Cash," he says.

Saban would end up staying at Michigan State for five years, the longest stint in his career as an assistant coach. East Lansing became the place where he finally dug in his heels and stayed long enough to have a lasting impact on a program. The Spartans, though not necessarily college football heavyweights at the time, were a solid Big Ten team with loads of potential. During those five years, Saban grew as a coach and a recruiter, and developed into a legitimate candidate for a head-coaching job. He and Terry loved the collegiate atmosphere in East Lansing, and it's where they started a family together.

Perles played a big role. He became Saban's first true coaching mentor since Don James. He rescued him from the Navy job and gave him the opportunity to get back into major college football in what was then perhaps the country's strongest conference. He taught Saban the intricacies of the 4-3 stunt defense, a version of which Saban would employ as a head coach down the road. It was from Perles that Saban learned the "twenty-four-hour rule," in which a team—players, coaches, and staff—was given twenty-four hours to celebrate a win or mourn a loss, no matter its significance, then had to move on. Perles also showed Saban the importance of off-season conditioning for his players. All of Saban's subsequent strength and conditioning coaches—Ken Mannie, Tommy Moffitt, and Scott Cochran (who currently runs Alabama's notorious "Fourth Quarter" conditioning program)—are, in one way or another, disciples of Carl "Buck" Nystrom, who was in charge of the Spartans' punishing conditioning program under Perles.

Most important, Perles gave Saban both responsibility and freedom. In year one at Michigan State, Saban coached the secondary as he absorbed the intricacies of Perles's defense. "I didn't name a defensive coordinator the first year," says Perles. "But after that season, it was obvious to me that Nick would be a great coordinator. He worked hard, was in early, and stayed late. He was a teacher. And he was interested in moving up. He was good at what he did, and the kids who played for him respected him and liked him. He was everything you wanted in a coach."

From 1984 on, as Perles took more of a big-picture role with the team and the program, Saban finally got his chance to implement the sophisticated defensive schemes he'd dreamed of running. His task then became finding the players who could pull it off.

After Saban's first season at Michigan State—in which the team went 4-6-1 as it began recovering from years of neglect, in both recruiting and in discipline—Saban dug in on the recruiting trail, where he continued to burnish his growing reputation. Recruiting at Michigan State wasn't as hard as it had been at Navy or West Virginia, but it certainly wasn't easy. The Spartans competed with their bigger-named Big Ten rivals, Michigan and Ohio State, as well as the traditional powerhouse Notre Dame. Michigan State had not been a hot spot for attracting talent since the mid-1960s, under coach Duffy Daugherty. Saban was no longer at a place where he could merely twist a ring on his finger and woo a player.

His main area of focus was Ohio, still a stronghold of Ohio State's. "Nick always did such a great job in the homes," says Perles, who accompanied Saban on many recruiting visits. "He'd go for the mothers. He'd charm them and they'd bite. When he left the room, those mothers would turn to their kids and say, 'You go with him, he's so nice.'"

Sometimes he even had to reach back to an earlier generation. Andre Rison, the wide receiver who would play twelve years in the NFL and make the Pro Bowl in five of those seasons, was a star recruit from Flint, Michigan, in 1984. Early during his recruitment, he was leaning toward signing with Wisconsin or Michigan. Saban was assigned to Rison, and he wanted him badly. In his research, Saban discovered that Rison's grandmother was a woman named Alberta Brown from Fairmont, West Virginia—the same Alberta Brown whom Saban had known all his life (she drove a garbage truck in town).

During the Christmas break that year, Saban and Terry went home to West Virginia. They were expected to attend a Christmas Eve party at Terry's mother's house. Instead, Saban paid Brown a visit that night, and he stayed at her house, drinking beer and talking to her about her grandson, until 3 a.m. Though Terry and her mother were not pleased at all that he missed the family get-together, Saban's visit to Brown worked. Rison enrolled at Michigan State.

As a recruiter, Saban—who was assigned an area and not necessarily one side of the ball—found and delivered some other key offensive players for Michigan State during those years, like lineman Tony Mandarich, and another receiver named Mark Ingram, whose son, Mark Ingram Jr., would later play for Saban at Alabama and win the Heisman Trophy. He also made sure to beef up his defense, especially in the secondary, bringing in defensive backs Harlon Barnett, John Miller (the number-one recruit in Michigan), and Todd Krumm. "When I was being recruited, I had all of these people telling me how good their programs were," says Krumm. "Then Nick came in and he told me that it was going to be hard and that if I was up to the task, I should come. And that if I didn't think I would be, I should go somewhere else. I found that appealing. I liked the challenge."

"Challenge" might have been an understatement. On the field and at practices, Saban drove his defense hard, and was often quick-tempered and profane. His players had to develop thick skin or they'd get demoralized. A few refused to buy in. "I watched him challenge a defensive back to a fight behind the football field one day," says Miller. "The guy was being disrespectful, and Saban said, 'Let's settle this man-to-man.' The guy backed down then, but he never did listen. I ended up with that guy's job."

Most of his defensive players learned to adapt. "You had to filter out the yelling and the screaming," says Barnett. "And when you did, you learned." Saban was big on fundamentals, especially with his players in the secondary: As they set up before the snap, their feet were never to be wider than the shoulders. At the snap, they were instructed to hit the receiver on the inside pectoral muscle with their palms (so they wouldn't break a finger). And they never were to fall for an inside fake as they drove their man out wide. Everything was drilled over and over in practice. Film—both of the opposing team and of his own players—was meticulously combed over. ("If he saw that you made a bad step on film, he'd call you out and say, 'You run like a broke-dick dog,'" says Krumm.)

Saban was approaching the same age his father was when he started to ride his son, hard, and Saban became like him, demanding an impossible perfection from his players. "After practice, we'd have to run ten forty-yard dashes and they had to be perfect or we had to run more," says Barnett. "Everyone would run as hard as they possibly could, but we never ran just ten." Miller recalls a game they played against Illinois in his sophomore season. "I graded out at one hundred percent on the film of the game," he says. "Saban never gave out a perfect grade, though, so he took a point off. I think my jersey came untucked at one point in the game."

Saban's desire for perfection leaked into areas off the football field, as well. "We had a charity softball game one day on campus, us against the hockey and basketball teams," says Miller. "We lost, and Saban was pouting like we'd just lost the Super Bowl. I went over and put my arm around him and said, 'Smile, Coach, it's for charity.' He just looked at me with those eyes."

It all paid off. Michigan State gradually crawled back to national relevance. In 1984, Saban's second season, the team finished the regular season with a winning record and went to the Cherry Bowl, the program's first postseason appearance since the mid-1960s. The Spartans made another bowl game in 1985, finishing 7-5. The defense improved every year. The offense, with Rison, Ingram, and running back Lorenzo White, was solid. After a 6-5 season in 1986, everything finally came together.

Michigan State was unranked in preseason polls heading into the 1987 season. It faced a daunting trio to begin the season—USC, Notre Dame, and Florida State were all ranked in the top twenty. The Spartans ended up beating USC, but lost the next two games. That put all of the pressure on the fifth game of the season, against the number-twelve team in the country, Michigan.

Saban prepared his defense flawlessly the week before that game. "We scripted everything in practice, and had our scout offense running Michigan's offense, all based on what Saban had seen on film," says Krumm. "When we got in the game and had their routes totally covered, Miller and I just looked at each other and were like, 'We've seen this a million times in practice.' That was all Nick's doing." Michigan State intercepted seven Michigan passes that day (Miller had four of them) and won, 17–11. "After that, we knew we had something special that year," says Krumm.

Saban's defense was led by linebacker Percy Snow and a stingy secondary. Perles, to the annoyance of some fans, nearly always punted on fourth down and short, even when the Spartans were close enough for a long-range field goal attempt, figuring his team had a chance to score more points by putting the defense—which ended up ranked number two in the country that season—on the field.

Perhaps the most satisfying win for Saban in that season came in the eighth game, when Michigan State went on the road to Ohio State, coached by his old boss, Earle Bruce. The Spartans shut down the Buckeyes' passing offense, thanks in large part to Saban's safeties, whom he had recruited and trained to stop the pass—exactly the type of safeties that Bruce never let him have at Ohio State. The Spartans won, 13–7; it was the start of a three-game losing streak for Ohio State that ended up costing Bruce his job. "Nick didn't say anything about the game, but I could tell how important it was to him," says Perles. "You could see it after the game with how emotional he was." Saban did later admit to the *Columbus Dispatch* that the win left him "maybe some feeling of redemption."

Michigan State finished the regular season 8-2-1 and won the Big Ten, which earned it an invitation to the Rose Bowl. There it would play USC, the team it had defeated back in the first game of the season. USC had become a different team by then, though, with a more potent offense, led by Rodney Peete, who had matured as a passer. Michigan State's defense allowed a few long drives but, in the end, pressured USC enough to force four turnovers. The Spartans won, 20–17.

Jack Ebling, then a beat reporter for the *Lansing State Journal*, remembers entering the Spartan locker room after the game. The players and coaches were all going wild . . . all except for one of them. "I looked in the corner and there was Saban, slumped, all alone, taking huge drags from a cigarette. He looked like someone had shot his dog. He was miserable," recalls Ebling. "I asked him what was wrong. He looked up at me and said, 'Did you see what they did to my defense?' "

Despite his post–Rose Bowl misery, Saban appeared to be outwardly content at Michigan State. Terry had made many close friends in East Lansing. The couple adopted their first child, a son they named

Nicholas. (They adopted a daughter, Kristen, four years later.)* Privately, though, Saban was restless and ready for something bigger. For a brief moment, it appeared that he might get that opportunity at Michigan State. After the 1987 season, the Green Bay Packers made an offer to Perles. "It was pretty obvious that if I left, Nick would become the next head coach here," he says. Perles actually did accept the job for two days before Michigan State gave him a new ten-year contract. "It was disappointing to Nick that I stayed," he says.

At around that same time, the head-coaching job came open at Kent State. Saban went after it, and most reports listed him as the front-runner. Saban believed that because of his connection to the school, he would get the job, and was surprised when Kent State ended up hiring Dick Crum, an older, more established coach from the University of North Carolina. It marked perhaps the only time in Saban's career that he was on a list for a job that he actually wanted, then was turned down.

Saban settled for the next best thing: a job in the NFL with the Houston Oilers, led by an eccentric, free-spirited coach named Jerry Glanville.

The story of how Glanville found Saban goes something like this: In January 1988, the Oilers' head coach went down to the Senior Bowl (the annual showcase for graduating collegiate players in Mobile) to scout talent for the upcoming NFL Draft and to find a new coach for his secondary. He wasn't having much luck with the latter. One night he went out for a late dinner with two of his NFL coaching brethren: Tony Dungy and "Mean" Joe Greene, the defensive coordinator and defensive line coach, respectively, for the

---

* In 2010, Terry told an Alabama booster club that the couple tried to have children for fifteen years. "Nick's recruiting area was everything west of the Mississippi River," she said. "When you're at a little school and don't have a big budget, you're on the road a lot. So he was in California recruiting and he'd call home and say, 'Hi, honey, what are you doing?' And I would say, 'Ovulating.'"

Steelers. Though Glanville was almost robbed after dinner—when he and Dungy left the restaurant, they were surrounded by a group of would-be thieves who scattered only when the massive Greene walked out of the door—he did leave that meal with a name. Both Dungy and Greene said they were very impressed with the young defensive coordinator at Michigan State. It didn't hurt, either, that Belichick later put in a good word for his friend.

Saban showed up for his interview with Glanville wearing a suit and tie and a pair of gleaming wing-tipped shoes. "I told him to take off the coat and tie if he wanted the job," says Glanville. Then Glanville had Saban walk up to a chalkboard and sketch out some defensive plays, to show him what he could do with his secondary. As Saban dutifully grabbed the chalk and started writing out some X's and O's, Glanville wadded up a spitball and threw it at him. "Nick turned around and was like, 'What?'" says Glanville. "And I told him, 'That's going to happen to you in meetings with my guys. What are you going to do about it? You need to have a plan.'" It would not be the last time the freewheeling Glanville would needle the ultraserious Saban.

Indeed, the Oilers' secondary was an infamous group, as nasty off the field as they were on it. (The team's stadium—the Astrodome— was nicknamed "the House of Pain" in large part thanks to the defensive backs.) "I told Nick during the interview that this might be the toughest coaching job he'd ever have," says Glanville. "These weren't the kind of guys you took home for dinner. They couldn't care less about you. But come Sunday, they'd line up and play."

Glanville also interviewed Pete Carroll for the job. Though Carroll had four years of NFL experience by that time, Glanville says he "took a chance" and went with Saban because he liked the techniques he taught and thought he could improve his secondary. The thirty-six-year-old Saban accepted the job in March 1988 and moved to Houston. It was his first job in the NFL, and one that required some serious adjustments for the former college assistant: The somewhat uptight Saban had to get used to the off-the-cuff style of his new boss. He also had the challenge of trying to reach professional players as opposed to wide-eyed nineteen-year-olds. Saban would ultimately harness the Oilers' secondary and indeed make it better, just as Glanville had hoped. It wasn't an easy task, though, and a few of the unbridled players would fight back—literally.

In the 1988 NFL Draft, Houston took two players from Saban's old Michigan State team—running back Lorenzo White in the first round and punter Greg Montgomery in the third. In the fifth round, the Oilers selected a cornerback from Purdue named Cris Dishman, whom Saban had scouted and coached against in the Big Ten.

The Oilers' most talented players were on the offensive side of the ball: quarterback Warren Moon, running backs Mike Rozier and White, and wide receiver Drew Hill. The offense was potent: Glanville ran an early version of the spread offenses that are in vogue today. The defense "had a chip on its shoulder," says Kim Helton, the offensive line coach, and it showed, both in games—where it was aggressive and blitz-minded—and in practices, where it liked to do things its own way.

Glanville was right. This wasn't like college for Saban—he wouldn't be taking his Oilers players home for dinner with Terry. They were too unruly. Finally, though, Saban had the secondary of his dreams. Jeff Donaldson, Keith Bostic, Richard Johnson, Dishman, and, in Saban's second year, Bubba McDowell, were all big and athletic men who could play press man-to-man coverage. Bostic was that ideal safety that Saban had coveted during his days at Ohio State. He could stop the run and was nimble enough to cover receivers. Clearly, the talent was there. "But the big question for Nick coming in was could he confront pro footballers and get their respect," says Helton. "It's not like intimidating some college kid. These guys had to believe what he was saying."

Saban refused to adapt his style. He expected his players to do what he said, or they wouldn't play. He was on them constantly. "I thought my name was 'Fucking Asshole' for a long time," says Dishman. "First name 'Fucking,' last name 'Asshole.'" Dishman says he would even occasionally check the back of his jersey to make sure it had his real name on it. "The thing was, he treated the rookies and the veterans the same way. A lot of the vets didn't like that. He was cussing out me and Bostic, who was a Pro Bowler, the same way."

Bostic, who'd been in the league for six years, didn't like that very much. He openly quarreled with Saban in practice, frequently told his coach to "fuck off," and fell asleep during Saban-led meetings. Saban never laid off Bostic, but he did grow tired of the antics of perhaps his most talented player. Eventually, he went to Glanville, who told him to call out Bostic the next time he went astray. In one meeting, Saban finally did just that and Bostic, who towered over Saban, reacted by jumping out of his seat and attacking his position coach. The two wrestled on the floor for a few moments before the other players broke up the fight.

In the end, Saban's coaching got through. Though they would remain overshadowed by the offense, the Oilers defense became a solid unit, especially in the secondary, where they were often left in one-on-one coverage and open to attack because of the frequent blitzes. They mostly held their own.

Saban was competitive off the field, as well. He often played racquetball against Helton. "He was very physical," says Helton. "One day we were playing and he drilled me in the back. I turned around and looked at him and he said, 'You gotta move your feet.' I wanted to go back and hit him in his little mouth. But he was a good player, and you had to know that you were going to get hit with the ball. Nick was fun to be around in a nonwork environment if you were one of his friends. But when you went to work, Nick was so disciplined. 'F-U-N' was just not part of the equation."

It was for his boss, though. By that time, Glanville was nearly as famous for his off-the-field antics as he was for his coaching. For Saban, football—everything about it—was deadly serious. Not so for Glanville. "We worked hard and practiced hard but, boy, we played hard, too," Glanville says.

Glanville famously dressed in all black on the sidelines, in homage to Johnny Cash. He owned a 1950 black Mercury because that's what James Dean once drove. He left tickets at the Astro-dome's will-call window for Elvis Presley. He once left tickets in Seattle for D. B. Cooper, the man who in 1971 had hijacked a Boe-ing 727, parachuted into the Washington State mountains with two hundred thousand dollars, and disappeared. ("We got into a bit of trouble for that one because the FBI showed up to see if he'd actu-ally come," says Glanville.) Glanville once cut an off-season film session short to take Saban and his fellow assistants to the Houston Motor Speedway to race cars. Later in his career, Glanville would stop a scrimmage and put the singer James Brown in at running back. (Brown, in boots and street clothes, took a toss sweep around the end for a touchdown.) Glanville ran practices seemingly by the seat of his pants, with no written scripts, a highly unconventional tactic for a head coach in the NFL or in college, for that matter. "I think Nick was a little shocked at the way we did things here," says Glanville. "I do think I remember him smiling twice."

In the last regular season game of the 1988 season, the Oilers trav-eled to Cleveland to play the Browns in the stadium with a section nicknamed the "Dawg Pound" for its famously rabid fans. Though the Oilers lost that game on a fourth-quarter touchdown pass, they finished the season 10-6 and headed right back to Cleveland the following week for a wild card playoff game on Christmas Eve. Be-fore that game, Glanville had some fun with the Cleveland fans. He told the media: "I don't think Santa Claus really wants to come to Cleveland." A picture of him taking a bite out of a dog biscuit ran in the Cleveland newspapers. On the morning of the game, Glan-ville received a death threat. The coaching staff all wore bulletproof vests under their jackets.

Saban was in the press box for the game, overseeing his sec-ondary. He later told the *Houston Chronicle* that he felt safe. The coaches on the field, however, attempted to stay as far away from Glanville as they could. Over the headset, Saban kept telling Floyd

Reese, the Oilers' linebacker coach, to go ask Glanville about something. Reese replied: "I'm not asking Jerry about anything."

Despite three Warren Moon interceptions, the Oilers won the wild card game, 24–23. Saban's secondary allowed the Browns just 192 passing yards. The next week, the Oilers went to Buffalo to face the high-powered Bills' offense in the divisional round of the playoffs. Saban's secondary again played well, limiting Bills quarterback Jim Kelly to 237 passing yards, but the Bills ended the Oilers season, winning the game, 17–10.

Midway through the next season, Saban believed he was ready for a college head-coaching job and began to send out feelers to various programs. Glanville not only encouraged the search, he actually helped. "It was pretty clear to me that he wanted to be a head coach in college," says Glanville. "The fun of coaching for me was when one of my assistants could get a better job." In December 1989, Saban got an interview at the University of Toledo, which happened to be a place where Glanville had also interviewed a few years before. "I practiced with Nick for the interview, got him prepared," says Glanville. "He came back and said, 'Every question they asked me was one we had practiced.'"

In late December, Saban took the Toledo job, but he had to finish with the Oilers first. That year, the Oilers made the playoffs again, this time facing the Steelers, a team they'd defeated twice already that season by a combined score of 50–16.

The Oilers had some locker room trouble heading into the game. Richard Johnson, a defensive back and the Oilers' first-round draft pick in 1985, had been a malcontent throughout the season, missing meetings and pregame walk-throughs. On December 28—three days before the Oilers' playoff game—Saban and Johnson got into a heated argument during a meeting before practice. Johnson went ballistic, tearing up the meeting room. He was suspended for the game. Saban caught some flak from the local media for making such a drastic move right before the playoffs. Perhaps because he felt the freedom of already having a new job, Saban took the unusual step of publicly defending himself. "This year Richard has done nothing to deserve to play," a visibly worked-up Saban told a Houston television station. "If anybody in this town thinks I would jeopardize my professional integrity by not playing the best guys to give us the best chance to win and be fair to our football team, you've got to be crazy."

Johnson's absence appeared to have no impact on the game. The Oilers held the Steelers to 112 passing yards, but the offense struggled, and they lost, 26–23, in overtime.* Saban packed up his belongings and was in Toledo the next day. Glanville later told the media that Saban was "the best thing that ever happened to me."

The conventional wisdom is that Saban didn't learn anything of much significance from Glanville during his two years in Houston, and that the chaos was driving the punctilious man mad. Glanville himself joked some years later to the *Palm Beach Post*, "I think he's been so successful because he listened to me. I always said, 'Remember how I did things, and do the opposite.' " †

In truth, though, Glanville had a significant impact on Saban and, along with Big Nick, Don James, George Perles, and, later, Bill Belichick, he became part of the holy quintet of Saban coaching mentors. Glanville gave Saban his first exposure to the professional game and let him earn his way—with all the bumps and bruises—to running an aggressive secondary. "Saban to this day still talks about himself as a secondary coach," says Chris B. Brown, the editor of the website Smart Football and the author of *The Essential Smart Football*. "Glanville was a real influence on him. His view was to play press man coverage all day. Saban is not quite willing to do

---

* The Steelers would be a bugaboo for Saban throughout his career in the NFL.

† Glanville was forced to resign from the Oilers after the 1989 season. He got the head-coaching job at the Atlanta Falcons shortly thereafter and offered Saban a job as his defensive coordinator. Saban declined.

that, but that philosophy is at the core of what he does, of challenging every single pass play."

Saban also took lessons from Glanville's disorderliness. When he finally became the head coach of his own team in 1990, his philosophy was the antithesis of Glanville's. He demanded absolute discipline and organization. There would be no frivolity.

5

The Front Porch

"**A** LOT OF people want to know why I want to come back to college football," Saban said at a press conference upon taking the Toledo Rockets job. He was thirty-eight years old, sporting a pair of large rimless eyeglasses and thick, dark leonine hair. "I think college football is a lot more fun. The involvement you have with the players, the influence you have on their lives at a time in their lives which is critical to their development, is a lot more fun and a lot more rewarding than the professional athlete."

It all sounded good, true, and from the heart at the time. Saban signed a three-year contract with Toledo, with a base salary of $65,000. The contract came with a buyout provision: Saban owed the school money if he left to take another college job before his contract ended. The buyout clause, however, did not say anything about him taking a job in the NFL, a stipulation that would come back to haunt the school and its athletic director, Al Bohl.

Saban stepped into a bit of a hornet's nest at Toledo. Just a few months before he arrived, Bohl had fired Dan Simrell, Toledo's all-time winningest coach, an alumnus of the school and a popular man on campus who had just posted a 6-5 record and finished in a tie for second in the MAC. His firing prompted protests on campus and attracted national attention in a scathing article in *Sports Illustrated* that slammed Bohl for what was described as misplaced priorities. Protestors delivered a petition with 22,500 signatures to the school's president, demanding the rehiring of Simrell.

In his own defense, Bohl told the media he was simply sick of mediocrity (Simrell had gone 22-21 in his last four seasons). Toledo was in the MAC (the same conference as Saban's alma mater, Kent State), so they weren't necessarily expected to compete for national titles. But Bohl wanted a winner. He also had another pressure to deal with, something he didn't highlight in his discussions with the press: The school had embarked on an $18 million renovation of its stadium, the Glass Bowl, complete with 26,000 new seats and corporate boxes. Bohl needed to sell tickets in 1990, and he believed Saban could help him.

Bohl says the entire situation back then was "an Excedrin headache." Saban went to the media and pleaded for the school and community to rally around the team, to let go of the past and concentrate on the present and the promising future. He eventually made Bohl's headache go away, at least temporarily.

Most first-year coaches inherit a poor team and face a major rebuild. That's why they're hired. Saban, instead, was taking over a team with some promise, one that was coming off two just-better-than-mediocre seasons and one that was loaded with juniors and seniors who were hungry for something more. The offense—the strength of the team—had eight returning starters, which included Kevin Meger, an athletic if somewhat unpolished quarterback; Richard Isaiah, a talented wide receiver; and Jerry Evans, a big, soft-handed tight end who would go on to play for three years in the NFL. Saban didn't think much of the talent level on defense, but he liked their attitude, describing them to a UPI reporter as a bunch of "junkyard dogs." The football media thought highly enough of Toledo's returning talent—and its first-year coach—to name the Rockets the preseason favorite in the MAC.

David Walkosky, a senior safety in 1990, remembers the team's first meeting with its new coach. "When Saban walked into the room, everything just stopped," he says. "He started in right away. He told us there were no freshmen, no sophomores, no juniors, and no seniors on the team. There were no starters. Everything was open.

I thought it was just lip service. But then a player named Dan Williams, a starter and a guy who would play in the NFL, stood up and openly questioned him. Saban kicked him off the team right then and there. He was our best defensive player, and he was gone. That set the tone right there."

When Saban became too demanding of his players on the Oilers, or went on one of his frequent tirades, they could effectively tune him out. They were pros and he was merely an assistant coach. Saban's college players didn't have that option. For the most part, they were on the one-year contracts known as scholarships, which could be revoked on a coach's whim. (Saban's assistants later successfully lobbied for Williams's reinstatement, with the appropriate disciplinary actions, of course.)

Saban instituted strict new academic policies for his players, which included mandatory study halls and required work with a troop of academic advisers. He gave each member of the team a three-ring binder with hundreds of pages. Along with the playbook, it included a guide on how the players would treat their fellow classmates and women on and off campus, and dietary instructions for players who either needed to gain or lose weight. The booklet was illustrated with some of Saban's favorite sayings (many cribbed from his father) about toughness, effort, and attitude, and pictures of Vince Lombardi and Paul "Bear" Bryant.

Shortly after that first meeting, the team began its winter conditioning program, modeled after Buck Nystrom's at Michigan State, and run by a man named Ken Mannie. "It was brutal, all blood, guts, and vomit," says Tom Amstutz, the Rockets' linebacker coach. Practices in the spring took on a new tenor, too. Simrell had been an offensive-minded coach, and "he screamed at us if we even touched a receiver in practice," says Walkosky. "Saban had us hit the receivers and try to knock the ball loose. It made everyone better." Some of the older players left the team, deciding they didn't want anything to do with this new coach. "Nick was fine with that. He figured it was better for them to quit now rather than at fourth-and-one at the one-yard line in a game," says Amstutz.

The kids who stayed were, for the most part, glad they did.

"Saban was able to simplify everything," says Darren Anderson, a junior defensive back. "He had his hands on everything. He had a strong personality, but you just trusted he knew what he was doing. So we just let our guard down and let him lead."

Saban got a late start on recruiting because of the Oilers' play-off game, but he hustled and turned out a respectable class in one month's time. He resorted to some unusual recruiting methods. Amstutz remembers one time when they were together recruiting a talented but troubled offensive lineman. During one visit, Saban put the kid on probation, before he'd even committed to Toledo. "As we walked out of the house, I turned to Nick and laughed and said, 'I've never seen that done,'" says Amstutz. "Nick just shrugged and said, 'The kid needs it.'" The lineman signed with Toledo and became a three-year starter.

Saban had a solid young coaching staff. Amstutz would later become the head coach at Toledo for eight years. Dean Pees, Toledo's defensive coordinator, now holds that same position for the Baltimore Ravens. The secondary coach, Phil Parker, who also played for Saban at Michigan State, is now the defensive coordinator at Iowa. At age fifty-eight, Ellis Rainsberger, the offensive line coach, was the oldest member of the staff, and he always called Saban "boy." "He was the only guy maybe ever to get away with that," says Walkosky. In practice, Saban couldn't help but get his hands on the secondary. "Phil [Parker] would recruit on Fridays, so Saban would coach the defensive backs that day," says Walkosky. "And he would inevitably change everything Phil did. When Phil came back from his trip, he'd come to me and say, 'Okay, what the fuck did he change?'" (Being Saban's secondary coach has always been the toughest coaching job on his teams.)

The Rockets won their first six games in the 1990 season. They didn't overwhelm anyone, but they played solidly on both sides of the ball. Saban had come to Toledo with visions of installing a wide-open offensive attack with the quarterback, Meger, similar to what Glanville had run with the Oilers. "But I was young," says Meger. "I was an athlete who was learning to play in a pro-style set and I struggled." So Saban simplified the offense, relying on a strong running game and an experienced offensive line.

On October 20, the Rockets traveled to Central Michigan for what appeared to be the quasi–conference championship game. Both teams were undefeated coming in. The Rockets led the game 12–7 in the fourth quarter, but Central Michigan scored a touchdown after a controversial call on a critical third down that sent Saban into a fit on the sidelines. Toledo missed a fifty-one-yard field goal attempt as time expired and lost by a point.

On the bus ride back to Toledo, Saban called Meger up to the front to talk. "Everyone got really quiet," says Meger, who had played an inconsistent game. "They thought he was going to ream me out. But he was calm. He talked to me like a father would. He asked me what he could do to help me get better. He was always calm after a loss. Calm and analytical."

Saban's fatherly relationship with Meger also extended off the field. Meger came from a broken home and didn't have much of a relationship with either of his parents. Earlier in the season, Saban had discovered that Meger had not invited his parents to the Rockets' opening home game, so he called them and invited them on his behalf. "It initially pissed me off," says Meger. "I didn't think it was any of his business." His parents ended up coming to the game, and Meger says it "turned out to be the bridge me and my family needed. I wasn't listening to my parents and they weren't listening to me, but we were clearly both listening to him. Things got smoother after that."

The Rockets lost only one other game that season, to Navy on a last-minute touchdown pass. They ended the season at 9-2, with the two losses by a combined five points. When Central Michigan was upset by Ball State late in the season, Toledo became the co-champions of the MAC.*

---

* Central Michigan, and not Toledo, got to go to the California Bowl because of its head-to-head victory.

In the 1990 season, after nearly two decades in the game, Saban finally accomplished what his father once had: He'd become a head coach and gained total control of a program. His players respected him. He had driven them and his coaches hard, and they had responded. And he'd won. His father never seemed far from his mind during that season, according to Amstutz. "It was clear that he really missed him," he says. "I've thought about this a lot since then, and I realize now that you could sense that in some part of his heart he felt driven because of his father, that part of what he did was dedicated to his father."

Bohl had every reason to believe that this was just the beginning for his coach and the Toledo program. Saban had recruited well during the season, convincing running back Casey McBeth, an all-AP Ohio high school player, to choose Toledo over some bigger programs. Bohl knew full well that budding young coaches used the MAC as a springboard to bigger and better jobs, but he also knew that most of those coaches stuck around to build and establish a program—and reputation—for at least a few years. Don James, after all, had stayed at Kent State for four seasons.

Then Saban's old friend Bill Belichick came calling.

In late January 1991, Belichick had crafted a masterful game plan in the Super Bowl as the New York Giants' defensive coordinator, holding a superb Buffalo Bills offense in check in the Giants' 20–19 upset win. Shortly thereafter, he was named the head coach of the Cleveland Browns and was given free rein to hire his assistants. One of his first calls was to Saban, whom he wanted as his defensive coordinator. The two men met and discussed the job at the NFL Scouting Combine. Saban then told Bohl that he was considering the job offer.

Bohl suddenly found himself in a bind. He had fired a popular coach the year before and put his reputation on the line for an unproven career assistant (Bohl's son also played defensive back for Saban on the 1990 team). That unproven coach had delivered in spades. Now he was possibly leaving. "We were 9-2, we were selling tickets, and then he comes in and tells me about

Belichick," says Bohl. "When he was in my office, he didn't want to go to the Browns. He made me feel, anyway, like he was really distraught."

Bohl tried to get Saban to stay, offering to increase his salary. Saban wavered, something he would do in an even more painful fashion a few times later in his career. He told the *Toledo Blade* that he didn't make his final decision until half an hour before what would become his final press conference at Toledo.

In that press conference, Saban broke the news that he was accepting the job as the Browns' defensive coordinator. As he spoke, he pursed his lips and frequently looked down at the podium he gripped with two hands. His eyes were puffy and red. He told the assembled members of the media: "I haven't cried for eighteen years—since my dad died—but I cried all afternoon. It was something I just couldn't pass up. . . . It's probably not fair to the University of Toledo. It's a little bit of a selfish decision. But I have a responsibility to my family." Saban would be more than doubling his salary in his new job.

Meger says he and his teammates knew something was up over the preceding days when Saban wasn't present for a few of the team's 5 a.m. winter workouts. "He never missed those," says Meger. "Then one day he gathered us together and told us he was leaving. He told us first. I can remember after he spoke, I was walking across the street, from the health center. He saw me and walked up and asked me if I was mad at him. I said, 'You're damn right I am.' We'd just come off a championship season. Later on I was okay with it, but I was pissed then."

Richard Isaiah, the team's best receiver, says he was surprised, but understood. "It was the Browns. If it had been Bowling Green, I would have had a problem. But some of the guys resented it. The community resented it a bit. We'd just gotten rid of our guy, he comes in, and then he jumps to the NFL. It didn't look good."

Bohl says now that he, too, understood, but that it was "a sad moment." Back then, though, he seemed a little more defensive. When asked about that critical lack of a buyout clause for the NFL

in Saban's contract, Bohl told the *Blade*: "You learn. The next football coach's contract will cover the pros, too." *

In the aftermath of Saban's departure, the *Blade* ran dueling edi-
torials. One condoned Saban's move and put the blame squarely on
Bohl. The other excoriated the coach: "It is not unusual, though,
that Nick Saban would want to leave. That is his history. Nine different stops in 18 years. . . . A guy like Saban gets a better offer and
he skedaddles."

To Saban detractors, leaving Toledo after just one year into a three-
year contract is merely the first betrayal of many to come. It's where
his reputation as a mercenary for hire is first revealed. It's one thing
to skip around as an assistant—that's expected. Assistant coaches
are essentially migrant workers, and moving around is often the
only way up. At Toledo, Saban was the *head* coach. He had made a
heartfelt plea for the support of the community, and had projected
the image of a man who would be sticking around for a bit, who
was committed to, at the very least, his initial contract and to building a sustainable program.

It's easy to see how Bohl could forgive and forget now, twenty-
five years later. Bohl is now known as the first athletic director to
hire Saban, as the man who first took a chance on an unknown
coach who has since won five national titles and is perhaps the
best in the business. In retrospect, Bohl looks like a genius. That
revision in history took a while to develop, though. At the time, it
certainly seems like Saban's leaving—after just one year and with
no protections afforded to the university—stung both Bohl and
the community, regardless of whether they could see his reasoning
or not.

What's also clear in retrospect, though, is that Saban gave
everything he had during his short stint at Toledo, in recruiting

---

* Bohl's next coach was Saban's old teammate at Kent State, Gary Pinkel, who
ended up staying at Toledo for a fruitful ten years before becoming the head coach
at Missouri.

and coaching and in the community, where he and Terry were always available for social gatherings and fund-raisers. He certainly didn't act like a man who was intent on skipping out after just one season.

In the end, he was made an offer that he believed he couldn't refuse, to coach with a man with whom he had shared those many front porch sessions. Saban and Belichick were two men who loved football and shared many of the same philosophies about the game. When they hung out together, they fed off each other and took the level of discourse about a rough-guy game to some higher plane. Though Saban is six months older, then he considered his friend as a more accomplished mentor, with the more pertinent experience. Belichick had spent his entire career to that point—sixteen years— in the NFL, and he had just guided a ferocious defense to one of the most famous upsets in Super Bowl history.

Saban and Belichick's relationship had continued to grow after Saban's year at Navy. They made it a point to visit each other a few times a year. Sometimes those meetings were clandestine, almost like a couple having an affair. When Saban was with the Oilers, he flew up to meet Belichick, despite the fact that Glanville had a strict rule about his assistants talking to other NFL coaches while under his employ. "We'd have these meeting spots," Saban recalled in a press conference in 2006. "West Point seemed like a place that we could hide out. So we went there and stayed for weekends, stayed in a hotel up there, and talked ball."

Glanville says now that had he known about these secret meetings, "I would have fired Saban on the spot."

The Cleveland Browns team that Belichick took over was a bit of an enigma. Just two seasons earlier, they'd made an inspired run to the AFC Championship game—their third trip in the past four years—and lost to John Elway and the Denver Broncos. The 1990 team, however, had been a disaster. The Browns had won only three games and their coach, Bud Carson—a key coaching figure in the 1970s Steelers dynasty (and someone whom Saban had gotten to know during his early-career visits to the Steelers)—was fired midway through the season. The 1990 Cleveland Browns gave up 462 points, more than any other defense would in the decade of the 1990s. Saban's task in 1991 was to fix that.

Though only 120 miles from Toledo, the Sabans' new home in Cleveland seemed worlds away. The professional game was a colder, less personal one. Saban and Terry had been a part of the community at Toledo, two of the most visible representatives of the school, a role Terry in particular had cherished. Defensive coordinators' wives and families in the NFL didn't take on those roles. It was neither expected nor desired of them. For Terry, especially as she raised their two young children, a college campus held much more allure, a preference she'd already formed by this time and would continue to hold throughout her husband's career.

At the time, her husband was also going back and forth about what his career goals indeed were. During his years as an assistant at Michigan State and with the Oilers, he believed that becoming a college head coach was what he wanted. Taking the Toledo job seemed only to solidify that feeling. Now, though, he was telling friends and the media that the Browns job appealed to him, mainly because it was a possible avenue to a head-coaching job in the NFL. His internal tug-of-war between the college game and the NFL would never be decisively settled, and there are those close to him who believe that even with his prodigious successes in the college ranks, the NFL still holds some allure for him to this day.

Working with Belichick was something Saban was eager to do, though. Finally, all of those enlightened discussions about football theories could be put into practice. The two men could build something together. What Saban didn't know going into the job was the level of exhaustion and frustration he would face. During a talk at the American Football Coaches Association convention in early 2014, Saban recalled his years with the Browns as the worst in his coaching life. Many assumed that the statement was likely some inside joke between him and Belichick, but it may have had a ring of truth to it. Though Belichick says today that Saban "is a great friend and there is no one that I have more respect for in the game of football," it is likely that their friendship has held up over the years in part because they don't work together anymore. The front porch would always remain their most comfortable place together.

One month before the 1991 season, Paul Brown, the namesake of the Cleveland franchise and its first coach, died. His death cast a pall over a team that seemed destined to repeat the misery of the season before. Bernie Kosar, a gangly quarterback with an unorthodox sidearm throwing motion, led the offense and was adored by the fans. He was a fairly accurate passer when given enough time, but he was limited by his lack of mobility. Elsewhere on offense, the Browns lacked playmakers.

The defense, as bad as it had been the year before, had a few bright spots. That year's first-round draft pick, Eric Turner, was the kind of big and athletic safety that Saban adored. Two promising young players, Michael Dean Perry and Rob Burnett, anchored the defensive line. Behind them, the linebacker corps featured Clay Matthews Jr., already a grizzled vet heading into his fourteenth year with the Browns (he would play for nineteen years in the NFL and is the father of Green Bay Packers star Clay Matthews III). The Browns ended up 6-10 that year, doubling the number of wins from the season before. The biggest reason for the improvement was the defense, which moved from the league's cellar to fourteenth.

Though Saban seemed committed to Belichick and the Browns, he never stayed too far off the radar screen of college athletic directors. In January 1992, Perles again began talking to an NFL team (this time the Indianapolis Colts). It seemed a foregone conclusion that if Perles left Michigan State, Saban would be offered the job, something he would have had a hard time passing up. Perles ended up again staying with the Spartans, but his various flirtations with NFL teams would wear on the patience of Michigan State administrators and play a role in his eventual dismissal.

Saban was also offered the job at Northwestern around that

time, but he declined it, an easy decision for him. The academics-first school had finished at or near the bottom of the Big Ten since the 1970s. A far more intriguing rumor surfaced toward the end of the 1992 season when John Cooper's job at Ohio State seemed in peril (Cooper had taken over for Earle Bruce). Taking that job would have brought Saban back in a full redemptive circle after being fired there in the early 1980s. Saban downplayed the reports, though, telling the *Columbus Dispatch* that he was happy with the Browns. "Someone told me once, 'You should get your ducks in line for the Ohio State job,'" Saban told the paper. "To be honest, I don't have any ducks." That same year, Belichick brought in Al Groh to coach the linebackers. Groh had been the New York Giants' defensive coordinator in 1991 and had worked with Belichick there earlier. The move seemed like a precautionary one on Belichick's part, taken because of the burgeoning interest in his defensive coordinator.

Though Saban publicly proclaimed himself happy, it was in his second season, in 1992, that the strain of the Browns job began to show. Belichick turned out to be the most demanding boss Saban had ever had, a man wholly consumed with the game who expected the same level of intensity and focus during those eighteen-hour days from his assistants. For four years, Saban basically didn't see Terry and his kids from July through January. Louis Riddick, an ESPN analyst who played for Belichick and Saban for two years, says Saban would often talk about the demands Belichick put on his coaches. "Nick would say that coaching for Bill didn't leave time for anything else," he says. "He would look at me and say, 'You ever watch film with Bill?'" Belichick was notorious for the amount of film he watched, of other teams and his own players, taking the time to pore over some things that would seem to be of little consequence. "I'd come in at ten p.m. and Nick and Bill would be watching film of our bag and agility drills from practice," says Ed Sutter, a linebacker on the team. "It was amazing."

Saban worked tirelessly on improving the defense while adding to his own workload by also coaching the secondary himself. At one point during the 1992 season, Saban's defense didn't allow a touchdown for thirteen consecutive quarters, a foreshadowing of the dominant force they would become a few years later. After pulling a few all-nighters in preparation for a game against Houston and their unusual "run and shoot" spread offense, an exhausted Saban told the beat reporter at the *Dispatch,* "I don't know how many more of those I have in me." Later in the season, that same reporter would write that Saban was "running himself into the ground."

Part of the strain was caused by an unexpected clashing with his boss. Belichick was an open-minded coach who always considered well-thought-out ideas, and he let Saban pretty much run his defense in practice. However, Belichick also always had the final say on game plans and schemes, especially on defense, where he had earned the reputation of being something of a genius.* Saban and Belichick differed in their visions for that side of the ball. Saban believed, particularly as his defense matured in his last two years with the Browns, that it could become more complicated and dynamic. "Bill was more conservative," says Rob Burnett, a defensive end. "Nick wanted to let the dogs loose, but Bill held him at bay. Bill would override him. You could see the look of frustration on Nick's face."

Burnett says the team actually had two defensive playbooks— Saban's and Belichick's. "Nick's was a lot more aggressive," he says. "But we didn't use his much. I honestly think if we had, we'd have been a better team defensively."

In 1992, the Browns ended up 7-9, in third place in the AFC Central. The defense improved to tenth best in the league. Despite the improvement, the team's owner, Art Modell—perhaps sensing

---

* In David Halberstam's book *The Education of a Coach*, Belichick's father, Steve, had a rather funny riposte to his son's oft-awarded "genius" label. "You are talking about someone who walks up and down a football field," he said.

Saban's exhaustion—asked Belichick to hire a secondary coach so Saban could become more of a "roving" defensive coordinator. Saban was reluctant to give up the hands-on role of the secondary. Eventually, he and Belichick convinced Modell that, because the secondary heading into the 1993 season was so young and raw, Saban needed to continue to coach them. Modell relented.

That 1993 season was a calamitous one for the Browns. They began with three straight wins, and were 5-2 heading into the half-way point of the season. During that season, Belichick benched—then released—Kosar, one of the most popular players in the franchise's history (Belichick believed his quarterback had taken too many hits and had "lost it"). The Browns dropped seven of their last nine games. It was hard to tell at the end of another 7-9 season that the Browns—and particularly their defense—were poised for a special season in 1994.

As has been the case throughout his coaching career, Saban's players had varied opinions about him. He had a hot temper and a never-waning intensity. His nickname on the team was "Grumpy." Some players, like Burnett, loved him. "I got along great with Nick," he says. "He knew how to teach. He was the best defensive backs coach I was ever around. He'd take guys back there who were mar-ginal at best, or guys who otherwise wouldn't have made an NFL team, and turned them into players."

Others, like Sutter, didn't like him much at all. "He wasn't very personable, which is okay because he wasn't paid to be personable," he says. "But he tried to intimidate and threaten players, even vets like Clay Matthews. That works in college, but not in the pros. He was kind of a little tyrant walking around out there. And because he was just a coordinator, you could blow him off, and sometimes guys did just that."

For most players, though, the opinions were somewhat mixed. Harlon Barnett had been a defensive back for Saban at Michigan State and was already on the Browns team the year before Saban arrived (Barnett now coaches the secondary at Michigan State). "I was so interested when he came to the Browns," says Barnett. "His approach just doesn't work that well in the pros. Vets don't like to be yelled at. They say, 'I'm a grown man!'" Saban's demeanor with professional players never did change, which would come back to haunt him in his later stint in the NFL.

Saban's knowledge of the game was the only thing that kept some of his players from tuning him out completely. "The guys would slowly start to realize that he really knew what he was talking about, and that got him the respect," says Barnett. "The man is a nut, but he can coach football."

Riddick, a safety who signed with the Browns in 1993, felt the Saban wrath more personally. "From the first practice on, he was all over me. He gave me no break, just pressure, pressure, pressure. For a small guy, he has this booming big-man voice. I could never tell if he even liked me," he says.

Riddick didn't play much in his first season, but halfway through 1994, Saban told him he'd be on the field for some of the team's pass-defense packages. "From that point on, he kind of took a different tone with me. It was almost like because I never went into the tank, because he never broke me, I earned his respect. And he can break you. I never let him see what he did to me. I didn't break in front of him. But there were times I would go home to my girlfriend, who is now my wife, and tell her, 'I don't know if I can play for this guy, he's so demanding.'"

Riddick adds a sentiment shared by many of Saban's players, past and present: "The players, if they're being honest and whether they like him or not, will tell you that the guy flat-out knows what he's talking about. The question is, can you wade through the bullshit and get the message, or does the bullshit prevent you from hearing it?"

Saban was equally demanding of the coaches who worked under him. In 1994, Modell finally got his wish when Belichick hired Rick Venturi to coach the secondary to free up Saban for a bigger-picture role with the defense. When Venturi arrived, Saban insisted that they meet on early Saturday mornings in the off-season to go over the secondary schemes. "He just put me in a clinic," says Venturi. "I sat there and took piles of meticulous notes. I still have them. And you know what? He never really stopped coaching the secondary anyway."

When Pat Hill arrived as the Browns' offensive line and tight ends coach in 1992, he ran the scout teams in practice against Saban's defense. "I had to draw up the cards for Nick," he says. "Usually it's not that big of a deal, they don't have to be that detailed. But with Nick, they had to be drawn up with the exact alignments and splits, and if they weren't, if I was half a man off in alignment, he let me know it. It took me a little while to figure out exactly what he needed, but I did, and I took great pride in making those cards right. It didn't seem like a big deal to me at first, but it turned out to be a big part of our success, getting those details exactly right."

Chuck Bresnahan, Saban's former player at Navy, was the linebacker and quality control coach under Saban for one year at Cleveland. "We had an inside joke on the staff that whenever we entered the football building, it was like we had to get ready for war. Nick was different outside of the building, more personable. But once inside, it was all business all the time," he says. "Most of us [defensive assistants] sat in a big room. We knew when Nick was coming because he always jingled the change in his pocket when he walked. If we were bullshitting and we heard that, we'd all quickly pull out our playbooks. There were certainly times when I wanted to punch Nick in the nose but, at the same time, I knew I was getting better as a football coach."

Saban didn't ever seem to relax on the practice field or in meetings. "I just remember him in meetings just sitting there and rocking," says Kirk Ferentz, the offensive line coach for the Browns from 1993 to 1995. "He would go faster and faster if he was getting excited about something." On the practice field, Saban was always worrying a plug of Red Man in his cheek. "He could never sit still," says Everson Walls, a veteran defensive back who finished his career with the Browns. "At practice he just paced back and forth. It reminded you of a lion in a cage." *

Saban did calm down, at least when it came to football, only during the actual games. "On game day, he was really different," says Riddick. "He was cool and analytical. He never had some of those fits like he does on the sidelines now at Alabama. We never saw that. But he would explode at practice. We couldn't wait to get to Sunday."

Off the field, as Bresnahan said, his fellow coaches got a glimpse of a more relaxed Saban at the annual Kentucky Derby party that he and Terry hosted for them and their families. "We'd all take numbers out of a hat and bet on the race," says Hill. "We really had a great time at those parties. Those were some of my most memorable times on the team."

By 1994, Belichick had assembled what, in retrospect, was a truly remarkable coaching and personnel staff. Along with Nick Saban, his assistant coaches were:

- Kirk Ferentz (current head coach at Iowa)
- Pat Hill (head coach at Fresno State from 1997 to 2011)
- Kevin Spencer (a former special teams coach with the San Diego Chargers, Indianapolis Colts, Pittsburgh Steelers, and Arizona Cardinals)

---

* Walls relates a story about Saban that happened after the 1993 season. That year, Walls, a fourteen-year player who had been one of the better defensive backs of his era, was let go by the Browns. Walls says that like most veterans who are basically forced to retire, he was angry, not wanting to face the facts of his own physical decline. At the time, he says, he blamed Saban, his hard-assed coach. After the season, Walls says he was on a flight leaving Cleveland when he suddenly looked up and there was Saban walking down the aisle toward him. "He had this huge smile on his face and he was like, 'Hey, Everson!' He was with his family. I'd never seen him like that. I'd never seen him smile. He was so engaging. It actually caught me off guard. I was so shocked I kind of blew him off. But later on I realized that that might have been the real Nick, that sometimes when you're a coach you have to separate emotionally. I realized that I didn't treat him the way I should have that day, so a few years later, I called him and I apologized for the way I acted."

- Chuck Bresnahan (former defensive coordinator at the Oakland Raiders and current defensive coordinator at Central Florida)
- Scott O'Brien (a former special teams coach with the New England Patriots)
- Rick Venturi (longtime defensive assistant in the NFL, for the Browns, New Orleans Saints, and St. Louis Rams)

The personnel staff included:

- Ozzie Newsome (current general manager of the Baltimore Ravens)
- Michael Lombardi (former general manager of the Browns and now a personnel assistant with the Patriots)
- Jim Schwartz (former head coach of the Detroit Lions and current defensive coordinator of the Philadelphia Eagles)
- Scott Pioli (former general manager of the Kansas City Chiefs and now the assistant general manager of the Falcons)

The Browns' weekly Tuesday staff meetings during that year in particular have gained legendary status. "I wish I had tapes of them," says Venturi. They functioned as extended versions of the Saban-Belichick front porch meetings, with the addition of ten more football-savvy participants. "Bill encouraged different views and he was a great listener," says Ferentz. "So many great ideas came out of those meetings."

Those were also the meetings when some of Saban's more extravagant ideas for the defense were shot down.

There is some truth to the conventional notion that Saban and Belichick are alike, in demeanor and as coaches. Both men love defense and are systematic and detailed taskmasters. Both are perfectionists. And neither seems to enjoy dealing with the media very much. "Philosophically, they look at football the same," says Riddick. "They think the same type of players work on defense. They want to be strong down the middle, a big middle linebacker and big physical safeties, then go from there. They always want to defend the middle of the field first, to make the offense throw the ball outside, and if they come across the middle, then they'd get the hell knocked out of them."

Despite the fact that Belichick never let Saban do all he wanted with the Browns' defense, Saban did absorb a lot of lessons from his boss. He learned how to better evaluate players, especially in the secondary, where both men stressed athleticism and the ability to play man-to-man and ball skills (that is, being able to knock away or intercept a pass). Later, when Saban got head-coaching jobs, he drove his staff as hard as Belichick did at Cleveland. "Nowadays, everyone wants to learn the tricks of the trade rather than learning the trade," says Bresnahan. "It wasn't like that with Bill and Nick. Everything was so detailed." Perhaps the biggest lesson Saban learned from his friend was how to run an entire organization. Belichick was a master at getting everyone involved with the team on the same page by outlining exactly everyone's individual responsibility. Saban has often publicly noted that his favorite saying of Belichick's, which was posted on the wall of the Browns' locker room, was the simple but powerful "Do your job."

There are some significant differences, though, which went beyond Saban's desire to run a more complicated defense. Saban had a hot temper. "He could fly off the handle in meetings," says Venturi. "Bill was more methodical and consistent every day. He was more even-keeled." Belichick wasn't much of a yeller, either. "Bill would get his point across by being sarcastic, by questioning your intelligence. It got on your nerves sometimes," says Riddick. "Sure, Nick would yell a lot, but at least he was more straightforward. You did it his way or he got someone else in there who would." There was also a difference in motivation. Belichick grew up in relative comfort and attended private schools. "I always got the sense that Nick seemed like a guy with a big chip on his shoulder," says Bresnahan. "Going back to his childhood, he's always had to work for every single thing he's gotten."

The 1994 season was the high-water mark of the Belichick-era Browns, thanks mainly to the defense. Belichick and Saban had assembled a roster with an effective mix of veterans (the now-seasoned Burnett and Perry were joined by linebackers Carl Banks and Pepper Johnson, two stalwarts of Belichick's Super Bowl–winning defense with the Giants) and younger players, like safety Eric Turner and the team's first-round draft pick in 1994, cornerback Antonio Langham. The first sign that something special was in the works was in the third game of the season, at home against the Arizona Cardinals, when the Browns won, 32–0, and forced three turnovers. The shutout, though, wasn't good enough for Saban, who was fuming after the game, believing his defense should have had three more turnovers and demonstrating for the first time—to the public, at least—that wins left him far angrier and nervous than losses. The victory over the Cardinals began a five-game winning streak that got the Browns off to a 6-1 start.

Despite the fast start and the stellar play of the defense, the Browns had some concerns. Even as Saban whipped his defense into a world-class unit, the mediocre-at-best offense remained a heavy anchor. "If we'd had an offense that was even above average, I seriously believe we'd have gone to the Super Bowl," says Riddick. The middling offense left Saban frustrated. Rumors again began to swirl that he was in line for various head-coaching jobs, most notably at Stanford, where Bill Walsh was on his way to a 3-7-1 season and leaving the coaching profession for good. This time, the rumors seemed more significant. "We knew Nick was eventually going to leave because of his frustrations with Bill," says Burnett. "They had a good relationship, but with their differences, it was just a matter of time."

That time came on November 8, 1994, when Perles was fired at Michigan State, after failing to lead the Spartans to a winning season for four straight years, and as rumors swirled of a possible grade-tampering scandal. (Perles was allowed to coach the team's remaining two games.) Saban immediately pursued the job with the full support of Belichick and the rest of the Cleveland staff. "We didn't want to break up what we had here, but everyone was in his corner," says Venturi, who drove Saban to the airport to fly up for his interview with Michigan State, then picked him up later that night.

Saban was the front-runner for the job right away. At least he believed he was. A week or so after his interview, however, media reports indicated that Michigan State was leaning toward hiring Fran Ganter, an assistant under Joe Paterno at Penn State. A few days later, the *Philadelphia Inquirer* reported that Ganter was actually offered the job but declined it. "That was an interesting week," says Venturi. "Nick came into my office and looked pretty disappointed, but I told him not to worry about it."

Ultimately, Saban was offered the job and accepted it on December 3, 1994, telling the media that he felt like he was "coming home." According to Sutter, when word of Saban's hiring filtered back to the locker room, several of his players stood up and clapped, happy to be getting rid of the "tyrant."

They'd have to wait a little bit longer, though. Modell declared Saban "untouchable" until the end of the Browns' season, which had four games to go, plus a likely spot in the playoffs. This left Saban in a tough spot regarding his new job. According to NCAA rules, he couldn't recruit for Michigan State while he was employed by the Browns, which meant—if Cleveland made the playoffs and continued to advance—he'd have to condense his first year of recruiting into just a few weeks. It also left Saban totally exhausted as he worked the two jobs at once. He handled his Michigan State business on the phone during his twenty-five-minute commute to and from the Browns' facility and during quick flights to East Lansing whenever Belichick gave him a free afternoon (which wasn't often), and he continued to push himself to the limit with the Browns' defense. The strain manifested itself physically: Saban's hair started to go gray and he looked haggard for the first time in his career. (He arguably looks younger today than he did back in late 1994.)

It didn't help that the 9-3 Browns lost a sloppy game to the 5-7 Giants the day after Saban took the Michigan State job. They bounced back quickly. In the next game, they traveled to Irvine, Texas, to take on the 11-2 Dallas Cowboys, a team led by the formidable offensive trio of quarterback Troy Aikman, running back Emmitt Smith, and receiver Michael Irvin. The Browns held Aikman to just 177 yards passing in a 19–14 upset win, their finest of the season. When the last second ticked off the clock at Texas

Stadium, Belichick, in a rare show of emotion, jumped into Saban's arms. Their collaboration—a memorable one, even if it wasn't always smooth—was coming to an end.

The Browns finished the year 11-5. The defense—the best in the league by far—allowed only 204 points, exactly 258 points fewer than they'd allowed the season before Saban arrived. The Browns made the playoffs for the only time during the Belichick era. The good news for Saban: His defense had led them there (and he used his $8,000 playoff bonus to pay off his in-laws' mortgage). The bad news was that the victory cost him more invaluable time for his new job.

In the wild card game, the Browns hosted the New England Patriots, a team coached by Belichick's former boss Bill Parcells. Cleveland won, 20–13, harassing Patriots quarterback Drew Bledsoe into throwing three interceptions. Cleveland's next task was to travel to Pittsburgh to play the Steelers in the divisional round. Though the Browns that year had handled most of the teams they'd faced, the Steelers had been the hump they couldn't get over—they'd lost to them twice.

On the day of the game, a cold sleet fell on the hard Astroturf at Three Rivers Stadium. "I remember coming out for pregame warm-ups and Greg Lloyd [a Steelers linebacker] was out there in a cutoff gray T-shirt with his belly button showing," says Riddick. "He just stood there and glared at us when we came out and started barking at [quarterback Vinny] Testaverde and our offense, and I was like, 'Oh, no, this isn't good.' The Steelers defense just intimidated the shit out of our offense."

The Steelers crushed the Browns, 29–9. Saban was in East Lansing that evening, having dinner with a dozen potential recruits.*

---

*Though the Browns were preseason favorites to reach the Super Bowl the next season, the franchise went straight downhill after that playoff loss to the Steelers. The next year, Belichick appointed Venturi to replace Saban as his defensive coordinator. Venturi—pushing himself to replicate Saban's success—was forced to take a leave of absence before the season began because of exhaustion. Midway through that season, Art Modell infamously announced that the franchise was leaving Cleveland for a new home in Baltimore. The team ended up going 5-11 on the season, and Belichick was fired.

———————

Venturi says he remembers near the end of the 1994 Browns season when Saban was working the two jobs nearly to the point of collapse. One evening, Saban walked into Venturi's office, slump-shouldered and hollow-eyed, lamenting the fact that he just didn't have the time to properly set up his staff and recruit at Michigan State. Venturi, trying to lighten his friend's mood, told him: "Just send Terry up there to do it."

The remark—a humorous nod to Terry's rapidly growing presence in her husband's football life—turned out to be prescient.

PART II

6

"Why Can't He Be Happy?"

BEFORE BECOMING the president of Michigan State University in 1993, M. Peter McPherson had fashioned for himself a pretty impressive résumé—special assistant to President Gerald Ford, the head of the U.S. Agency for International Development (USAID) under President Ronald Reagan, the deputy secretary of the U.S. Treasury from 1987 to 1989, and an executive vice president of Bank of America, where he managed $600 million in assets. That experience left him well prepared for his role at Michigan State, especially when it came to fund-raising and handling the endowment, and academic affairs and public outreach. The only attribute he lacked was a familiarity with athletics, which happens to be an important (and lucrative) facet of the university. In fact, when it came to the sport of football, according to Joel Ferguson, a longtime trustee of the school, McPherson "didn't know shit." Nonetheless, when the school needed to find a replacement for the fired George Perles, McPherson installed himself as the point man in the search.

Nick Saban was not his first choice. Depending on whom you ask, he wasn't his second one, either. McPherson says the first man he reached out to was Nebraska's coach, Tom Osborne. Though Osborne was in the midst of an undefeated season when the offer was made in late 1994, at the time he was known as a coach who could get his team to the brink of a national championship, but no further. McPherson was prepared to make Osborne the first million-dollar coach in college football. "We came really close to getting him," he says. Osborne declined the offer and went on to win the first of his three national titles at the end of the 1994 season. (A few months later, Florida State's Bobby Bowden became the first million-dollar college football coach.)

Fran Ganter, the coordinator of Penn State's record-breaking offense (in 1994, Penn State averaged 477 yards and 47 points a game), may also have been offered the job. McPherson says now that he only had "close discussions" with Ganter. Terry Denbow, Michigan State's spokesman at the time, says he remembers actually handing Ganter a contract at one point, just as the *Philadelphia Inquirer* had reported. "After that, I'm not exactly sure what happened," says Denbow. "I just remember Peter calling me a few days later and telling me, 'I want Nick Saban.'"

Though not Michigan State's first choice, Saban ultimately won the job because of his interview with McPherson. The day after the Cleveland Browns lost to the Kansas City Chiefs in the eleventh game of their 1994 season, Saban flew to Detroit at 5 p.m., after a practice. He met McPherson, Denbow, and Merrily Dean Baker, Michigan State's athletic director, in a conference room in the Detroit airport. It was dinnertime, so McPherson arranged for food.

McPherson's main worry with Saban was that the young coach was merely a disciple of the man whom he'd just fired. Saban allayed that fear, with his words and his demeanor. He placed a yellow legal pad filled with pages of handwritten notes on the table, and immediately took control of the interview. He described his connection to the school and his love for the program, but distanced himself from Perles. "He basically said he had his own way of doing things," says Denbow.

Saban laid out a detailed plan for turning around the program, both on and off the field. One by one, he listed the assistants he was going to hire. Above all, he made this single point: He didn't want just any job in football—he wanted this one. "Nick was very impressive," says McPherson. "He sat there with that yellow pad and explained how committed he was to Michigan State, how he knew the place, and how much he wanted the job. He was very definitive about his interest and commitment."

Denbow takes it a step further. "It was the best interview I've ever seen and I've seen a lot of them," he says. "He was well prepared and focused. He looked everyone in the eye. He conveyed a sense of getting things done. There wasn't a phony thing in that interview."

Nearly three hours later, Saban stood and picked up his yellow pad. He had a plane to catch back to Cleveland, where he had to begin to prepare his defense for a game against the Oilers. As he was leaving, Baker glanced down at the untouched plate of food in front of Saban and said: "Do you want me to wrap that up for you?"

The Michigan State head-coaching job would turn out to be Saban's proving ground, his postgraduate degree in coaching. Though his overall record wouldn't necessarily demonstrate it, in Saban's five years there he completely turned around the performance and attitude of the entire program. He learned—sometimes the hard way—how to navigate some of the off-the-field matters that a good coach must master: the administrative duties, the various power struggles that occur within the chain of command, the glad-handing of boosters and the media. Saban made some friends for life at the school. He lost a few, as well. His stay at Michigan State would be punctuated by his dramatic and agonizing departure.

During his time at Michigan State (1995–99), three key figures emerged in Saban's life. They helped form him then, and continue to do so to this day. The first person was Terry, who, of course, had always played a big role. It was in East Lansing, however, that she began to get involved in more than just his home life, and where they formed a true professional partnership. The second person was a backwoodsy-looking professor of psychiatry who would become the unlikely coarchitect of what's now known as "the Process." The third—who appeared late in Saban's tenure at Michigan State—was a portly, affable, and aggressive man named Jimmy Sexton, who became an avatar for Saban's continued desire for approval and eventually—thanks to his most famous client—the most powerful agent in college football.

Saban officially started his new job at Michigan State the evening of January 7, 1995, a few hours after the Browns lost their playoff game against the Steelers. His contract paid a base annual salary of $135,000, with a bonus of up to $150,000 if the grades of his Spartan players improved, he stayed away from NCAA infractions, and he won a majority of the games he coached. Saban and Terry would eventually put some of that money into the construction of a new house, though when they first arrived in East Lansing, they lived for a spell in the home of a Michigan State film professor named Jim Cash, who was perhaps better known as the screenwriter of the Hollywood films *Top Gun* and *Turner & Hooch*. At his first press conference, Saban was asked if he was merely a short-timer at Michigan State, as he had been at Toledo. He replied: "I'm committed to staying at Michigan State for as long as it takes to be a championship team." He wouldn't quite get that far, in part because of the dreadful state of the program he was taking over.

At his first head-coaching job, at Toledo, Saban had inherited a solid team. This time, he did not. The cupboard was bare, enough so that Saban, a few months into his new job, couldn't help but express some thinly veiled criticism of his old boss. "George [Perles] gave me a great opportunity professionally in 1983. We took over a 2-9 situation and in five years built it to a top-ten team, a Big Ten championship, and a Rose Bowl victory. I think George did an outstanding job," he told the *Sporting News*. "What has happened since that time, I really don't know. I wasn't here, but we certainly don't have the quality of players."* The Spartans were particularly weak on the offensive and defensive lines, positions that Saban would put much focus on during his abridged, three-week recruiting period.

It turned out that many of those returning players also had seri-

---

* Saban's statements only further inflamed an already bitter Perles, who had filed two lawsuits against Michigan State after he was fired, for breach of contract and age discrimination. By midseason, though, Perles had dropped the lawsuits and patched up his relationship with his former protégé, when Saban invited him to attend practice and watch some film.

ous academic issues, something Saban discovered only after taking the job. It appeared that he also would be facing a potentially serious obstacle when it came to recruiting more talented players: The Spartan football program was facing possibly serious NCAA sanctions for alleged academic fraud and cash payments made to recruits, all of which happened under Perles. (Saban *did* know about this before he took the job.) The loss of several scholarships was among the feared punishments.

Saban cobbled together a staff that he believed would help turn things around, mixing in some former colleagues with some new blood. His old friend Gary Tranquill was hired as the offensive coordinator; Dean Pees, Saban's defensive coordinator at Toledo, came in to run the defense; Mark Dantonio, a bright up-and-coming coach, left Kansas to oversee the Spartans' secondary; and Saban's former strength and conditioning coach Ken Mannie was poached from the Toledo staff. "When the job opened up, I got a call at three a.m.," says Mannie. "I jumped out of bed and picked up the phone. It was Nick. He said, 'Ken, did I wake you?' "

With his staff in place, Saban set about to reverse the downward course of the program. He set up mandatory study halls and training meals for his players. "It was amazing. He was physically there to make sure we checked in," says Flozell Adams, an offensive tackle. Saban also created what he called "peer intervention programs," essentially leaving some of the disciplinary measures on the team to a handful of players who had been selected by their peers to be leaders. He believed that when his players had a say in the rules, and in the creation of those rules, it provided them with a more meaningful stake in the fate of the entire program. From his first meeting with his players, says the quarterback Tony Banks, Saban "put it all on us, the consequences and the repercussions if we didn't do things the way he wanted." Some players balked at the changes, and paid the price during the season. "We had some preseason All-Americans who rode the bench," says Muhsin Muhammad, a wide receiver. "Saban was interested in winning and not in making a bunch of friends. If you did your job, the guy loved you."

Saban's point to his players was made most emphatically with the implementation of the brutal "Fourth Quarter" winter conditioning program, done under the command of Mannie. It involved running, punching, jumping and sidestepping, power workouts, and agility drills. Some days were dedicated to the mechanics of sprinting, others to working on honing quick-twitch reactions to visual or verbal cues. The idea, like boot camp in the military, was to break the players down, then gradually build them back up. "It's really more mental than physical," says Mannie. "We try to get to a point where there's nothing they will face in a game, from a physical and effort and discipline and toughness standpoint, that they haven't faced before." Brian Mosallam, an offensive lineman who had played for two years under Perles, says Saban's conditioning program was "probably the two toughest months of my life."

The strength and conditioning coaching position remains one of the most important on a Saban-led staff. He wants these coaches to be alpha dogs. ("I show the players the weight room and tell them, 'I pissed in all four corners. This is my territory,'" says Mannie.) The strength and conditioning coaches—along with the trainers— spend a lot of one-on-one time with the players, and Saban relies on them to become critical liaisons. When Saban and the rest of the field coaches are out recruiting, these guys effectively run the team. Like Mannie (who stayed at Michigan State after Saban left), Saban's subsequent strength and conditioning coaches, Tommy Moffitt (LSU) and Scott Cochran (Alabama), have been invaluable contributors to his success.

The first off-season in Saban's Michigan State head-coaching stint contained some memorable moments. On February 21, he was greeted with raucous cheers as he took the microphone at halftime of a Michigan–Michigan State basketball game. Saban made some brief remarks about the upcoming football season, punctuated by a rare act of public bravado when he proclaimed: "We're going to kick Michigan's ass!" The crowd ate it up.

On May 5, Saban had his workday interrupted when a posse of Secret Service men knocked on his office door. President Bill

Clinton was in town to make Michigan State's commencement address. The Secret Service men told Saban that the president needed a couch. They then requisitioned his office, and Clinton took a twenty-minute catnap.

Later that month, Merritt Norvell, a former IBM executive who had played on Wisconsin's 1963 Rose Bowl team, replaced Merrily Dean Baker as Michigan State's athletic director. Norvell and Saban's relationship, cordial in the beginning, would rapidly deteriorate, and the two men would eventually "post up," in the words of Norvell.

Through it all, Saban's focus on the football team remained absolute, which was illustrated perfectly in an incident that happened that summer, one that remains one of Terry's favorite stories—perhaps partly apocryphal, but nonetheless true in spirit—about her husband:

One early evening, Saban met a friend at an East Lansing bar. The two men sat on some stools, twenty feet or so away from the cash register, and fell into a deep conversation about football. As they talked, a man walked through the door, pulled out a gun, and robbed the bar. Saban, in Terry's telling of the story, never once looked up from his conversation.

Some moments later, as he stood up to leave, Saban finally noticed an unsettled air about the bar. He turned to the bartender and asked him what was up. The bartender stared at him incredulously. "You didn't notice that we just got robbed?" he asked.

Michigan State was picked to finish near the basement of the Big Ten in 1995. That prediction seemed accurate after Saban's first game as a head coach, when his Spartans were pummeled, 50–10, at home by Nebraska, which was coached by Tom Osborne, the man whom McPherson had initially desired as a coach. The Michigan State defense gave up an astounding 666 yards in the loss. After the game, Saban called out his team, telling the Associated Press: "I was disappointed in the way we competed in the second half . . . to put it bluntly, I felt our players quit."

The loss was an instructional one, however. In that Nebraska team—which would go on to win its second consecutive national title that year—Saban got a glimpse of his future. The Cornhuskers had a suffocating defense and a collection of talented running backs led by Ahman Green and Lawrence Phillips. They dominated teams into submission. Osborne's mid-1990s Nebraska teams would become the blueprint for Saban's successful teams at LSU and, particularly, at Alabama.

In the ninth game of that season, the Spartans didn't exactly kick ass, but they did upset the seventh-ranked Michigan Wolverines, 28–25. Saban would later tell Jack Ebling that he actually regretted that win since it prematurely—and unreasonably—raised expectations for his program.

After beating Indiana the following week, the Spartans entered the last game of the regular season—a home game against fouteenth-ranked Penn State—at 6-3-1, with some hope of gaining a berth in at least a midtier bowl game. By that time, the Saban mystique was in full bloom on campus. During the game, a fan sitting in the end zone held up a sign that read, "Saban is God," recalling the guitar-hero graffiti that once followed around a young Eric Clapton. The Spartans lost, 24–20, on a Penn State touchdown with eight seconds to go in the game, which left them in fifth place in the Big Ten, and matched up in the Independence Bowl in Shreveport, Louisiana, against LSU, which was coached by a man named Gerry DiNardo. The Tigers crushed the Spartans, 45–26. Saban would make note of the sheer athleticism of the Southeastern Conference (SEC) team and, four years later, he would have DiNardo's job.

Michigan State ended the season at 6-5-1, the program's first winning record in five long years.

Terry Saban thrived in the Michigan State community. "People loved her here," says Norvell. She was the extroverted part of the Saban duo, performing even the most perfunctory social role with a smile and easy grace. Like Mary Saban had done with Saban's father, Terry ironed out any wrinkles made by her at times irascible husband. McPherson calls her "a positive for Nick, an anchor." Her importance when it comes to her husband's career and success cannot be overstated. They are truly a team. "When you deal with Nick, you really have to deal with two people," says Norvell. "Terry is a strong woman and she's heavily involved in Nick's affairs. He trusts her judgment."

Norvell learned of her importance firsthand. In the second game of Saban's first season, the Spartans traveled to Kentucky to play Louisville. As the athletic director, Norvell generally had the final say about where the Michigan State VIPs watched the games, even at "away" stadiums. The Thursday before the game in Louisville, Norvell says he called Terry and invited her to sit in a stadium box with him and his wife. "Terry tells me that all the coaches' wives are traveling for the game, so she'll just sit in the stands with them," says Norvell. "So I said, 'Okay, but feel free to come up.' "

On the morning of the game, it began to rain. "Then it turns to a gusher, raining like you couldn't believe," says Norvell. "It's not cold, but it's cool enough." Norvell says he spent the pregame hours mingling at various alumni events. "I didn't have time to take care of Terry Saban," he says. "It wasn't my job." Michigan State won the game easily, 30–7. When it was over, Norvell made his way down to the locker room. "I'm standing there right by the door and Terry walks in. She's drenched and her son is with her and he's the same way. I thought to myself, *This is going to be a problem.*"

Later, the players and coaches and VIPs all loaded onto the plane. McPherson, Norvell, and the trustees—with their spouses—sat in the first-class cabin. The players were in the back. In the front row of that section, in three seats, sat Nick, Terry, and Nicholas Saban.

"Terry's hair was all messed up," says Joel Ferguson, the trustee who was one of Saban's closest confidants at Michigan State. "Nick comes looking for me. He tells me he's going to kick Merritt's ass. I realize that he didn't really want to, and that's why he's talking to me, so I could talk him out of beating the shit out of him." Ferguson believed he'd calmed down Saban.

However, as the plane took off, Norvell kept a wary eye on his coach. "Nick has clues when he's getting ready to go," says Norvell.

"He rocks back and forth when he's agitated. He ticks. Usually if I saw him like that in the office, I'd just keep walking by." He didn't have that option on the plane. "Then Nick gets up and starts screaming at me, 'Why the fuck did my wife have to sit in the rain and my kid is probably going to get pneumonia!' The president is there. The trustees are all there."

That was pretty much the end of Saban's relationship with his athletic director. It was also the beginning of Terry taking matters into her own hands.

Throughout her husband's career, Terry had always artfully played the role of the coach's wife, especially when it came to off-the-field issues. "She was great at getting Nick lined up with thank-yous and invitations and phone calls," says Bob Knickerbocker, the Michigan State equipment manager, then and now, and a former golf and paddleball partner of Saban. As time went on at Michigan State, however, her influence began to grow. Terry became interested in the inner workings of the equipment room, among other smaller details of the football program. She even interviewed prospective coaches. "Nick allotted time for her," says Knickerbocker. "He'd be in the room with a possible hire, then he'd get up and leave and say, 'This is my wife and she'd like to talk to you.' She'd want to know about their families. She was just as thorough and prepared as Nick was."

Terry was also very protective of her husband. Rick Audas was an active member of the Downtown Coaches Club, a Spartan booster organization, during Saban's years at Michigan State. Early on, his family and the Sabans became close. They both had cottages in northern Michigan on Higgins Lake. "Terry had a lot of influence on him," Audas says. "He got pounded by her." He says she was just as detail-oriented as her husband—especially when it came to an issue regarding him. Audas helped sponsor Saban's coaching TV show in East Lansing. "She'd call in all the time and say that Nick's hair was out of place and things like that," he says.

Audas and Saban eventually had a falling-out that was caused in part by Terry's protectiveness. After the Spartans' spring practice game in early 1997, the Sabans hosted a gathering at their house.

Audas and Knickerbocker, Saban's uncle Sid, and fifty or so other people attended. "We got there at four or five o'clock and started drinking," says Audas. Five hours later, the party started to wind down. Audas says he was preparing to leave when Saban asked him and Knickerbocker to stick around and "have a few more beers." (Saban's beer of choice at the time: Miller Lite.) "So he's sitting at the bar in his basement, and his leg starts going and he's chain-smoking cigarettes," says Audas. "Terry's in the back singing Patsy Cline on the karaoke machine. And Nick said, 'Rick, I gotta ask you a question: What do people really think of me?'"

Audas says at first, he said nothing. At this point Saban was entering his third season at Michigan State. It was clear to most people in the know—including Audas—that he had the program headed in the right direction. For many people involved, it hadn't always been a pleasant experience. Saban demanded that the entire organization, from top to bottom, demonstrate loyalty and support of his mission. When things didn't go exactly as he liked, he let people know, usually by screaming at them. On the practice field, to avoid his wrath, the football support staff often played a game of cat-and-mouse with him: When he was on one side of the field, they'd move to the other, in the hopes of avoiding any confrontation. Assistants in those three years had left the Michigan State program for lesser positions. Saban was so focused and intense that when people said hello to him in the offices, he'd sometimes not even acknowledge their presence, a trait he had apparently inherited from his father. His staff had to learn quickly not to take anything personally. They could pretend that they weren't intimidated but, deep down, most of them were. "I often wondered how successful he could be acting like that, being that negative," says Knickerbocker. "But, gosh darn, everywhere he goes, he wins."

Audas knew all of this. He finally broke his silence that night in the Sabans' basement because, he says, "I'd had about fifty beers.

"I said, 'Nick, I gotta be honest with you, people think you're a miserable prick.' Terry suddenly stopped singing. Then I got on a roll. I said, 'Nick, you get a hard-on getting on people beneath you, ripping them and undressing them.' I gave him example after example. And Bob [Knickerbocker] turns to me and says, 'Hey Rick, watch it.'"

The damage had already been done, though. Audas says that Terry made a beeline for them and slammed her wineglass on the bar. "She said, 'I knew you were always against us,'" says Audas.

Audas and the Sabans were supposed to go to a party for the base-ball player (and former Spartan) Kirk Gibson a few days after the incident. Audas says Saban called him and told him Terry no longer wanted to go with him. Sometime later, Audas says Terry spotted him on the field during a game and attempted—and failed—to get his field pass revoked. "After that, we didn't talk much anymore," says Audas.

Saban's players at Michigan State didn't seem to have as much of a problem with him as his coaches did. Sure, he rode them just as hard, but they could see the improvement, as individuals and as a team. The holdovers from the Perles era wanted to win, and the newcomers—the Saban recruits—pretty much knew what they were getting into before they came. And, well, college football play-ers seem to be more inherently accustomed to being yelled at than most humans.

Saban recruited extremely well at Michigan State. Among his recruits that made the NFL from those years: the flaky but tal-ented receiver Plaxico Burress; Julian Peterson, the hyperathletic linebacker; and T. J. Duckett, whom Saban converted from a high school linebacker to a battering-ram running back. Saban went to extraordinary lengths in pursuing recruits. While after Duckett—who was also being recruited by Florida State, UCLA, Michigan, and Notre Dame—he attended his high school basketball games and track meets. "I remember the night he was supposed to come by my house, there was a huge snowstorm. I thought there was no way he'd make it," says Duckett. "But there he was, walking up the stairs in his tan jacket and white mock turtleneck. He came across as someone who was going to coach you about life. He said, 'Here's the truth. You either like it or you don't.'" Duckett's mother loved Saban.

Aric Morris, a strong safety, had already committed to Michigan when Saban came knocking. "He was really respectful," he says. "He did his homework. He somehow knew that my mom liked to keep a clean house, so when he walked in, he asked her if he should take his shoes off." Saban wrote letters to Morris, offering encouragement to him before his big high school games. "No other coach ever did that," says Morris, who eventually flipped to Michigan State. Tranquill says that the depth of Saban's research on a prospect—done by talking to teammates, friends, teachers, coaches, parents, and grandparents—was like nothing he'd seen before. "When we walked into that house, he literally knew what brand of chewing gum that kid preferred," he says.

Saban also helped the players he'd inherited, as long as they bought in. "He made me mature as a player and a man," says Muhsin Muhammad, a senior on the 1995 team who went on to play for fourteen years in the NFL. Tony Banks was the Spartans' quarterback in Saban's first year. He had NFL aspirations, but he wasn't sure how far he could go. Saban gave him the confidence. "We were in practice one day before the season," he says. "Saban never gave out compliments. Instead, he'd just chew your ass out when you did something wrong. But that day I made a throw to the back of the end zone. Immediately he turned to me and said, 'That's an NFL throw.' I hadn't even played a real down for him yet. When I look back at him and his staff, I realize they were the reason I got drafted so high." (Banks was taken early in the second round of the 1996 NFL Draft.)

Saban also helped Banks in another way that seemed unintentional. "Before he came, I was used to being close to my coaches, joking around," he says. "Saban was pretty distant. That got me prepared for what the pros were like."

Ike Reese, a linebacker, was at Michigan State for two years under Perles. "George was a players' coach. You could relax a bit under him," he says. "When Nick came in, it was like a culture shock." Reese and Saban's relationship got off on the wrong foot when Reese was arrested and charged with disorderly conduct during a fight outside of a bar in the summer of Saban's first season. "I hurt a kid. Saban let me stay, but he said this was my one shot. I had to get my grade-point average up, I had to be the first one in the weight room and in the front of the line during winter conditioning," says Reese. "He wanted me to be accountable for my actions. I responded to that tough love."

Midway through the 1995 season, Saban went to his weekly meeting at the Downtown Coaches Club. As reported in the *Sporting News,* he brought along Reese, who told the boosters that "we have another good game plan" for the upcoming week. Saban turned to look at him, then said: "It's very encouraging to me that Ike has approved the game plan." The audience broke out in laughter. Reese nervously chuckled, too. Saban stared at him. "Better get your laughs in now because when we watch film on Monday, I'll either approve or disapprove of the execution of that game plan." Then Saban started laughing.

"He thought he was the funniest guy when he said that," says Reese. "It was hilarious to just watch him."

In the 1996 season, his fellow players voted Reese as a captain of the team. "I think Saban started to see me differently then," he says. "I was walking on eggshells around him until then." Reese says he eventually felt so comfortable around his coach that he started to even joke with him. "He used to come out to the practice field with his coach's shirt on," he says. "It was unbuttoned, and there'd be this fistful of hair and I'd say, 'Coach, this ain't 1970 anymore. This ain't *Saturday Night Fever.*'"

Even as they grew closer, though, Reese says there remained a line. Reese had lost his own father when he was three years old. He says Saban wasn't the type of coach who filled that void. "He's one of the few coaches that you don't get the fatherly vibe from," he says. "You get the disciplinary side of the father, yes, but not the other side." Reese played in the NFL for eight years.

At the beginning of the 1996 season, the NCAA handed down its ruling on the infractions that had occurred under Perles. The football team was put on probation for four years, lost nine scholarships, and vacated its wins from Perles's last year, in 1994. As harsh as the sanctions were, the prevailing feeling within the program was a sense of relief. "It could have been worse. To us it was good news," says Denbow. "After that we felt like, 'Okay, we're on our way.'"

Michigan State won its first game that year, 52–14, over Purdue. Then they traveled to play Nebraska and again got whipped by the Cornhuskers, 55–14. Saban didn't call out his players this go-round. Instead he asked them to merely evaluate themselves in comparison with Nebraska. The Cornhuskers, he believed, had showed them what true domination looked like.

Michigan State entered the ninth game of its season, against rival Michigan, at 4-1 in the Big Ten, and there was talk around campus of a possible league title. It turned out to be a bit premature. The Spartans were easily handled, 45–29, and later ended the regular season at 6-5. Michigan State accepted an invitation to play in the Sun Bowl against Stanford, who had what appeared to be their own up-and-coming coach at the time, Tyrone Willingham.

During the 1996 season, Saban's name had popped up on various coaching search lists. He'd been mentioned as a candidate for the St. Louis Rams, the Detroit Lions, and the New York Giants. The last team on that list turned out to be more than just a rumor.

By the end of the season, McPherson had caught wind that something was up with his coach, and noticed that Saban had begun acting strangely a week or so before the bowl game. Neither Saban nor his coaches showed up for an arranged golf outing with the Stanford coaches (Saban sent boosters instead). McPherson remembers that, during the bowl week, Saban holed up alone in his hotel room. "I went to Nick's room and said, 'You can't just sit in here. You've got to go see your players,'" he says. "Nick was depressed."

On New Year's Eve, Michigan State lost to Stanford in the Sun Bowl, 38–0.

Saban's dalliance with the Giants was much more serious than

McPherson knew. Before the bowl game, Saban had secretly met with George Young, who was the general manager of the Giants. Young had come back from that meeting and told Wellington and John Mara, the father-son duo who owned the Giants, that Saban was "the best candidate he'd ever interviewed," according to John Mara.

In early 1997, after the bowl game, the Maras arranged another clandestine meeting with Saban, this time in an off-the-radar office in New Jersey. "We were very impressed with him," says John Mara. "We offered him the job."

In the course of the next week, Mara says he had numerous conversations with Saban directly, and a few with Neil Cornrich, who was Saban's agent at the time. Saban wanted control over personnel and staffing decisions. "We could never really come to terms with his role, and he was never entirely comfortable with our structure and the power he would or wouldn't have," says Mara. "We offered him a sum, but we never really started negotiating it, and we soon both agreed to walk away." The Giants hired Jim Fassel instead. A few years later, they'd be in contact with Saban again.

As various media outlets began to get wind of the Giants' interest—the *Boston Globe* even reported that he'd taken the job— McPherson grew angry. The university was forced to issue a statement on Saban's behalf, saying that he would stay. McPherson says he only found out about Saban's meetings with the Giants well after they happened. "It certainly was awkward," he says.

The flirtation—as so many of them have during his career— earned Saban some more money. In 1997, Michigan State renegotiated his contract, upping his base salary to $190,000 and loading it with incentives that could easily get it to $650,000.

That off-season, Saban seemed a bit more relaxed. He enjoyed some of the fruits of his celebrity status, playing in a Pro-Am golf tournament with Tiger Woods, who had just won his first Masters that year. During the round, Saban knocked one of his shots deep into the surrounding gallery and plunked a woman (she turned out to be okay). "Nick seemed a little nervous," Woods said afterward.

Saban played tennis frequently with Denbow. "Nick was tenacious. He ran everything down and called the lines close, and there was never any talking between points," says Denbow. "He never beat me. He was just starting. But I liked playing against him because he got a lot of balls back."

Yet, some of the trappings of Saban's new status seemed to befuddle the son of a service station owner. One year, his childhood friend Donnie Evans came with his two sons to Saban's summer football camp. After a session one day, Saban pulled up to Evans in a brand-new Cadillac and offered him a ride. "I said, 'Nice car, Nick,'" says Evans. "And he said, 'Yeah, I get a new one every year and I don't know why. I only put two or three thousand miles on it.' He wasn't bragging, it didn't seem like. He was just thinking it was sort of senseless."

The 1997 season seemed set up to be Saban's finest yet at Michigan State. He told the media that he had his "best team on paper." Saban had seventeen returning starters, ten of whom were on defense. Todd Schultz returned as the starting quarterback. The 6'7", 330-pound Flozell "the Hotel" Adams anchored the offensive line. The Spartans were ranked as high thirteen in one preseason poll.

They jumped off to a great start, winning their first five games, including an impressive 23–7 victory at Notre Dame. Michigan State entered its game against traditional Big Ten weakling Northwestern at number twelve in the nation, its highest ranking since the late 1980s. And then the year unraveled.

In the Northwestern game, the Spartans were behind, 19–17, late in the fourth quarter. They drove the ball to Northwestern's nine-yard line with seconds remaining in the game, only to have an attempted game-winning field goal blocked. Michigan State then lost 23–7 at home to Michigan, and had six passes intercepted by a defense led by Charles Woodson, who would win the Heisman Trophy that year. The next week, Michigan State was dominated by Ohio State, losing 37–13. The most crushing loss came a week later, against Purdue. The Spartans had the lead with less than three minutes left when Purdue blocked a field goal attempt and ran it back for a touchdown, then recovered an onside kick and scored another touchdown. Michigan State lost by one point after missing a forty-three-yard field goal attempt as time expired. It was their fourth loss in a row. "We just didn't have much maturity back then," says Reese. Saban took a measured tone in his remarks after the game. "I'm very disappointed, but I'm not discouraged about the program," he said.

Michigan State rallied to win its last two games, which included a 49–14 blowout of fourth-ranked Penn State, finishing the season 7-4. In the Aloha Bowl against Washington (Don James had retired by then), played on Christmas Day, the Spartans were smothered, 51–23. Saban's bowl record at this point was 0-3, and his teams had been outscored, 134–49. Before the next season, a writer for the Associated Press would call him "the most overrated coach in the country" and wonder why his name kept popping up whenever a big school or NFL job opened up.

He remained a hot commodity anyway.

In early 1998, the Indianapolis Colts came calling. Saban released another statement through the university, declaring: "I have the job I want." Behind the scenes, though, Bill Polian, the general manager of the Colts, met with Saban. Polian believed he was interested. "I was prepared to offer him the job," he says. The talks eventually broke down, again over Saban's desire for control over personnel and staffing. The Colts ended up hiring Jim Mora and choosing Peyton Manning with the first overall pick in the NFL Draft.

In the first game of the 1998 season, Michigan State cruised to an early 16–0 lead over Colorado State midway through the second quarter, but lost the game, 23–16. The following week, against Oregon in Eugene, the Spartans lost 48–14, and their starting cornerback and one of the most popular players on the team, Amp Campbell, broke his neck. Shortly thereafter, Saban demoted his defensive coordinator.

Before the Michigan game, freshman wide receiver Plaxico

Burress told the media that "going down there will be like taking candy from a baby." Michigan State lost, 29–17.* At the three-quarter mark of the season, Saban's team was a disappointing 4-4 and seemingly in total disarray. And next up, they had to travel to play the number-one-ranked team in the country, Ohio State. The Spartans were 28-point underdogs.

From this chaos, though, came clarity, provided by a man who would forever change the way Saban approached his job as a football coach.

Saban had long taken a keen interest in the mental aspects of both life and sports. He had taken twenty-four credit hours of psychology courses while working on his master's degree at Kent State. So it's not too surprising that he would eventually befriend a professor of psychiatry at Michigan State. What *is* surprising is how much influence this professor would have on him.

Lionel "Lonny" Rosen is a grass-blade-thin man who wears large-framed eyeglasses and has a shock of gray hair and an unruly beard that reaches down to his chest. He looks like someone who has just wandered back into civilization after seven months on the Appalachian Trail. He likes to accessorize his wardrobe with a wood-chip belt buckle that's impaled by a large nail. The players on various Saban teams through the years have referred to him as "the head-shrinker," "the wizard," "the wizard dude," "Lonny Graybeard," or, when they're feeling particularly wordy, "the wooden belt buckle man." It is from this unlikely source that Saban's famous "Process" was born.

Rosen, now seventy-eight, is still a professor at Michigan State and maintains an outpatient practice from his campus office. He received his MD from Jefferson Medical College in 1965, and did

---

* Since then, Saban has not allowed freshmen on his teams to speak to the media, except when they are required to by the NCAA before championship games.

his psychiatry residency at Temple University Hospital. During the Vietnam War, he was a doctor in the U.S. Military Special Forces.

Rosen has worked with Saban ever since the Michigan State head-coaching years. Some of that work has been in the more traditional realm of sports psychology—of getting athletes to focus on peak performance. He meets and counsels the teams as a whole, and the players individually as needed. The media-shy Rosen has, for the most part, shunned any interview requests, though he did talk to the *Lansing State Journal* in 2003 and explained some of his views on athletes and performance. "Motivation itself generally lasts about two plays—it's highly overrated," he said. "Give me a team that has a business-like attitude, a team that can deal with adversity when it comes." He added: "The most destructive phenomenon in sports is relief. It's typically followed by a decrease in performance." This, of course, jibes exactly with Saban's philosophies about football teams. Most of what Rosen does with Saban's teams, though, goes much further than just sports psychology.

In his sessions with players, Rosen usually talks about anything but football. He probes them about their families and lives. "Rosen helped me get a different perspective on things," says John Parker Wilson, Saban's first quarterback at Alabama. "He's not a football guy, he's just the wizard spitting truth at you."

Rosen also assists Saban with player evaluations, helping him get a read on mental makeups. He watches the players practice and will scrutinize their body language and observe how they interact with their coaches and teammates. Off the field, he has sat in on player interviews with Saban.

Rosen has, over the years, crafted profiles of Saban's players, to help him coach them. "Lonny figures out how a player thinks, what's the best way to reach him," says Curt Cignetti, the recruiting coordinator and wide receivers coach for Alabama from 2007 to 2010. A few of Saban's players have wondered if, at times, Rosen and Saban have shared too much information. "Lonny was basically Saban's snitch," says Matt Mauck, the quarterback for Saban's national championship team at LSU. "It's Saban's way of finding out what the players are thinking." Mauck says he didn't mind that too much, because it led to a useful two-way street. "I looked at Lonny as a way to say things to Saban without actually having to say things to his face."

Where Rosen has made his biggest impact on Saban, though, is in getting him to completely buy in to what's known as "process thinking," that is, the breaking down of things—like meetings, practices, games, and seasons—into smaller pieces that can be handled without anxiety. It provides a way of functioning without being overwhelmed by the bigger picture, a "momentary stay against confusion," in Robert Frost's words. The world is complex, Rosen told Saban. So is football, with twenty-two men on the field, the coaches, the fans, the referees, the pressure. Process thinking keeps players and coaches anchored to reality, allows them to make sensible choices, and helps induce more repeatable outcomes. This step-by-step thinking mechanism is nothing new— it's a prominent part of cognitive behavioral thinking, stemming back to the famous psychiatrist Aaron Beck. It also happens to be a significant component of the Alcoholics Anonymous recovery program. However, it had never before been so systematically applied to a football program before Saban did it. And it all started in early November 1998.

Leading up to the game that year against Ohio State, Saban was having a crisis of confidence. He saw fear in his players' eyes, and felt that same fear himself. The Buckeyes had been ranked number one all season, and were annihilating their opponents by an average score of 38–9. The fact that Saban was facing the only program to have fired him didn't help with his anxiety. His old boss Earl Bruce would be in the press box, calling the game for a local radio station.

So Saban turned to Rosen, who walked him through a new approach. The Spartans, and their coach, would, starting in practice that week, take it one step at a time. Each player would focus on his individual responsibility. Rosen emphasized that the average play in the football game lasted about seven seconds. The players would concentrate only on winning those seconds, take a rest between plays, then do it all over again. There would be no focus at all on the scoreboard or on the end result.

The idea resonated for Saban in some deep place. In a meaningful way, what Rosen was preaching was merely a reinforcement of the lessons Saban had learned early in his life from his father. The only way to deal with the impossible perfection that Big Nick demanded was to learn to love—and master—the steps taken in its pursuit. Take care of the individual details and the bigger goals will come. It's the seed from which what's now known as "the Process"— Saban's much-written-about systematic approach to managing a football program—blossomed and became a key component to his success. Jason Garrett, who coached the quarterbacks for Saban at Miami and is the current coach of the Dallas Cowboys, says Saban relies on Rosen so much "that you can hear his language in Nick. He's a big part of what Nick does."

Bill Burke, Michigan State's quarterback in 1998, says that he and his teammates noticed a big change in their coach the week before the Ohio State game. "He was more relaxed, he wasn't always on top of everybody, and we had a little more fun." The game itself couldn't have gotten off to a worse start for the Spartans. Ohio State jumped out to a 17–3 lead in the first quarter. With ten minutes left in the third quarter, the Buckeyes returned an interception for a touchdown to go up 24–9. At that moment, it appeared that the game would be just another blowout for Ohio State. Saban's players, though, remained eerily calm. "It was such a strange game," says Burke. "It really felt like the score didn't matter, that no deficit was too big, and that we had an infinite amount of time to come back. Psychology played a large part in that game."

Three minutes after Ohio State's interception return for a touchdown, Burke threw for his own touchdown (Michigan State missed the extra-point attempt). A Spartan field goal on the next drive made the score 24–18 in favor of Ohio State. Burke then calmly led the team on a ninety-three-yard touchdown drive to take the lead, 25–24. Michigan State tacked on another field goal. Ohio State got the ball one last time, and drove down to the Spartans' fifteen-yard line. On fourth down, with just over a minute remaining, Renaldo

Hill, a Saban recruit who played cornerback, intercepted an Ohio State pass on the goal line to cap a 28–24 victory, one of the biggest upsets in Michigan State's history.*

Ever since then, Rosen has never been further than a phone call away from Saban, his most famous patient.

The Spartans finished the 1998 season at 6-6, and missed out on a bowl game for the only time during Saban's time there. By the beginning of the 1999 season, several media outlets proclaimed that Saban's job was in jeopardy, which wasn't the case, according to McPherson. "There was never any pressure on Nick in that way. We knew we were getting better and better." Saban's nemesis, Norvell, had been forced out ("I think they thought getting rid of me would be better for Nick," says Norvell) and was replaced by a man named Clarence Underwood. Trouble was coming, however.

Near the end of every season, according to McPherson, "something would come up" with Saban, in the form of a job offer from another team or a request for a raise. To McPherson, the annual rite was getting a bit tedious by 1999. "My wife always said, 'It's Christmastime, we need to go over to the Sabans,'" says McPherson.

For some time, Saban hadn't felt fully appreciated by the school. "The fissures in their relationship were already there in 1999," says Norvell. "Nick had gone up the hill so many times to the president with different kinds of issues. He wanted this and that, and wondered when things were going to happen, and his patience started to wear thin."

The issue in 1999 was a pay raise. McPherson's perceived lack of urgency on the issue led to that patience eventually wearing out altogether.

---

* Saban's old friend and fellow former Ohio State assistant Denny Fryzel was on the sidelines for that game. When it ended, he jumped into Saban's arms and planted a kiss right on his lips.

In the first game of the 1999 season, Michigan State hosted Oregon, the team that had embarrassed it the year before. The Spartans won the rematch in a game that was highlighted by an eighty-five-yard fumble return for a touchdown by Amp Campbell, who was back on the field after his frightening neck injury, which had occurred in the previous year's game. Michigan State was 5-0 and ranked number eleven heading into its game against Michigan, which was ranked number three in the country and was also undefeated. It was the most-hyped Michigan–Michigan State game in decades, and the Spartans responded. Michigan State's defense held its own in the game, taking on the Wolverine quarterback platoon of Drew Henson and Tom Brady. "[Julian] Peterson and Robaire Smith [a defensive end] were all over Henson in particular," says Burke. "You could see it in his face." Burke threw for 400 yards, and Burress had 255 yards receiving in a thrilling 34–31 win.

Michigan State proceeded to lose its next two games, to Purdue (quarterbacked by Drew Brees) and Wisconsin. Outwardly, it appeared that Saban's team was unable to handle its success and had begun to flake yet again, just as it had in years past. The players didn't believe that, though. "We had a mature bunch of leaders on the team by then," says Duckett. The Spartans won their last three games of the regular season to finish at 9-2 and number nine in the national polls. Saban believed his team worthy of one of the marquee Bowl Championship Series (BCS) New Year's Day bowl games.

Instead, Michigan got the invite to the Orange Bowl, even though it had finished with the same overall and in-conference records as Michigan State and had, of course, lost the head-to-head game. Saban was livid, but not exactly surprised. He'd long believed that Michigan State was perceived as a second-class program, in the state and in the Big Ten. The belief held more than a grain of truth: Michigan State didn't come close to the prestige held by its in-state rival (Michigan didn't even consider Michigan State its true rival; that distinction went to Ohio State). To Saban, Michigan's Orange Bowl invite was merely the latest demonstration of that status, and he would ultimately point to that snub as the main reason he left the program. There was much more to it than that, however.

Saban, who made close to $700,000 that season, believed that McPherson had promised him a $100,000 bonus. McPherson says that Saban misunderstood the planned payment and that he had worked out a "figurative payment of $1 million" for Saban that he put in an endowment fund and that would gain earnings if Saban stayed at the school for a certain amount of time. "I don't think Nick was fully comfortable with what I was doing with the money, but I was comfortable, as a banker and finance guy, understanding and working the resources to work out right," says McPherson. Saban merely believed he was being stonewalled.

One of the difficulties McPherson says he faced was the emergence of a new agent for Saban, a Memphian named Jimmy Sexton. Saban and Sexton had first met in 1993, when Sexton brought his first big client—the NFL defensive end Reggie White—to the Cleveland Browns for a free agent visit. Saban and Sexton, two men who lived for their work, immediately hit it off. Saban had parted ways with his previous agent—Neil Cornrich—because he didn't like the way he had handled his flirtation with the New York Giants in 1996. Sexton quickly became "one of my best friends," Saban told *Sports Illustrated*.

Others didn't feel quite so warmly toward him, though. "Sexton was impossible," says McPherson. "There was no way to cut a deal with him." Next to Terry, there is no one Saban trusted more with his professional decisions than Sexton. A former equipment manager for the University of Tennessee who had then just started representing coaches, Sexton would eventually help convince Saban that he could be more successful—and more appreciated—in another job.*

---

* Sexton, who now works for Creative Artists Agency (CAA), represents much of the top tier in college football coaching, including Auburn's Gus Malzahn and Florida State's Jimbo Fisher.

On November 15, 1999, Gerry DiNardo—the man who had so soundly beaten Michigan State in Saban's first-ever bowl game—was fired at LSU. DiNardo's overall record at LSU (32-24-1) was eerily similar to Saban's at Michigan State (34-24-1). The difference was in the trajectory: In his last two years at LSU, DiNardo had registered six wins against fifteen losses. Immediately, rumors began to surface about his potential replacements. No one mentioned Saban. The belief was that he finally had things rolling with his 9-2 Spartans, and that leaving the program then would have been an imprudent decision. Behind the scenes, something different was playing out.

In retrospect, the signs of Saban's unhappiness were readily apparent—the disagreement on the bonus, Michigan State's inability to get into a top-tier bowl game, and Sexton's recent involvement in Saban's affairs. Saban believed that some things had even gotten personal. Sometime later, he told the *Detroit News,* "[i]t seemed like, for whatever reason, there came a negative attitude around here about Nick Saban."

Saban had thinner skin back then, and was a little less sure of himself. He'd gotten the earful from Audas about the way he was perceived, of course, which told him more than he wanted to know. Even in the 1999 season—Michigan State's best since 1987—he didn't feel like he received the adoration he deserved. Just before halftime of Michigan State's home game against Ohio State that year, Saban's Spartans were up a comfortable 17–0 and had completely shut down the Buckeyes' running game (Ohio State rushed for zero yards in the game). With just seconds remaining in the first half, Michigan State had the ball in Ohio State territory, and Saban decided to take a knee rather than go for more points. As he jogged off the field to the locker room, a few drunken fans booed him and called him a coward. The day after what turned out to be a dominating 23–7 win, Saban called Jack Ebling and asked him, "Why don't they like me?" Ebling replied: "What are you talking about?" Saban mentioned the drunken fans. "I heard those guys booing," he said.

Saban, it seemed, was like the baseball great Ted Williams—another sensitive man who seemed to hear only the catcalls and would have preferred to operate in a state that John Updike described as a "perfectionist's vacuum," apart from the fans and media.

Saban was further wounded at a banquet for coaches and players after Michigan State's November 20 win over Penn State to end the season. Ferguson says that McPherson made a long speech that night, congratulating the team on its 9-2 finish, but didn't mention Saban by name. Afterward, Saban turned to Ferguson and said: "Joel, the president never said how we had moved the program and never said what I'd done."

"Nick is a sensitive guy," says Ferguson.

What ensued after that banquet was one of the most bizarre ends to a college coaching tenure in the modern era. In the week that followed that last regular season game, Saban went on the recruiting trail and started preparations for the Citrus Bowl—or at least that's what the Michigan State administration believed. One night that week, the Sabans went to dinner and a movie with Ferguson and his wife. Ferguson says there was no indication that Saban was going anywhere at that point. LSU appeared to be going after one of Saban's old coaching mates, Glen Mason, the coach at Minnesota. Mason suddenly fell out of the mix for the job. Ferguson says McPherson called him a few days later. "He told me, 'LSU is after Nick,'" says Ferguson. "I was surprised."

Rumors of Saban's potential departure eventually reached the Michigan State players. So Saban called a meeting with them and acknowledged that he had indeed been in contact with LSU. "He told us not to think about the rumors," says Duckett. "He didn't say he was leaving, but there also wasn't a hard 'I'm staying.' It was just eerie and weird." According to Burke, "the feeling on the team was that he was staying."

Ebling says that the fact that Saban even seemed interested in LSU was surprising. "When they got back from that first bowl game [in 1995] in Shreveport, I talked to Terry," he says. "I didn't get the impression that she liked Louisiana or Louisianans at all. It seemed like the last place she'd go."

Yet, one day in late November, she was there, in Baton Rouge, checking out potential homes, something McPherson and the trustees would learn about the hard way. That same evening, McPherson called Ferguson and Underwood and asked them to go over to Saban's house to figure out what was going on.* "When we got there it was just Nick, an in-law, and his kids," says Underwood. "It looked strange because he was getting dinner ready for the kids, which I don't think he ever did. They looked hungry."

Underwood says Ferguson asked Saban where Terry was. "And Saban says, 'She's at the store.' Joel asked him again and again, and Nick gave the same answer."

Ferguson kept pressing, asking Saban what it would take to get him to stay at Michigan State. "Nick just didn't answer him," says Underwood.

Then the phone rang. "Nick answered it and he was just mumbling, 'nope, yep,' which seemed strange," says Underwood.

After Saban hung up, says Ferguson, "someone in the room slipped up and said, 'Is her plane on the way back?'" There was a silent pause. Ferguson then asked Saban if Terry was in Baton Rouge. He finally admitted it, but claimed "she was just checking things out," says Underwood. Ferguson asked Saban again what they could do to get him to stay. Saban replied: "Nothing." Underwood and Ferguson left.

Ferguson, who was accustomed to late-night arm-twisting (he'd been a key part of Jesse Jackson's 1988 presidential campaign), says he went home and called Tom Izzo, the popular and successful coach of Michigan State's basketball team. Izzo and Saban were good friends—the Sabans had helped Izzo through the process of adopting a child. Ferguson and Izzo returned to Saban's house later that night. They rang the doorbell, but Saban wouldn't let them in.

Saban later told the media that he made the final decision to leave Michigan State at 5 a.m. on November 30. He didn't tell his assistants anything until afterward. That morning, he called a meet-

---

* The *Wall Street Journal* first reported a slimmed-down version of this story in 2013.

ing with his players. "We knew something was up, but even at that point, I didn't think it was anything major," says Burke.

Saban was brief with the players, thanking them for their work and asking for their understanding. He stood at the doorway as they all filed out, shaking hands, one player at a time. "That was an awkward moment," says Aric Morris. "We felt betrayed and abandoned, but that's human nature. At the end of the day, I understood. But I never got an opportunity to talk to him again. We used to talk sometimes about things other than football. I would have liked to talk to him more, to talk about my track outside of football."

Amp Campbell, the cornerback who returned to the team after breaking his neck, says: "I bawled like a baby when he left, and I'm not an emotional guy. If you didn't know him, he could come off as a jerk. But once you got to know him, you learned from him. He's one of the best guys I've ever met in my life."

Saban flew to Baton Rouge and was introduced as the new coach at LSU later that day. The drama wasn't quite over, though. Saban wanted at least six of his assistants to come with him to LSU. He held formal interviews with them, and was so confident that at least some of them would be joining him that he had LSU send a plane up to East Lansing to retrieve them.

The night before the plane arrived, though, his Michigan State assistants had stayed up late together, discussing the offer. They talked about how Michigan State, at the time, had the superior program, and things seemed like they were only going to get better. Some of them didn't want to move their families to Louisiana. Others were still a bit taken aback by the fact that Saban took the LSU job without telling them first. Bobby Williams, Saban's associate head coach at Michigan State, was appointed the interim head coach for the bowl game (and was later given the full-time job). Williams was an easygoing man, well liked by the players and his fellow coaches. Life with him as a boss seemed as if it would be, well, a little easier.

The plane that was supposed to be occupied by a handful of men who were loyal to Saban and believed in him—disciples, really—

flew south and returned to Baton Rouge empty. Though the men all had legitimate reasons for staying at Michigan State, the fact that not one of them followed him to LSU was a striking—and somewhat embarrassing—gesture. Pat Ruel, Michigan State's offensive line coach and now the offensive line coach for the Seattle Seahawks, says, "Nick took it personally."

A day or so after taking the job, Saban himself seemed to have a dramatic change of heart. He called Ferguson late one night with some startling news. "He was down there by himself in a hotel room," says Ferguson. "He was lonely without Terry there and seemed fragile. He told me that he didn't like it there, and that he didn't think he wanted the LSU job and he wanted to come back." Ferguson immediately called McPherson, who says at the time he was "open to Nick's return." Denbow says he remembers getting a call that night from McPherson. "He said, 'You'll never guess who wants to be our next head coach: Nick Saban.' I was shocked."

Saban called Underwood early the next morning and reiterated what he'd said to Ferguson. "It was five thirty in the morning," says Underwood. "He just said, 'I made a mistake and I want to come back.' He said he was lonely. He was crying."

Ferguson, with the go-ahead from McPherson, tried to reach Saban throughout the day, without success. "I couldn't find Nick to tell him he could come back," says Ferguson. When he finally did reach him, Saban had changed his mind yet again. "He told me, 'Joel, this won't work. The first time I have a mediocre season up there, they'll remember this.'"

In the end, of course, Saban stayed in Baton Rouge. He agreed to a five-year contract with LSU that paid him $1.25 million a year, making him the third-highest-paid coach in college football behind Bowden and Steve Spurrier.

The Michigan State community was stunned. Soon that emotion turned to hurt and vitriol. Bob Traxler, a Michigan State trustee, said publicly: "Nick Saban's conduct is totally unacceptable." The media had a field day. The *Detroit Free Press* ran a banner across its front page that read: "So Long, $aban." In his *Free Press* column,

Mitch Albom wrote that what Saban "seems best at is leaving at the right time. . . . Where is the genius coaching?" Some of his former players even chimed in. Sedrick Irvin, a running back who left Michigan State early for the NFL, told a newspaper: "When I left I wanted to fulfill a lifetime dream, but he called me selfish. Now the team finally has a good year and he leaves, so I guess that makes him selfish." (Years later, Irvin would walk back those words, saying: "That was just me being a boy.")

The anger left behind when a coach like Saban leaves one program for another can seem almost unreasonable, though it *is* understandable. First and foremost, Saban is an extraordinary football coach. When he leaves a program, there is an enormous hole to fill. Football coaches enter the same sort of covenant as a marriage with the fan base, and the hurt felt when one runs off is a bit akin to being left unexpectedly by a spouse for another lover.

When a head coach voluntarily leaves a football program like Michigan State, Norvell says, the pain is felt by more than just the fans. "For a place like Michigan State, the head football coach and the football team is the biggest element that a university has in terms of maintaining relationships with its constituents, whether they are in East Lansing or Hong Kong. The football team is the single most important department on campus with people who relate to Michigan State. It's the only unit of the university that gets it in the public eye on a day-to-day basis, in the newspaper, on the radio and TV. English departments and physics departments don't do that, even though they are way more important. If you're an alum thinking about giving money, if what you hear about the football team is positive, you'll write a check."

Norvell believes that Saban's departure may have spurred more hate in part because of his demeanor. "Nick was stiff then, stiffer than he is now. He wasn't warm and cozy. So when things went south, there was a reluctance to support him, even though many people knew he left the program in better shape than it was before he got here."

A month after Saban left, Michigan State played Florida in the

Citrus Bowl. It won on a last-second field goal, 37–34, which meant that Williams was able to accomplish something Saban never could: win a bowl game at Michigan State.*

McPherson says he sometimes ponders Saban's stint at Michigan State, his constant flirtations with other jobs, and his messy departure from the school. "That was Nick then and Nick ever since, every place he's gone," McPherson says. "He's such a wonderful coach. Why can't he be happy?"

Saban was forty-eight years old when he was hired by LSU, no longer a young coach, and two years older than his father was when he died. LSU got a man with lots of promise (and a decent amount of hype) without a sterling résumé. Saban's overall record as a head coach (including the year at Toledo) was 43-26-1. Though he joined Bowden and Spurrier as the only million-dollar college football coaches, he was the sole member of that trio who hadn't yet won a national title (Bowden had two; Spurrier had one). What he was, at the close of the twentieth century, was a bundle of potential energy.

In the twenty-first century, that potential would become kinetic.

---

* Williams would go 5-6, 7-5, and 3-6 in nearly three seasons at Michigan State before getting fired. He's been with Saban pretty much ever since—as a wide receivers coach at LSU, a tight end coach with the Dolphins, and the current special teams coach at Alabama.

7

On the Bayou

IT TURNED out that things were just as strange on the LSU side during Saban's hiring.

As agonizing as his departure from Michigan State turned out to be, it was Saban, through Jimmy Sexton, who first made contact with LSU, not the other way around. Sexton had a rough go of it at first. LSU's athletic director, Joe Dean, was a notoriously parsimonious man who fervently disliked agents. He wouldn't take Sexton's calls, so the Memphis agent got creative. He knew that Dean had once been a close friend of a man named Edward "Skeets" Tuohy Jr., who'd been the longtime basketball coach at Isidore Newman, a high school in New Orleans. Skeets had died in 1982 at the age of fifty-one. Sexton knew his son, Sean Tuohy, a former basketball player at the University of Mississippi, a prominent businessman in Memphis, and the broadcaster for the NBA's Memphis Grizzlies.* Sexton asked Tuohy to call Dean on his behalf and tell him that Saban was interested in the LSU job. Tuohy did, and Dean finally took Sexton's call.

Saban wasn't LSU's first choice, though. Butch Davis, the coach at the University of Miami, was. Davis "had a great interview and was a first-class guy," says Charlie Weems, an LSU trustee and a

---

* Sean Tuohy is, of course, the man who, along with his wife, Leigh Anne, adopted the football player Michael Oher, who was the subject of Michael Lewis's book *The Blind Side*.

member of the university's coaching search committee. "We wanted him and we would have hired him."

Davis, though, had designs on getting a head-coaching job in the NFL, and he figured that his gig at Miami paved a surer path to that goal than one at the downtrodden LSU program did. The search committee (which, along with Weems, included Dean, trustee Stanley Jacobs, Tiger Athletic Foundation head Richard Gill, and LSU chancellor Mark Emmert) also, of course, interviewed Glen Mason, Saban's old assistant coaching mate and, at the time, the head coach at Minnesota, but nothing came of it.

A week after Michigan State's last regular season game, against Penn State, the LSU search committee hopped on a plane and flew to Olive Branch, Mississippi, a suburb of Sexton's hometown of Memphis. By then the LSU men had grown anxious about their hunt for a new coach. LSU was in the midst of a $55 million, 11,600-seat addition to Tiger Stadium. The school needed to sell tickets, no simple task after a couple of horrendous seasons. After striking out in their first few interviews, "we had to hit a home run with the new coach," says Jacobs.

When Tuohy greeted the men at the Olive Branch airport, he had a little surprise in store for them. "I had a van and I filled it with Ole Miss balloons and cups," says the Ole Miss graduate with a laugh. "I certainly didn't want LSU to succeed." Nevertheless, Tuohy dutifully drove them to Sexton's house.

When they walked in, Saban was already there, sitting in a chair. The men each took their positions: Sexton sat on Saban's right, Gill and Weems on his left, and Dean, Emmert, and Jacobs took seats across from him. On the table in front of Saban: a yellow legal pad, of course, with pages of handwritten notes. Saban was wearing a green sport coat and a tie. "He looked kind of wired," says Jacobs. "He was ready."

It was Saban who started the meeting. "His first words out of the box were 'Joe [Dean], why can't you guys win?'" says Jacobs. "Joe said, 'Well, Florida never won until they found [Steve] Spurrier. We've never found the right guy.'" Saban was off, once again about to win over a school during an interview with his calm, methodical, take-charge approach. "He was interviewing us hard, and we were interviewing him less hard," says Weems. Jacobs was impressed right away. "It was clear that Nick had done his homework," he says. "He was like a really good chess player. He could see what needed to be done with the program and, in his mind, he could see how he could do it."

The state of Louisiana had some of the best high school football talent in the country (it traditionally has had one of the highest number of NFL players per capita) and LSU had no in-state competition from another major college football program. So Saban wondered: Why couldn't DiNardo keep those guys? He also asked about academics. DiNardo had constantly run into problems with academically ineligible players. Saban wanted to know what kind of resources the school had in place to address that problem. Dean and Emmert tried to answer his questions as best as they could. "But the truth was, at the time, we didn't really have any good answers," says Weems.

Dean eventually shoehorned in a question of his own: Why would Saban leave Michigan State just when everything seemed to be coming together? Saban didn't mention any rift with McPherson. He simply replied: "Michigan." Gill then asked Saban about his plans for assistant coaches. "Saban said that Jimbo Fisher would be his offensive coordinator and John Thompson would coach the defense," says Jacobs. "He said he didn't really know those guys, but he knew they were good and that they were familiar with recruiting in the South." Saban said he would round out his staff with more guys who knew the SEC, and a handful of his best assistants from Michigan State. (This last part was the only thing he said in his interview that didn't eventually come true.)

The meeting went on for four hours. As it progressed, Dean gradually receded and Emmert took over as the voice of LSU. Sexton, seemingly not wanting to show his cards, remained mostly quiet. Near the end of the interview, Saban made some bold proclamations: "He said that within three years he would win an SEC championship, and that within five years, he'd win a national one," says Jacobs, who also remembers a comment Saban made during the interview that would become hugely significant in a few years' time: He said that, someday, he wanted to coach in the NFL. The LSU contingent, by then wholly enraptured, paid that comment little mind.

Earlier that day, on the plane ride up to Olive Branch, the LSU committee had decided that if they liked Saban, they would caucus before making any moves. That plan went out of the window, though, late in the interview when Emmert suddenly blurted out: "Nick, we want you to be our coach." Weems says he cornered Sexton and asked him what it would take to get Saban to LSU. "Jimmy choked out '$900,000,'" says Weems. "I said, 'If we pay him $1.1 million, can we stop talking and get it done?' Sexton's eyes got huge."

Saban and Sexton had happened upon LSU at a particularly fortunate time. The trustees, tired of losing and eager to sell new tickets, were ready to make a big commitment to a new coach. The Tiger Athletic Foundation, a nonprofit booster club that raised money for athletics—including coaching salaries—had the necessary funds in place to make that happen. Perhaps most important, Emmert, the chancellor, was looking to transform his university, and he viewed the football program as the way to do it. (Emmert's favorite description of the university's athletics—and football, in particular—was as the "front porch" to the greater school.) "We all knew the potential of LSU," says Weems. "All the pieces were in place. We had commitment at all levels to see how good we could be. We had to take a big step. We couldn't tiptoe in. And Saban was the last best chance to make that statement."

Before Saban even started to negotiate, he demanded a few commitments from the university: He wanted a new academic center for student-athletes and, with it, a host of new academic support programs for the football players. He also wanted the players' academic lives to be run by the provost and not the athletic department. Sure, Saban wanted his players to actually get an education, but he also didn't want to face the same problems DiNardo had when it came to player eligibility. He also said he needed a new, centralized football operations center—with offices, meeting rooms, locker rooms, and training facilities—built near the team's practice fields, to replace LSU's somewhat antiquated football facilities. "He wanted to make sure we had a full commitment to excellence in football," says Weems. The two sides agreed to start working on a contract.

When the interview ended, Tuohy shuttled the men back to the airport. As the plane ascended, Emmert turned to Dean and said, "This is how you negotiate with Sexton: Ask him how much it will cost for Nick to become our new head coach." Emmert knew he had to stress this point to Dean, who was always worrying over the budget. In the end, Sexton squeezed another $150,000 annually out of the school, and Saban agreed to a five-year contract that paid him $1.25 million a year. Sexton masterfully negotiated some stranglehold additions to the contract: There would be no buyout should Saban leave, and the school would owe Saban $2 million if they fired him.

On November 30, LSU sent a plane to bring Saban down to the press conference announcing his hire. By then Weems and his colleagues had begun to worry about the ultimate consummation of the deal. Saban had seemed a bit hesitant and distant in the days leading up to the press conference. "I agonized about getting him on that plane," says Weems. "I had the pilots call me when he boarded and when they took off. I was still panicking." Weems met Saban at the airport and took him to the campus but still couldn't get a read on him. Minutes before the scheduled beginning of the press conference, Weems and the others got word that Saban was waffling, pacing back and forth in another room, and openly wondering if he'd made the right decision. "To this day I believe that had the Michigan State president called Nick at any time up until the moment he stepped up to the press conference, he could have had Nick back," says Weems. "Nick makes these decisions reluctantly." (At the time, Weems and the others had no idea that Saban would later call Ferguson and Underwood at Michigan State.)

When Saban did eventually stand up and face the media ("I can't tell you the relief I felt," says Weems), he told them he looked forward to the challenge of coaching in the SEC and that, yes, the security provided by his contract was nice, but that he hadn't made the decision because of money. The money became a hot topic anyway. Mike Foster, Louisiana's governor, told the press that Saban's salary "boggles the mind." Sexton optimistically boasted, "Our deal will help every other coach in America." Jacobs would later tell anyone who asked that the money spent on Saban was the best deal in the state since the Louisiana Purchase. "And I still feel that way," he says.

The local media, which Saban would eventually come to dominate, expressed optimism in the hire, but couched that with a hint of uncertainty. Saban was still a relative unknown in these parts, remembered mostly for Michigan State's big loss to LSU in the 1995 Independence Bowl in Shreveport. They constantly referred to him as a "Yankee." Stories about him that originated in other SEC locales weren't quite so benign. In the summer of 2000, the *Arkansas Democrat-Gazette* became perhaps the first media outlet to refer to him as "Satan." The LSU fan base, however, tossed any skepticism aside. "C'est Bon" stickers were plastered on car bumpers all over the state, and season tickets to LSU's refurbished Tiger Stadium sold out in days.

As promised, Saban did indeed hire Jimbo Fisher, who had coached the quarterbacks at Auburn for six years in the mid- to late 1990s, as his offensive coordinator, and John Thompson, who'd been an assistant at a slew of southern schools, as his defensive coordinator. He filled out the rest of his coaching staff with some experienced hands, like defensive line coach Pete Jenkins, who'd been with LSU for eleven years in the 1980s and 1990s, and some younger men, like Derek Dooley, a tight end coach and recruiting coordinator, who had just four years of coaching experience.

Dooley says that he initially felt like he had no chance to make Saban's staff and was even less sure of his status after his interview. "A coach he'd worked with mentioned me, so I flew in, and he grilled me for five or six hours. It was an early lesson in how little I knew about football," says Dooley. "And it was classic Nick when I left the interview. He just said, 'All right, it was good to meet you,' not 'I'll call you' or anything like that. But he hired me and gave me a shot, and I was really grateful."

Dooley and his fellow assistants had no idea what was in store for them, though. They'd waded into a cesspool of a program, which had posted only three winning seasons in the last eleven years. The graduation rate for LSU football players—40 percent—was dead last in the SEC. Some of their top recruits had been unable to play because of poor grades, and others simply failed out of school altogether. Under DiNardo, LSU players couldn't seem to stay out of trouble. They'd been arrested for, among other things, purse snatching, stalking, and drug trafficking. A few players had been caught talking to agents. At one point under DiNardo, nearly thirty players on the team had children. Rosen, who continued to work for Saban even though he remained an employee of Michigan State, clearly had his work cut out for him.

Saban demanded change and went after it, hard. He took a lot of pride in the fact that no one could outwork him—in the office, on the practice field, and on the recruiting trail. He started his days at 5 a.m. and didn't get home until 11 p.m. He expected his staff to match his effort, and made them feel like wimps if they couldn't. In Saban's first year at LSU, the coaching staff worked an astonishing forty-eight weekends. Even though they were weekends, there was nothing casual about them. Saban expected every moment of every day to have some sort of meaning, and for every minute to be used efficiently. When things didn't go his way, he exploded.*

"That first year, there was no time to think," says Dooley. "If you asked the nine of us in staff, we would all say that we had no other year like that in coaching, that it was our toughest year in the profession. We hadn't been on staff with Nick, and he was detailed and demanding. Usually, when you're new, you can rely on some of the guys who've been on the staff to fill in the blanks. Well, we didn't

---

* One former Saban assistant says that the coach made only one exception when it came to screaming at his underlings: He never raised his voice when talking to female staffers. Saban would later tell a newspaper that his yelling was part of his "tension relief," and that anytime he did it, it was calculated.

have any of those guys. It was impossible for Nick to communicate exactly how he wanted everything done in such a short period of time, just impossible. Every single day was just a disaster of screw-ups. But as hard as it was, I saw early on that everything he was saying I believed in philosophically, and I knew that this guy was going to be good. You could look past all the stuff that upset you because you knew you were going to win. We just had to sit tight. I'd bet a lot of the coaches who left early because he was so difficult might look back and wish they'd stuck it out."

One of Saban's biggest hires didn't stick it out. Thompson, his defensive coordinator, left LSU just twenty-eight days after being hired. The rumored reason was that he and Saban had fought after Thompson got lost while driving the two of them to a recruit's house. Thompson says that story is untrue. "We were recruiting Chad Lavalais [a defensive tackle] and it was the driver who got lost, then started getting nosy and chatty with Nick, and Nick went off on the guy," he says. "Nick and I never got in a fight."

Thompson does admit that Saban's demands were beating him down, though he says the only reason he left is that his dream job opened up in the state where he had played his college ball. Houston Nutt, the head coach at Arkansas, offered Thompson a job as his defensive coordinator in early January 2000. Thompson accepted it. "Then I asked Houston if he would call Saban and break the news to him. He said no," says Thompson. "So I did it, and Saban went off on me, and deservedly so. It wasn't a conversation. I just listened. I understood his anger. He had to find a new coach and take time away from recruiting and deal with the media."

A few days later, Thompson met with Saban in his office for an exit interview. During the meeting, Thompson says, something very odd happened. "His phone rang and it was Roy Kramer [the commissioner of the SEC]. Saban laid out the whole situation right there to him while I was sitting there. Nick was talking about how business had been done, and how he didn't like it at all. I'm not sure it was a coincidence. I don't even know if it was really Roy on the phone. But it was uncomfortable for me. Nick was right about everything, though. I didn't handle it the right way."

Saban hired Phil Elmassian, a former defensive coordinator at Virginia Tech and Boston College, to replace Thompson. Elmassian would only make it a year.

Saban pushed the administration hard to follow through on the promises made to him when he was hired. He and Terry kicked off the fund-raising for the school's new student-athlete academic center with a $50,000 donation, to help move that project along. (The Cox Communications Academic Center for Student-Athletes would be completed in two years' time.) He also hounded first Dean, then Skip Bertman—who became the athletic director at LSU after Dean retired in 2000—to start the new football operations center. When Saban got to LSU, his players, with no locker rooms or facilities next to the practice fields, were forced to dress for practice at the stadium, then hop on a bus to get to the practice field. Saban believed LSU's football facilities were lacking and out-of-date, and that if they weren't modernized, it would start to affect his ability to attract recruits. He wanted the new center right next to the practice fields. "He told me, 'Every fucking team has that,'" says Bertman.*

The most significant problem facing the LSU football team—at least from an on-the-field perspective—was something Saban had mentioned in his interview: the school's frustrating inability to convince in-state high school football talent to stay home. The list of top-shelf recruits who had fled Louisiana in the 1990s included Peyton Manning, Marshall Faulk, Warrick Dunn, Kordell Stewart, and Travis Minor. Saban told his new staff that their first order of business was to "build a wall around the state of Louisiana."

The foundation for that wall, in Saban's estimation, was Louisiana's high school coaches. "He needed to patch up LSU's relationship with the high school coaches. It had gotten pretty bad," says Tim Detillier, the head coach at Lutcher High School in south-

---

*The center—after some foot-dragging—was eventually started during Saban's time as LSU, but he left before it was completed. It is now nicknamed "Saban-Land." "There's even a terrace outside of the head coach's office that was supposed to be for Nick, but he never saw it," says Bertman.

eastern Louisiana. Right after he was hired, Saban began barnstorming the state, dropping in to meet every high school coach he could. "He wanted to look eyeball-to-eyeball," says Dennis Dunn, the former coach at Evangel Christian Academy. "He wanted to know why kids were leaving the state." (Brock Berlin, a highly touted quarterback at Evangel, had signed with Florida the year before Saban arrived at LSU.) The coaches were impressed with him. "When Saban walked into a room, you could hear a pin drop," says Kenny Guillot, the former coach at Parkview Baptist in Baton Rouge. "When he started to talk, it was mesmerizing. He reminded me of Al Pacino." Eventually, Saban would hire a longtime Louisiana high school coach named Charles Baglio to become his liaison to the prep coaches.

Saban sometimes even took extra, more personalized steps with the high school coaches, which further ingrained their loyalty. He signed the son of longtime Notre Dame High School coach Louie Cook, even though the boy never played for LSU. Cook also got a letter after he lost the state championship in heartbreaking fashion. Saban wrote Guillot a congratulatory letter after Parkview won the state championship, which Guillot still has. Stacy Searels, who coached Saban's offensive line at LSU in 2003 and 2004, says part of Saban's magic is that "he goes into those high schools and makes that coach feel important."

Another part of his magic is his uncanny ability to evaluate talent. Throughout his career, Saban has demonstrated an innate gift for it. "He's like someone who can identify a Thoroughbred racing horse at a young age. He can just look at a high school player and say, 'That guy is a winner,'" says Glen Mason. Saban—then and now—never pays attention to the player rankings done by the recruiting services. Instead he trusts his own eyes, honed over the years, especially in his stops in the NFL. He's discovered several lightly regarded recruits over the years who eventually became stars. During his LSU years, he found a player named Jacob Hester, who was undersized and, at best, a two-star recruit according to the analysts. He didn't talk much, and he did whatever his coaches at Evangel asked of him, playing running back and nose tackle.

Saban watched him, saw some talent, and realized something more: Hester was a baller and a selfless player, the kind of guy who could become the team's glue. He reminded Saban a bit of himself.

Evaluating talent is only half of the recruiting equation, though. Once a college coach identifies a recruit he wants, he has to then hook the kid and reel him in. Saban's belief has always been that the first step is to win over the parents. He always dressed sharply, in two-piece Italian suits and pressed white shirts. He showed up for his visits with a driver. "He could see class, and not just in football players," says Dunn. "He'd go into a house and comment on the furniture and notice the curtains and the chinaware. That impressed those mommas."* The feeling Saban provided for the parents was that "your child would be taken care of," says Cook. "And you believed him. He was in charge, he has a plan, and he wants your kid to be part of the plan."

Throughout his career, Saban has always seemed uncomfortable and awkward in public settings. In smaller gatherings—with recruits and their parents, with administrators, and even with some journalists—Saban's natural shyness dissipates and he becomes quite charismatic. He doesn't leave all of his quirks behind, though. Beth Hitt, the mother of an LSU recruit named Lyle Hitt, says that during an in-home visit, Saban was "very businesslike and cordial, but he moved his leg the entire time."

Several Saban recruits and their mothers, in particular, also mention Saban's brown eyes, surrounded by subtle but still-punctuating crow's-feet. They contain within them both empathy and sympathy. It is with them that he smiles, and, as those recruits would find out if and when they played for him, it is with them that he glows with anger. (As Warren St. John reported in an article for *GQ*, Saban's

---

* There is, of course, the scene in *The Blind Side*—both the book and the movie— when Saban (playing himself in a cameo role in the movie) arrives at Sean and Leigh Anne Tuohy's house for a recruiting visit with Michael Oher, and he compliments Leigh Anne on her "window treatments." She swoons.

assistant coaches refer to the scornful look he sometimes gives them and the players with his eyes as "the bug zapper.")

When it came to the player he was recruiting, Saban was, as always, relentless. He once sat in the metal stands on a frigid day and watched an entire soccer game just to get a word in with Hester, who was moonlighting as Evangel High's goalkeeper. While at LSU, Saban also made a special appeal to the hearts of the boys he was after, something that had to do with that wall he was building.

In 2000, Saban went after a tight end at a Baton Rouge school named Marcus Spears, who was also being heavily recruited by Florida State, Florida, Miami, and USC, among others. "He really played up the staying at home and being around the family things," says Spears, who eventually signed with LSU, switched positions to defensive lineman, and played in the NFL for nine years. Rudy Niswanger, an offensive lineman, got a similar pitch. "He knew I had offers from Florida State, Texas A&M, and Nebraska," says Niswanger. "He came in and asked me where I was from, and I said, 'West Monroe, Louisiana.' He said, 'Not from Florida, right? Not from Texas or Nebraska, either, right?' He kept going through all these other states. At one point, I was wondering if he was okay. Then he said, 'You can go to one of those other schools in those other states, or you can come play for me and play for LSU and be part of a tradition in the state you love, where your pride is, and where you'll probably return. Those are your options.' It was pretty compelling stuff for an eighteen-year-old to hear." Niswanger signed with Saban in 2001.

What Saban did so well, according to Dooley, was tailoring his pitch and tactics to each individual recruit. "He doesn't have a cookie-cutter approach. He's out there prodding the aunt, the uncle, the mom, the coaches, the kid himself," says Dooley. "He always used to say, 'You gotta notice what you don't notice.'"

Recruiting with Saban, however, was a nerve-racking experience for his assistants. Everything had to go smoothly, or there was hell to pay. "It was not fun to be with him if you walked into a high school and the coach wasn't there, or you were driving around and you couldn't find a recruit's house," says Dooley.

In the car with his assistants on a recruiting trip, Saban usually had his head buried in a scouting report and rarely engaged in conversation. If he spoke at all, it was only to ask how much longer they had to go. That silence made his assistants uneasy.

Yet his work ethic—the hours, the concentration—demonstrated something: that for all of his social awkwardness and screaming, he gave everything he had to make his team better and win. It showed, in whatever unusual way, a sort of unselfishness, which is perhaps the most important part of leadership. He never asked for more than he gave, but what he gave was sometimes nearly impossible for his assistants to match.

Eventually, Dooley—Saban's recruiting coordinator for three years at LSU—figured out a way to at least start to even the scorecard. One month, he set up back-to-back-to-back meetings for Saban, with no breaks in between. "We started grinding him back," says Dooley. "We could do it because it was all nine of us against him. It was our way of saying, 'You aren't going to break us, and we're going to take you to the brink.'" A few weeks later, a worndown Saban finally cracked, just a little. "He bit at me," says Dooley. "He was like, 'Jesus, you guys drive my ass around for twelve hours and I can't even get an oatmeal cookie.' But deep down, you could tell he loved it. We backed down on him just a little after that."

Dooley says he had one more, slightly more devious way to push back at Saban. In southern Louisiana, spicy food is king, and the mothers of recruits would frequently put out huge pots of jambalaya when Saban came by for a visit. "Saban didn't take well to spicy food," says Dooley. "So I used to call the moms before he came and I'd tell them, 'Coach Saban really loves those spices, so load 'em up when he comes by.' I did it quietly. He really puts so much fear in guys. You can't forget we're human. I really always connected with Nick, but I had fun doing those things to him. Maybe that's why I stayed with him for so long." (Dooley, who is now the receivers coach with the Dallas Cowboys, remains one of Saban's longest-serving assistants, at seven years.)

Saban's first recruiting class at LSU was not ranked in the top ten by analysts, but the wall was beginning to take shape that year with the signing of two highly regarded Louisiana high school players, Devery Henderson and Derron Parquet.

Saban's first game as LSU's head coach was on September 2, 2000, in Tiger Stadium, against Western Carolina. The temperature at the 7 p.m. kickoff was 97 degrees. Saban believed his team was too casual during warm-ups, so he took the unusual step of ordering them to hit each other—before the game. LSU defeated the I-AA team, 58–0. A few games later, LSU faced another perceived lightweight, the University of Alabama at Birmingham Blazers, a program that had only recently joined the I-A ranks. UAB was so lightly regarded that LSU had paid them $410,000 to come to Baton Rouge and play. In one of the most bizarre games in Saban's career, LSU committed six turnovers and, stunningly, lost, 13–10. One national writer opined that Saban's "fat paycheck should help soothe his pain." LSU administrators and fans didn't panic, though. "Saban had a mystique about him, even then," says Jacobs. "People could sense his intensity. He got a free pass for that loss."

LSU recovered to end the regular season at 7-4. Through considerable behind-the-scenes lobbying done by Emmert and others, the school managed to wrangle a bid to the Peach Bowl to play against fifteenth-ranked Georgia Tech.

Saban, at the time, had never won a bowl game. At Michigan State, he'd driven his team hard in the weeks leading up to the bowl, an approach that clearly hadn't worked. "I remember him being pretty candid, saying he'd gotten his ass kicked in every bowl game at Michigan State, and that something had to change," says Dooley. Saban picked the brains of his assistants, and eventually came up with a new bowl preparation plan: He pulled back and let the team recover for a while, and had them lift weights and run and work on the same fundamentals they had in preseason camp. Only then would he start practicing for the bowl game. "Nick wanted to win this one badly," says Elmassian, who, in a highly unusual fashion, would play a big role in the game's outcome.

Saban had two significant issues with his team that had lingered from the regular season and would come to a head in the bowl game. One of them was Elmassian, the last-minute fill-in as LSU's defensive coordinator. Elmassian had never adjusted to Saban's demands during the 2000 season. "I slept at the stadium for six straight weeks," he says. "I'd go to bed at twelve thirty and wake up at four thirty. And as soon as I felt like I got my head above water, it felt like a whole dump truck of shit landed on top of me again." During the third game of that season—a loss to Auburn—Saban had stripped Elmassian of his play-calling duties. He did it again in the sixth game of the season, a 41–9 loss at Florida. Though Elmassian called the remainder of the regular season games, it was clear that he did not have the confidence of his coach.

The other issue was the play of the team's quarterback, Josh Booty. At halftime of the team's last regular season game, against Arkansas, Saban had wanted to pull Booty from the game. Jimbo Fisher had argued for continuity, and Booty had stayed in. He completed only six of the twenty-seven passes he threw, and tossed two interceptions, one of which was returned for a touchdown, in a 14–3 loss. It didn't help that Booty was not very well liked by his teammates.

During the Peach Bowl, Saban took drastic measures to remedy both issues, a sign of how badly he wanted to win.

Booty started the game, and the LSU offense went nowhere. It wasn't all Booty's fault: One of the Tigers' best offensive linemen, Brandon Winey, was injured and had not dressed for the game. Georgia Tech's offense was also having its way with LSU's defense. After the first quarter, Saban informed Elmassian that he'd be taking over the defense. ("When he did that, we were like, 'Oh, man,'" says Ryan Clark, a safety on the team.) At halftime, down 14–3, Saban made another change: He benched Booty in favor of a quarterback named Rohan Davey. Then, shockingly, Winey put on his pads and uniform and announced he was playing in the second half. In that half, behind a fortified offensive line led by Winey, Davey threw three touchdown passes. LSU's defense didn't surrender another point, and Saban finally won his first bowl game, 28–14.

Two days after the win, Elmassian left to join the staff at West Virginia. "Nick didn't fire me. It was my decision to leave," he says. "I wanted to please him and I was fried. I wasn't really his defensive coordinator. I was more like his defensive interpreter. He was tough on me, but good for me. One thing I knew for sure was that no one would ever stab me in the back to get my job when I was there. I used to taunt Mel [Tucker, LSU's defensive backs coach] and tell him I was going to give the job to him."

Saban finished that first season a surprising 8-4. Despite rumors attaching him to a few NFL jobs (the Washington Redskins and New York Jets), he seemed satisfied with life in Baton Rouge. The Sabans lived in a big French provincial house on Highland Road, not far from campus. Terry, despite her initial impressions of Louisiana back in 1995, was gradually becoming more comfortable there (she and Emmert's wife became fast friends). Saban's quality of life was improved even more near the end of the year when Skip Bertman became LSU's athletic director. Bertman, a towering man with a booming voice, had quite the coaching résumé of his own: He had led the LSU baseball team to five national titles in eighteen years of coaching. Bertman sized up Saban immediately, and knew he had something special, believing that he was "the best coach I've ever seen in any sport." He did everything in his power to keep Saban happy and on track. His football coach would repay him for that loyalty faster than he could have even dreamed.

8

The King of Louisiana

IN EARLY 2001, Saban said the following to the Associated Press about recruiting: "It's almost like picking puppy dogs. When you take the pick of the litter, it will always take two to three years to know what that dog is supposed to be like."

That year, Saban signed such notables as wide receiver Michael Clayton, running back Joseph Addai, defensive lineman Marquise Hill, and offensive lineman Andrew Whitworth. He also signed nine of the top-ten-ranked recruits in the state of Louisiana, pretty much completing his desired wall. That 2001 recruiting class—those puppies—would turn out to be show-winning dogs.

In the 2001 preseason polls, LSU was ranked as high as number ten in the country. They had seventeen starters returning. At his press conferences, Saban spoke at length about his desire to see his team truly dominate its opponents, and mentioned the mid-1990s Nebraska teams as the archetype. Those Cornhusker teams, years after the beatings they'd administered to Saban's Michigan State teams, never seemed to stray too far from his mind.

LSU easily won their first two games that season, over Tulane and Utah State. Then the terrorist attacks of September 11 happened. Word of the tragedies reached the football offices early in the morning, but Saban didn't pay it much mind. He kept working on his plan for his upcoming game against Auburn. The SEC initially decided to go ahead and play the following weekend's slate of games, but eventually bowed to public pressures and postponed them. The Auburn game was moved to the end of the season.

Though the attacks dominated public and private discourse, Saban—focused on game planning and recruiting—didn't talk to his players about them for the next week. He later admitted to a newspaper that he'd made a mistake and had his "head buried in the sand," and that he didn't initially realize the pain and confusion felt by both his players and his staff. Finally, he did talk to them, assisted by Rosen. Then they moved on.

Coming out of the layoff, LSU lost to seventh-ranked Tennessee and second-ranked Florida. Saban appeared happy with the effort against Tennessee and didn't even seem to mind the 44–15 blowout loss to Florida. In the press conference after that game, Saban said he was happy his team could see "how a really good football team dominates." Though he clearly wanted to win, Saban was staying true to one of Rosen's dicta: He wasn't paying attention to the scoreboard. Instead, he was patiently setting up the program with his guys and his system, his eyes fixed firmly on the future, which came a little faster than even he believed it could.

LSU won five of its next six games, losing only to an Eli Manning–led Ole Miss team. That set up its final regular season contest of the year, the 9/11 makeup game against Auburn. At stake was something that seemed completely unlikely after those early-season losses: The winner would claim the SEC West title and play in the SEC Championship game.

The game started on a strange note: Auburn was assessed a fifteen-yard penalty on LSU's opening kickoff, for dancing on the painted tiger on LSU's field during pregame warm-ups. Saban, with the field position leverage, opted for an onside kick, which his team recovered. LSU scored on that drive, and managed the clock throughout the game with a stout defense and 120 yards rushing from LaBrandon Toefield. The 27–14 victory sent Saban's 8-3 team to Atlanta for the school's first-ever appearance in the SEC Championship game, where it would meet 10-1 Tennessee, ranked number two in the country. The Volunteers had beaten LSU, 28–16, in the third game of the season and were expected to win again handily, then march right into the BCS National Championship game at the Rose Bowl in Pasadena.

Leading up to the game, nearly all of the focus was on Tennessee and its national title hopes. Saban's team felt slighted. They were further incensed when they arrived at the Georgia Dome and noticed boxes upon boxes of fresh rose petals, props to be used when Tennessee won the game and clinched a berth in the Rose Bowl.

Early in the game, it appeared that Tennessee would indeed see those petals falling from the stadium's rafters. The Volunteers scored seventeen points in the second quarter to take a seven-point lead into halftime. They had harassed Rohan Davey the entire half, and landed two brutal hits on LSU's starting quarterback that left him dazed. Saban pulled Davey from the game at halftime and inserted Matt Mauck, a twenty-two-year-old redshirt freshman, in his place. While Mauck didn't dazzle anyone with his passing (he completed just five of his fifteen passes), he ran the ball effectively, led LSU on four second-half scoring drives, and was named the game's MVP in LSU's 31–20 upset of Tennessee. The win gave LSU its first outright SEC title since 1986. Saban had delivered on his first promise to the LSU brass a year early. In the Sugar Bowl against Illinois, LSU stayed on its roll, winning 47–34, and finished the season ranked number thirteen in the country.

Near the end of the 2001 season and into the off-season, Saban's name once again came up in various coaching searches. He was a rumored candidate for Notre Dame, the Indianapolis Colts, the Chicago Bears, the Minnesota Vikings, the Carolina Panthers, and the Tampa Bay Buccaneers. It seemed that the itch had once again reappeared. However, Saban decided he hadn't yet accomplished his goals at LSU. That off-season, he was rewarded for staying with a $400,000 raise, which bumped his annual salary up to $1.6 million. His new contract carried with it an unusual provision: If he were to win the national championship, he would become the highest-paid coach in college football by at least one dollar. Only Oklahoma's Bob Stoops, Texas's Mack Brown, and Tennessee's Phillip Fulmer were paid more than Saban. In time, Saban would play a role in the ultimate demise of the coaching careers of two of those men.

One summer early in his LSU career, Saban invited a man named Bill "Brother" Oliver to host a clinic for his players. Oliver had played defensive back for Paul "Bear" Bryant's Alabama teams from 1959 to 1961. He'd been an assistant coach for Auburn, Alabama, and Clemson, and the head coach at the University of Tennessee–Chattanooga. He was a well-respected member of the South's old-school football fraternity, and he seemed like someone who could teach Saban and his players a few things about the game of football.

His clinic at LSU, however, was a disaster. Oliver was unprepared and distracted, and he seemed out of touch with the modern game and its players. The clinic ended up being a few wasted hours for Saban, which usually would have set him off. Instead, he was calm and extremely courteous with Oliver. "Saban respected him and respected the fact that he'd been around ball for a long time," says one LSU coach who attended the clinic and was initially surprised by Saban's reaction to it. "It really showed me something. Saban has this respect for older coaches who've made it through the ranks in one piece. He told me later that he learned to respect his elders as a kid, that if he didn't, he got his ass kicked."

Though Saban has more often than not filled his coaching staff with younger, less experienced coaches—especially in his first few years with a program, as the rebuilding effort gets under way—he has also kept at least one older hand around. At Toledo, that role was filled by Ellis Rainsberger, who, despite the fact that he addressed him as "boy," earned Saban's respect as a sounding board. Gary Tranquill—who had coordinated both sides of the ball, been a head coach in college, and had some NFL experience—was one of Saban's first hires at Michigan State. At LSU, Saban hired a defensive line coach named Pete Jenkins, who had started his coaching career when Saban was fourteen years old. "You won't find anybody who knows Coach better than me," says Jenkins. "He let me know him."

Jenkins was a smart addition to Saban's staff. He'd previously done an eleven-year stint at the university, and knew the ins and outs of the politics involving the administration, the boosters, and the alumni. "That first year, Coach had a lot of questions for me," says Jenkins. "But he's pretty sharp. By year two, he pretty much had it all down."

Jenkins became somewhat of a father figure. Saban even talked to Jenkins about Big Nick, as if still trying to figure the man out. "He told me there was no way to please his father," says Jenkins. "But you could really sense that somewhere deep down, he was still really trying to."

Saban enjoyed going on the recruiting road with Jenkins. On one particular trip, the two men visited the home of high school linebacker Cameron Vaughn. "Coach and I went over there, and Mama and Cameron and his twelve-year-old brother were sitting at the table. Cameron was a good student, and Coach was talking up the academic center," says Jenkins. "The mama and Cameron were eating it up. At the time, it was between us and Texas, and I'm thinking, *We got him*, and I'm relieved because it had gone so well. I'd done a lot of groundwork for the interview, and I was really hoping that it would go smoothly. Then Coach started to wrap it up and said, 'In case I haven't covered everything, please feel free to ask me any questions.' Cameron said he's good. The mama said she's good. Then the twelve-year-old boy raised his hand. 'I got a question,' he said. The mama looked embarrassed. Coach looked a little surprised, and I took a deep swallow and wondered, 'What's this kid gonna say?' The one thing I hadn't planned on was for a dadgummed twelve-year-old to ask a question. So the kid looked at Coach and asked him, 'How come you get so mad when they pour Gatorade on you?' Coach was stunned for a moment. He then smiled at the boy and said, 'Because the stuff is cold and sticky.' The kid seemed satisfied."

Vaughn chose LSU over Texas, started for three years, and made the SEC Academic Honor Roll.

Jenkins says that the thing that stuck out about Saban was his partiality to those who were troubled or down on their luck, the Pharisees of the program. Saban always told his players that they "wouldn't all be treated the same, but they would all be treated fairly," says Marcus Spears. The squeakiest wheels always got the most grease. "Nick was always about altering behavior," says Will Muschamp, Saban's defensive coordinator at LSU from 2002 to 2004. "If a person was willing to change, he'd help them. He'd do anything for them."

During his time at LSU, Saban developed a particular fondness for Shyrone Carey—a running back who frequently got into trouble and would eventually get suspended from the team—and for free safety Damien James, who habitually missed practices and was eventually dismissed from the team. Saban once told a newspaper that James was one of his favorite players ever. "The worst thing was when we had a kid who got into trouble and wouldn't straighten out and Coach had to kick him off the team," says Jenkins. "He would be hurt more than pissed."

That desire to help those in need extended to his coaching staff as well. Saban's relationship with his former assistant Bobby Williams was in serious disrepair after Williams took over for him at Michigan State. ("Coach was mad as hell at Bobby," says Jenkins.) Williams was fired from Michigan State in 2002, then coached the wide receivers for the Detroit Lions for a year and was promptly fired again. After that dismissal, Saban reached out to Williams, and the two men patched things up. Saban hired him to coach the wide receivers at LSU in 2004, and Williams has been with him pretty much ever since. The year before, Saban had hired an intern named Mike Collins, who had been fired as the head coach at the University of Louisiana at Monroe after being charged with driving under the influence. "Saban took a chance on me and I will always remember that," says Collins. (The charges against him were later dropped.) "You see it now in Kiffin, too," says Jenkins, referring to Lane Kiffin, who endured tumultuous and controversial stints as the coach of the Oakland Raiders, Tennessee, and USC before being hired by Saban as his offensive coordinator in 2014.

One of the closest relationships Saban formed at LSU was with a player who was down on his luck through no fault of his own.

Bradie James (no relation to Damien) was a linebacker who signed with LSU in DiNardo's final year. By Saban's first year, he'd become a key part of LSU's defense. A week before the Peach Bowl at the end of the 2001 season, James's father died. Saban allowed James to miss the entire week of practice leading up to the game, then was the first person to greet him when he returned. "From that point on, we started talking," says James. "And we weren't talking about the typical things a nineteen-year-old linebacker would with his coach. We were talking about life."

James says Saban choked up when he talked to him about his own father. He told James that Big Nick had expected his son to work for him. "Saban said he didn't want to do that, so he had to find something that he was really passionate about because he knew his dad would question the decision," says James. Saban's goal, he told James, was to prove to his father that he could be successful. "He said he wished his father was around to see his success," says James. On the day James's father was buried, "me and Saban were wiping tears off each other's faces."

Three months later, James's mother died. "On some days I was a zombie, others I was mad, and others I was all over the place," says James. He sought out Saban. "Nick was never really a father figure, I wouldn't call him that," he says. "But I would go to him and talk. He didn't say he had any answers. There were none. But he always listened."

A few days after his mother passed away, James was called into Saban's office. When he arrived, Rosen was there. "I was like, 'Dude, I don't want to see you. I don't want to talk to Lonny Graybeard,'" says James. He sat down anyway. Rosen told him a story about a young woman, an only child, who had just gotten a new job. One day, her parents, her husband, and her child got in a car to come surprise her at work, but they had an accident on the way, and all of them died. "I turned to Nick and said, 'What the hell?' He told me just to listen," says James. Rosen told James that the girl considered committing suicide after that day. Someone asked her whom she was living for. "And Lonny said she realized she was living for herself," says James.

When Rosen finished the story, James looked at Saban. "He was bawling," he says. "Then he started talking about his dad, and the next thing I knew, it was like me and Nick Saban were having a session together." What Rosen and Saban tried to make clear to James that day was that he had to live for himself, he had to find a passion. That passion became football. "It really became my outlet," says James. After graduating from LSU, James played in the NFL for ten years.

At various times during his LSU career—with his father never far from his mind—Saban turned the mirror on himself as a parent. He didn't like what he saw. Though he viewed himself as a parent to his players, and did a good job with most of them, the results at home with his actual two children, he surmised, were severely lacking. After the 2001 season, he told the *Shreveport Times*, "I really did a poor job with my kids this year. I put everything into this season and haven't paid attention to my family and kids like I should."

A few years later, when Nicholas and Kristen were teenagers, he told *USA Today*, "This business is not very family-friendly. Everyone's grown accustomed to me not being around too much. But I think I miss them a lot more than they miss me, and I don't say that in a bad way. They all adapt. I don't adapt very well to that. I see them grown up and the times I missed and then when I am home they're so used to me not being there, they all got things to do to entertain themselves. And when I ask them what they want me to do they look at me and say, 'But you're going to be here for about five minutes.'"

Muschamp, who would follow Saban to the Miami Dolphins,* says: "I don't think there's any question that Nick has regrets when it comes to his family. Nick and I had these conversations about missing family situations, how he'd miss Kristen's games or plays,

---

* Muschamp later became the head coach at Florida, where he was fired after four years, and is now the defensive coordinator at Auburn.

and how we put a lot of burden on our wives to be single parents. We talked about that a lot."

Saban only realized in retrospect, it seems, that he could never get those years back, a regret that has stayed with him. He had willingly entered the Faustian bargain that really all big-time coaches do. His drive, determination, and effort—and that greatness that has come with it—has a cost. It's what it takes.

Before the 2002 season, Gary Gibbs, Saban's third defensive co-ordinator in two years, left. Saban elevated Muschamp, his thirty-one-year-old linebacker coach, and finally found someone who would stick in the position. Muschamp, a keen defensive mind, was also particularly suited to work under Saban. "Nick's very honest and doesn't sugarcoat anything," he says. "I could handle the criticism and confrontations, and I realized that he was never asking me or anyone else to do something that he wasn't doing himself."

Besides, Muschamp had a ready outlet to take out any frustrations. On nearly a daily basis in the spring, Saban's staff played basketball. Saban called it the NBA ("Noontime Basketball Association"), and he pretty much forced his assistants to take part in the games. "He would walk by my office and tell me we were playing," says Muschamp. "He didn't ask." The games were ultracompetitive because, well, the commissioner of the league was that way. Saban chose the teams and also handpicked his own defender. More often than not, that defender was Muschamp. "He signed my checks, so I let him win most of the time," says Muschamp. "I threw some elbows during the games, and fistfights broke out pretty frequently. All in all, those games were really good for the staff."

They needed those games during the 2002 season, which was one of the most stressful of Saban's LSU career. In that off-season, LSU had been disciplined for three minor recruiting violations that involved Saban and two unnamed assistants. Someone had snitched on Saban for talking to a high school coach in the presence of a recruit when he wasn't supposed to. The penalties were light—LSU lost a few recruiting hours and had to stop recruiting two kids—

but the snitching sent a message: Saban's competitors had grown tired and fearful of his aggressiveness and success on the recruiting trail.

In 2002, LSU was picked to repeat as the SEC West champions and earned a preseason number fourteen national ranking. Matt Mauck, the unlikely MVP of the 2001 SEC Championship game, became the starter at quarterback, adding another chapter in his peculiar hot-and-cold relationship with Saban, which began in 1997. That year, Mauck had committed to play football for Saban at Michigan State but instead decided to pursue a baseball career. After three years of toiling in the Chicago Cubs' farm system, Mauck got back in touch with Saban and inquired about joining him in Baton Rouge. "He was great, very friendly, and said that he always honored his commitments," Mauck says. Mauck, who would become a premed major at LSU, says he always appreciated Saban's savvy and smarts. "He'd somehow figured out that I wanted to go into medicine, so he really focused on that with me and my parents when he was recruiting me. He was pretty cut and dry, and he always used excellent logic, which is something a lot of football coaches don't have."

That logic extended to the practice field. Mauck says Saban prepared his LSU players almost as if they were military recruits. "I'd be in practice and throw a pass and complete it and be pretty happy with myself when all of a sudden, ten coaches would start yelling and there'd be total chaos. I'd be like 'What the hell?' It was all by design. Saban wanted stressful practices, for it to be chaotic, so that when you were in the game, you'd be used to it and feel calm. He always was breaking us down mentally, then building us back up." That same intensity was brought into the meeting rooms as well. "His meetings were so focused. I had [coaches] Mike Shanahan and Jeff Fisher in the pros, and their meetings were jokes compared to Saban's," says Mauck.

However, Mauck says that shortly after he arrived in Baton

Rouge, his relationship with his coach began to cool. The extremely friendly man who had signed him seemed to suddenly disappear. "He'd walk right by me and not even say hello," Mauck says, echoing the complaints of many others who have worked with Saban. "I don't buy the 'He's just focused' thing. I just think it's not very nice."

In his first camp, Mauck was the fourth quarterback on the depth chart. A few days in, Saban asked Mauck to move to the safety position. Mauck wanted no part of that and asked his coach for a few more days of practice at quarterback. As it happened, two of the quarterbacks ahead of him got injured, and Mauck remained in his favored position. "That got us off on the wrong foot," he says. "He didn't ever really seem to see me as a good quarterback."

Mauck was also no fan of Saban's method of treating players differently. Saban sometimes seemed to revel in yelling at Mauck, and one time even kicked his starting quarterback out of practice because he thought Mauck was being disrespectful. After the practice boot, Saban called Mauck into his office to talk to him about it. "He basically asked me why I was being an ass. I told him that I couldn't believe he was treating guys who did the right thing like shit. Joseph Addai [the running back] was a perfect example. He was a fabulous guy and Saban treated him like shit. But he loved guys like Shyrone and Damien," says Mauck. "I think he likes being a father figure because either, one, he truly does think he can be a positive influence or, two, it gives him power. I would like to think it's one and not two." After that meeting, Mauck says, their relationship got a little better, good enough for Saban to trust him as his starter in 2002.

Though the season began with a thudding 26–8 loss to Virginia Tech, LSU followed that game with a string of convincing wins. Then Mauck tore ligaments in his foot in the sixth game of the season. He was replaced by Marcus Randall, an untested sophomore, who won his first game, at home against South Carolina.

LSU went into the eighth game of the season, against Auburn, with a 6-1 record, a number-ten ranking, and talk of possibly making it to the BCS Championship game. But Saban's team crumbled instead.

Early in the week before the Auburn game, Damien James left the team without any explanation and was later dismissed. Then Terry's mother, Linda Constable, died. On Wednesday, Saban flew home to West Virginia for the funeral, and flew right back to Baton Rouge that evening. On Saturday, Randall threw four interceptions and an unranked 4-3 Auburn team thrashed LSU, 31–7.

The next game, at Kentucky, was perhaps the oddest win of Saban's career, and definitely his least favorite. With eleven seconds remaining, Kentucky made a field goal to go up 30–27. The Kentucky players doused their head coach, Guy Morriss, with a bucket of Gatorade, as fans poured onto the sidelines from their seats. With the ball on their own twenty-five-yard line with just two seconds left in the game, LSU seemed done. Fisher, the offensive coordinator, sent in one last play, a Hail Mary pass attempt called "Dash Right 93 Berlin." As Randall took the snap, students stormed the field and began tearing down the goalpost behind him. He heaved the ball fifty-seven yards downfield, where it was tipped by multiple Kentucky players and somehow found the hands of LSU's receiver Devery Henderson, who broke one last tackle as he ran into the end zone to win the game. The play would become known as "the Bluegrass Miracle," but Saban found nothing redeeming about it. The fluky win didn't fit into his worldview. "We won the game, but we didn't defeat the team," he said at his postgame press conference. "If you want to be happy with the results, I'm happy with the results. If you want to be happy with the process, I'm not."

Going into the last game of the regular season against Arkansas, LSU somehow found itself in the hunt for its second straight SEC West title. A win would put it in the SEC Championship game again. LSU led for the majority of the game, but on Arkansas's last drive, quarterback Matt Jones—who had completed only two passes to that point—connected on two deep balls, the last of which went for the winning touchdown. The defeat was a heartbreaker, but Saban liked the way his players reacted to it: They became determined to get better. Saban believed that something clicked in that loss.

In the Cotton Bowl, against Texas, LSU lost again, 35–20, but Saban was upbeat after the game, telling the media that he was "proud of the way the players played." He was already setting the tone for the next season.

The 2003 off-season was Saban's smoothest at LSU, save for one incident that nearly rewrote the modern history of college football. Saban and his staff turned in one of their finest recruiting efforts. They lured quarterback Matt Flynn from his home state of Texas; nabbed another quarterback, JaMarcus Russell—who chose LSU over Florida State—from Alabama; and signed Dwayne Bowe, a talented wide receiver, from Florida. Saban also continued to lock down in-state talent, getting highly touted defensive back LaRon Landry, who was from Ama, Louisiana. The 2003 recruiting class was the best in the nation that year, according to the analysts.

LSU also had fifteen returning starters, including four players on the offensive line, which Saban believed was the most talented one he'd ever had. Mauck's foot injury from the season before had completely healed, and the team made it through the spring and summer with no off-the-field player issues. The fall camp, Saban told the media, was the "best in terms of attitude and work ethic." LSU was ranked fourteenth in the preseason AP poll.

However, the school came closer than most realized to losing Saban for good—and this time, it wasn't because another team was after him. On the Fourth of July weekend, Saban and Terry went to their vacation home on Georgia's Lake Burton. They were joined by a friend named Lenny Lemoine and his family. Lemoine was the chief executive of a construction company in Lafayette, Louisiana, that had built the student-athlete academic center at LSU.

Near sundown one evening, Saban returned to the docks after taking his kids wakeboarding behind his MasterCraft boat. Saban stayed behind to tidy up the boat as the kids ran back to the house. He was just about finished when he grabbed a wakeboard, started to walk off the boat, and slipped. "On the way down, I sliced my ear in half, hit my head on the deck, and was knocked unconscious, as I fell into the lake," he recalled in his book. "Fortunately, I awoke on the lake bottom cognizant enough to know I shouldn't be there, even though I couldn't recall how I'd gotten there. If not for a friend who was with me and pulled me to safety, I might not be here." That friend was Lemoine.

Lemoine later admitted that he wasn't quite as heroic as he'd been portrayed. "It happened so fast I didn't realize he hit his head as hard as he did," Lemoine told the sportswriter Dennis Dodd in late 2003. "In 10 seconds, when he wasn't back up I jumped off the boat and I started to dive in." Lemoine hesitated, though, worried that he might actually jump on top of Saban, who was in about eight feet of water. A moment later, Saban came to the surface, and Lemoine helped him onto the dock. Saban received twenty-five stitches in his head and ear. Afterward, he didn't talk much about the incident, and none of his assistants noticed any change in his demeanor.

A few folks did notice some other changes in Saban, though. As the years went on at LSU, "you just watched him get better and better at handling the stuff outside of football, the public and the boosters," says Weems. When Saban first arrived on campus, he'd ruffled a few feathers when he closed practices to boosters, who were accustomed to having carte blanche when it came to the football team. When trustees asked Saban to lunch, he would nearly always decline. "Nick would always ask me, 'Do they want me to eat with them or win here?' " says Bertman.

Eventually, as it became clear that his help was needed to get the academic center built and the football operations center funded, Saban—with some reluctance—began to glad-hand. "We'd get thirty people together for a fund-raiser and Nick would come to me and ask, 'How do I get out of this?' " says Bertman. "I begged him to get out there and mingle and just say, 'How you doin'?' He did, and it turned out he was good at it. People just started reaching for their wallets." *

Bertman says he had two pieces of advice for Saban when it came to dealing with the public and the media: Smile more and learn some jokes. "He did start to smile, but he was pretty awful at jokes," says Bertman. Saban became adept at controlling his own narrative in the media, however, and he worked hard on the messages he wanted to convey, writing down his thoughts well before a press conference and committing them to memory. Though he remained somewhat stiff and distant, Bertman says, Saban eventually excelled at getting the media "to write what he wanted them to write." The local Louisiana media seemed a bit cowed at times, especially when Saban glowered or snapped at them from the lectern. They put up with it, though, and did everything they could to keep their access to him, especially as he began his ascent onto the national stage.

After an opening 49–7 blowout over lower-tier Division I program Louisiana-Monroe, LSU traveled to play Arizona. Though they recorded another blowout, 59–13, the game became memorable for something other than the score. Late in the contest, with LSU up 45–0, backup running back Alley Broussard fumbled the ball. A few minutes later, with LSU up 52–0, Broussard fumbled again, and the ball was returned for an Arizona touchdown. Saban went ballistic on the sidelines—stomping his feet, screaming himself nearly hoarse,

---

* Saban, though, was never afraid to do things that were unpopular with the LSU money crowd. In the middle of the 2002 season, he brought in Jesse Jackson to speak to the team. Jackson, already a polarizing figure—especially among the white elite in the Deep South—had been out of the public eye for more than a year before his LSU visit after it had been discovered that he'd fathered a child out of wedlock. Jackson spoke to the players about David and Goliath, and how complacency and arrogance led to the fall of the mighty. The *Shreveport Times* reported that Saban "took heavy criticism from some conservative alumni," but his team—and in particular, his African-American players—loved it. "That meant a lot to us," says Marcus Spears. Saban has also said that Martin Luther King Jr. is "perhaps the man I most admire."

and reaching his hand back to grab his own butt cheek, which his LSU players later described as his go-to gesture when he was really angry. The rant was captured by television cameras. "I got so upset about what happened at the end of the game that I didn't remember what happened at the beginning," Saban said later at his press conference. His sideline eruptions were fast becoming almost an expectation at games—a signature move, like Michael Jackson's moonwalk—that the viewing audience waited for and usually got. The cameras always seemed ready. "People always asked me why he did this type of thing when the game was over, when it didn't matter," says Bertman. "And Nick would tell me, 'Skip, the players are screwing up. What do people want me to do, pat them on the back?'"

Mike Collins, the intern who would become Saban's linebacker coach the next season, says: "The thing you figure out about Nick real early is that it's fourth-and-one every second of every minute of every hour of every day." That held true for his fourth-string running back as much as it did for his stars.

By mid-October, the Tigers were 5-0 and ranked number nine in the country. The campus and media were abuzz with BCS title talk. A 3-3 Florida team with a freshman quarterback (Chris Leak) making only his third start was coming to play at Tiger Stadium. That week, however, LSU fans went into a mild panic. On the Thursday before the game, Chicago Bears general manager Jerry Angelo—Saban's longtime friend and former fellow assistant at Syracuse—attended an LSU practice. The Bears were 1-3 at the time and were coming off a 4-12 season. They were widely believed to be shopping for a new head coach, and Saban's name had been near the top of most lists. "It was pretty weird when he was there for practice," says Collins.

Saban dismissed the rumors and told the AP that he and his old friend only discussed LSU's players. "It would be wrong to make any assumption that it was about anything else, because there isn't anything else to talk about. I'm happy to be the coach here." Later in the year, at a speaking engagement in Mobile, Saban trotted out a memorable line about coaching in the NFL: "It comes down to this: Do you want to deal with a bunch of immature people or a bunch of college kids?" Though his denials and humorous manner calmed down things a bit, the anxiety felt by the LSU fans would turn out to be well founded.

In the game against Florida, LSU returned an eighty-yard punt return for a touchdown on its second possession, then never scored again in a 19–7 loss. The national title talk swiftly died. Saban, in contrast to his demeanor in the season's earlier blowouts, remained calm. "When we came back in that Sunday after the Florida game, Nick said, 'The sun's gonna come up, I'm not going to fire anybody, let's get to work,'" says offensive line coach Stacy Searels.

The measured approach worked. LSU won its next six games to finish the regular season with an 11-1 mark. It appeared, though, that it would be the odd man out of the BCS national title game. It was ranked number three, behind undefeated Oklahoma and one-loss USC. Saban told his team to focus on the SEC Championship game and the rest would take care of itself.

Indeed it did, thanks to some serious chaos. On the last weekend of the season, LSU crushed Georgia in the SEC Championship game, 34–13. Previously undefeated Oklahoma got blown out by Kansas State in the Big 12 Championship. The one-loss USC team beat Oregon State in its last regular season game. In the AP poll, USC ended up ranked number one, followed by LSU and Oklahoma. The BCS computers, though, kept Oklahoma in the top spot and ranked LSU number two, 0.16 of a percentage point ahead of USC, which meant that LSU would play Oklahoma in the BCS National Championship game. Adding a little salt to USC's wound: Saban later beat out Trojans coach, Pete Carroll, for the AP's coach of the year award.

According to Rodney Reed, an offensive lineman on the team, LSU's remarkable 2003 season actually began the year before. "It was the Arkansas game," he says, the one they had lost in the final seconds. "It set a tone. We figured out then what it took to win, what it took to be a dominant team for an entire game." Saban believed the same thing.

The 2003 LSU Tigers had a blend of experienced players and talented freshman recruits, like safety LaRon Landry, who started ten games that year and made second-team all-SEC. (Fifteen freshmen played for LSU that year. Seven of them played in every game.) The players and coaches by now had all bought in to Saban and Rosen's preaching. "We had no tangible goals of winning the SEC or the national title that year," says Reed. "The goals were all intangible. We tried to positively affect someone else every day, to get better every day, and to stop focusing on the outcome and instead focus on the process." Mauck says by that time, many of the players had been in Saban's system for so long that "you could hear his words when they spoke to the media. It wasn't necessarily intentional. We'd just heard it all so many times. Guys talked about dominating opponents on individual plays in the game, and of focusing on the moment and letting the outcome take care of itself."

Oklahoma, despite its loss in the Big 12 Championship game, became the media darling and was favored by 6.5 points. It had the far more decorated squad: Five of its players were AP All-Americans (LSU had one) and its quarterback, Jason White, had won the Heisman Trophy. The media also drew a sharp contrast between the coaches. Oklahoma's Bob Stoops, who'd already won a national title, was portrayed as the good guy, the warm-and-fuzzy coach who insisted that his assistants spend quality time with their children. Saban was given the black hat, described as the hard-ass, no-fun grinder. Stoops was, at the time, the highest-paid college football coach in the country. That designation would change, of course, by at least a dollar if Saban won, thanks to the provision in his contract.

Saban was unusually relaxed before the game. At one bowl week event he was cajoled into a dance-off with some of his players and did a reasonable impersonation of James Brown. "We'd never really seen him loosen up like that," says Reed. "In a weird way, it built up our confidence." The only time he almost lost his cool was at a practice in the Superdome in New Orleans, the site of the game. LSU was scheduled to get the field an hour after Oklahoma's practice was done. In a moment that perhaps confirmed the media caricature of the two coaches, Stoops didn't finish his practice on time, and the Sooners' practice started leaking into the hours set aside for LSU. "When Saban came out on the field and saw that Oklahoma was still out there, I thought he was going to blow up," says Sam Nader, LSU's longtime assistant athletic director. Instead, Saban pulled up a folding chair to a prominent spot on the sidelines and sat down and watched the practice, his arms crossed, his leg bouncing, his face set in a hard grimace. Oklahoma got the message and quickly left the field.

LSU dominated the first half of the national title game, holding Oklahoma's heralded offense to just thirty-two total yards. Still, it led only 14–7 at halftime. In the locker room, Saban cornered Spears, one of his best players on defense. "He said he needed me to figure out how I was going to affect this game, that I was a Baton Rouge kid, and that this was the biggest game of my life," says Spears.

Spears had gone through a transformation in his time at LSU. In his freshman year, he had played tight end, his preferred position, and made the freshman all-SEC team. Before the 2002 season, Saban called him into his office and told him he wanted to convert him to defensive end. "I didn't want to do it," says Spears. "Then Saban pulled out two sheets of paper and said, 'Marcus, this is what tight ends make in the NFL, and this is what defensive ends make in the NFL.' I said, 'Coach, lemme try this defensive thing out and see what happens.'"

Spears soon became a favorite of Saban's. He would frequently take his girlfriend (and now wife) to fish for catfish in the pond behind Saban's house in Baton Rouge. "Saban would tell me, 'Man, you gotta take this lady on better dates,'" says Spears. "I used to spend a lot of time there, with Miss Terry and Nicholas Jr." (During the LSU years, Saban's players—and Saban himself—began to address Terry as "Miss Terry," a moniker that carries with it a whiff of the Old South.)

On the first play from scrimmage in the second half, Spears sacked White for a loss of seven yards. On Oklahoma's next offensive play, he intercepted a White pass and ran it back twenty yards for a touchdown. "I came back to the sideline thinking Saban's going to be jumping up and down and excited," says Spears. "Instead, he just said, 'All right, I need you to go out and do a couple more things like that.' "

With 1:51 remaining in the game, and with a 21–14 lead, LSU stopped Oklahoma on downs and had the ball at the Sooner forty-yard line. All LSU had to do was simply run out the clock. Somehow, Mauck and his group failed to do just that, and they left nine seconds on the clock on fourth down. ("That was not a very pleasant time on the headset," says Searels.) LSU's punter, Donnie Jones, says he, like everyone else, had assumed that when LSU got the ball back, the game was over. Jones had his helmet off and was on the sidelines, deep into a conversation with David Toms, the PGA Tour player and former All-American at LSU. "The next thing you know, I hear, 'Punt team!' " says Jones. Oklahoma rushed everyone in an attempt to block the punt, but failed to reach Jones. The ball sailed high into the air, hit the ground, and rolled around on the turf as the game clock expired. LSU had won the national championship, its first since 1958.*

Saban, at the age of fifty-two, had finally made it to the apex of his profession, fulfilling his potential. He was in no mood to enjoy it, though. After the game, he gave Fisher and his staff an earful about the sloppy way the game had ended. ("Some people talk about the joy of victory," says Searels. "For us, it was more like the relief of victory.") Saban barely smiled after the win. Weems says he went down

---

*The title, for historical sake, is considered a split one. LSU won the official BCS title, but USC—which won its bowl game—was voted number one by the AP.

to the locker room after the game and found a brooding Saban sitting alone in his dressing room. "I asked him, 'What's the matter?' He says, 'What am I gonna do now? How am I gonna follow this up?'" Saban was already on to the next season. At his postgame press conference just forty-five minutes later, he lamented: "This year's accomplishments are next year's expectations." He was still his father's son, through and through.

Mauck says as he walked into the locker room after the trophy ceremony, strength coach Tommy Moffitt immediately grabbed him and wide receiver Michael Clayton and said that Saban wanted to see them. "I still had my game pants on," says Mauck. Clayton was the team's best receiver, and was expected to forgo his junior year to enter the NFL Draft. Mauck had already graduated but had one year of eligibility left. "We go into Saban's dressing room, and he's there all alone. He didn't say, 'Good game,' or anything like that. He just said, 'I need to know what you guys are doing next year.'"

Clayton did indeed choose to leave early, and Mauck decided that he'd had enough of a coach who never seemed to appreciate him, despite his success. He wanted no more run-ins, no more screaming. Mauck says he still has mixed feelings about the coach with whom he won a national championship. "Do I think he's a great person? No. Do I have a lot of respect for him as a football coach? Yes. Would I let my kid play for him? I don't know. There's a lot of shit to go through, but because of football and him, a lot of doors have been opened up for me."

Mauck was drafted in 2004 by the Denver Broncos and was in the NFL for four years. He is now the Broncos' team dentist.

According to one of Saban's friends, shortly after the national championship win, Saban called Rosen and asked him: "Why don't I feel happy?"

Saban had already begun to feel restless at LSU, and seemed to have an eye on the NFL. That season, Saban had reportedly talked to both the Jacksonville Jaguars and the Atlanta Falcons. A week before the national title game, he'd received a call from Ernie Accorsi, the general manager of the New York Giants. "I told him I just wanted to know if he was interested. I didn't want to bother him before the game, but I told him if he was interested, I would call him two days after that national championship," says Accorsi. "And he said he was interested."

Accorsi waited the prescribed two days after LSU's win, and called Saban. "I couldn't reach him then. I got Terry on the phone, and she said we'd all work together on this." But at the time, Accorsi was also talking to Tom Coughlin—Saban's former colleague at Syracuse—and it appeared that the Cincinnati Bengals were about to offer *him* a job. With no word from Saban, Accorsi says he went with Coughlin. "Had Saban called me back, I don't know what I would have done," says Accorsi. "We never got into the nuts and bolts."

The same day Accorsi called Saban, Bertman faxed a new contract offer to Sexton that would make Saban the highest-paid college football coach in the country. Bertman firmly believed that Saban would stay at LSU, despite the swirling NFL rumors. The reason was that he and Emmert were ready to give him just about everything he needed. After the contract offer, Bertman told the media: "The president of the university isn't going to get involved with him, and he has all the control he wants. We're supplying that, and love."

That last part was especially true. Bertman had pushed for raises for his football coach, had helped move the academic center along to completion, and had started building the football operations center (though that project was going slower than Saban would have liked).

Bertman's demonstrations of love went beyond just salaries and facilities, however. He did anything he could to keep Saban content. One day Saban went to Bertman's office and dropped a picture on his desk. It was of the University of Houston's offensive linemen, who, in formation, were spread five yards apart from each other, part of the team's somewhat gimmicky (at the time) spread offense. "Nick said, 'You see this fucking team? I can't play this team,' " says Bertman. It wasn't that Saban thought LSU would lose to Houston;

he just didn't want to waste a week of preparing his defense for an offensive attack that they wouldn't see again for years. "The thing was, we weren't even scheduled to play Houston that year," says Bertman. "They were on the schedule for the following season." Bertman eventually got LSU out of the game but says, "It took me about eight years to straighten it all out."

On another occasion, Saban called Bertman and demanded to see him. "I thought, *This doesn't sound good,*" says Bertman. Saban came in and again dropped something on his athletic director's desk. This time it was a handwritten letter from an LSU booster in Jackson, Mississippi, who was critical of some of Saban's coaching moves. "It was the kind of thing most people would have ignored and thrown away, but Nick is a very sensitive guy," says Bertman. Saban insisted on talking to the booster, so Bertman reluctantly set up a call between the two. "The guy got on the phone with Nick and was terrified," he says.

On other occasions, Saban requested that he help keep Terry happy. "He'd tell me that Terry was bothering him about something or other in the box, and that he didn't want to take any shit from her," says Bertman, who always promptly called Terry and did whatever needed to be done.

There was one thing that Bertman couldn't do for Saban, however, and it was the thing that worried Bertman the most: He couldn't tamp down the expectations that had been created. "After a national title, a few losses in a season can feel like a disappointment to fans, and that kind of thing can start to bother a coach," he says.

Despite the love shown, Saban and Sexton sat on the contract offer. The reason: Jerry Angelo was back in town.

Angelo had fired Bears coach Dick Jauron on December 29, 2003. Saban immediately became the presumed front-runner to replace him. A week after the national title game, Angelo flew down to Baton Rouge and met with Saban. The two men talked for nine hours, and Angelo stayed overnight at the Saban house. Saban kept Bertman and Emmert apprised of the proceedings. Bertman says that for the first time, he was genuinely worried.

Angelo wanted Saban, and this time Saban's dalliance with another team was serious.

Saban, as is his wont, had a hard time making up his mind about
what to do, and spent the night wrestling over the decision. Finally,
at noon the next day, he told Emmert that he was staying. At a
hastily arranged press conference, Saban said that his meeting with
Angelo had merely been an informational chat about coaching in
the NFL in general, and that they had not actually spoken about the
Bears job. Greg Gabriel, a longtime scout for the Bears who was involved in the courting of Saban, says: "I think it was real close. Jerry
thought we'd have the deal." The *Chicago Tribune* later reported
that Saban had rejected a deal for $2.5 million a year because it
was too low.

A month and a half later, Emmert and LSU approved the new,
seven-year, $18.45 million deal for Saban, which included $400,000
bonuses for making bowl games. It was the largest deal ever for a
college football coach.*

With Saban's new contract settled, all seemed ready for a promising future for the LSU football program. Saban again recruited an
incredible class in 2004—ranked number two by analysts—which
included receiver Early Doucet, running back Jacob Hester, and
defensive lineman Glenn Dorsey. The Tigers were ranked number
three in the preseason polls. The only notable change in Saban's
coaching staff was the addition of a young former Florida State
graduate assistant named Kirby Smart, who was hired to oversee
the defensive backs. (Save for one year, Smart has been with Saban
ever since and is currently the defensive coordinator at Alabama.)

The coming spring, however, brought with it some troubling
signs. Emmert, Saban's most powerful friend at LSU, left the university to become the president of the University of Washington.

---

* In giving Saban that contract, Emmert, somewhat ironically, played a significant
role in the hyperescalation of college football coaching salaries, an issue that, as
president of the NCAA, he is now frequently criticized for allowing to get out of
control.

At spring practice, the LSU players showed up overweight and out of shape. Saban spent the off-season warning both his players and the media that LSU had become complacent. Another big concern was at the quarterback position: No one had stepped up to replace Mauck. Saban eventually went with the two-quarterback rotation of senior Marcus Randall and redshirt freshman JaMarcus Russell.

In the first game of that season, LSU squeaked out a one-point win over Oregon State, with the Randall-Russell combination completing only sixteen passes in forty-four attempts. When the fans booed both quarterbacks during the game, and the media questioned their abilities afterward, Saban went on the attack. He blasted the fans and called the media "heartless," and said he'd no longer discuss the quarterback situation with them. A frustrated Saban was, at once, demonstrating his loyalty to his players—as he always has, even to this day—and lashing out at the expectations of the fans and the media, which he could not control.

After crushing Arkansas State, LSU lost 10–9 to Auburn, in part due to a missed extra point. The next week, LSU beat Mississippi State, 51–0. Then came the game that may have pushed Saban to finally make the jump to the NFL. In early October, LSU was blown out by Georgia, 45–16, the most points a Saban-led LSU team had ever allowed. "That was something we'd become unaccustomed to," says Weems. In his press conference, Saban—sporting a cut above his eye from an inadvertent elbow he'd taken from an assistant during the game—seemed genuinely befuddled with his team, saying: "We had a good week of practice . . . that was a curveball." The two losses had crushed any hopes of a national title defense.

Saban's team was wearing him out. On the eve of his fifty-third birthday, at a press conference after a win over Vanderbilt, an exhausted-looking Saban indicated that his disappointments were not contained to just his players or the fans or the media. He surprised the gathered media by talking, yet again, about his own fatherhood, saying: "I do a real bad job with my kids right now. I go home at night, I'm a little frustrated because things aren't going so well, and I don't go and spend time with my kids. That's bad. That's bad of me. Because that's more important than this."

Saban's discontent added fuel to a new NFL rumor. This time it was the Miami Dolphins, who had begun the 2004 season at 1-6. Dolphins owner Wayne Huizenga seemed to be growing impatient with his coach, Dave Wannstedt, and he was believed to be coveting the current coach at LSU.

The rumors gained some momentum when Sexton was spotted at the Dolphins' *Monday Night Football* game on November 1, without any convincing excuse for being there. Eight days later Wannstedt resigned, and a Miami newspaper asked Saban if he was interested in the job. "I'm happy with the job I have at LSU, and I'm not interested in doing anything else. I'm happy here and my family is happy here. I don't know anything about any other jobs. We have lots of challenges ahead of us, and I'm looking forward to playing the final three games of the regular season."

LSU won those three games, and finished the regular season at 9-2, earning an invitation to the Capital One Bowl in Orlando against Iowa.

The Dolphins rumor, at least early on, didn't seem to cause much concern for the LSU administration. Bertman told the media in early November: "I don't think he'll entertain any offers. . . . I don't think a team could pry him away."

A new set of factors was in play this time, however. Saban was unhappy with his complacent team, and with the displeased fans. Bertman had been right: The expectations for Saban had become burdensome. "Not too long before that at LSU, a 9-2 regular season would have been amazing," says Spears. "But that year it felt like we lost six games."

Most important, Bertman and the LSU administration had underestimated the will and charm of Huizenga, and just how far the Dolphins' billionaire owner was willing to go to get the coach of his dreams.

At an LSU home game during the 2004 season, Bertman unexpectedly ran into Huizenga in a press box. The two men briefly chatted. "Wayne told me there was no way we were going to keep this coach," says Bertman. "I told him that Nick really liked it here, but we had no chance to match him on money."

After LSU's regular season ended, Huizenga—along with Dolphins president Eddie Jones—made a much splashier entrance. On December 14, just after LSU's first practice for its January 1 bowl game, Huizenga flew to Baton Rouge on his private plane, which prominently displayed the Dolphins logo on its tail. That night, Huizenga and Jones had dinner at the Sabans' house. The next day, Saban released a statement through the university that called the meeting a "preliminary" one, and continued: "No decisions were made. . . . I will continue to be committed to LSU, our football program, and totally focused on our bowl game."

For LSU's administrators, as it had been for Saban's bosses at Michigan State, it was déjà vu all over again. They had dealt with Saban's flirtations with one job or another ever since he arrived. "Every year it was somebody and we'd have to go through it," says Weems. "[Richard] Gill and I were always concerned, and by that time, it was starting to get aggravating. We told Nick it was bullshit in no uncertain terms. He's such a complicated guy, it's hard to know why he does it. He was the king of Louisiana at the time."

After Huizenga's December 14 visit, Weems and the others finally began to realize that something was different this go-round. Bertman publicly changed his tune from just a month earlier, telling a local newspaper: "We hope he doesn't go anywhere . . . this one he is interested in." The LSU leaders, weary of Saban's constant threats to leave, had made the decision that they weren't going to enter into a bidding war. The contract they had given him that made him the highest-paid college football coach—which wasn't even a year old—was where they'd decided to leave it. Saban had all the leverage anyway, thanks to the lack of a buyout clause. It was now up to him to decide whether to stay at LSU and continue to build, or go to the Dolphins for an entirely new challenge.

Saban had immediately gravitated to Huizenga, the self-made billionaire. The former high school football player had, at age twenty-five, borrowed five thousand dollars from his father to purchase a single garbage truck and start a trash-hauling business. In time, that business became the mega-company Waste Management, the first of six Huizenga-built companies (including Blockbuster Video) that would end up listed on the New York Stock Exchange. He had bought the Dolphins in 1993 and had also, at one time, been the owner of Major League Baseball's Florida Marlins and the National Hockey League's Florida Panthers.

Huizenga had yet to replicate his business-world success with the Dolphins, however. He believed it had to do with coaching. Early during his ownership, he'd nudged legendary coach Don Shula into an early retirement. Shula, who had coached the team for twenty-six years and won two Super Bowls, had resigned rather than give in to Huizenga's demands to make widespread changes to his coaching staff. Shula's replacement, Jimmy Johnson—the former coach of the University of Miami and the Dallas Cowboys—lasted four years before resigning after an embarrassing 62–7 loss in a playoff game after the 1999 season. Then came Wannstedt, whose team was in a free fall before he left midway through his fifth season, in 2004.

That year had been a tough one for Huizenga off the field as well. He'd hired Dolphins legend Dan Marino to run the team's front office, only to have him suddenly resign after just three weeks on the job. His best offensive player, the running back Ricky Williams, was busted for pot and had decided to retire from football at the age of twenty-seven. And one of the team's best receivers, David Boston, was caught using steroids and got injured and missed the 2004 season. Huizenga wanted a clean slate. He believed Saban was the man who would provide it.

College coaches who jump to the NFL have always been hit-or-miss propositions. Jimmy Johnson won a national title with the University of Miami and went to the Cowboys and won two Super Bowls. However, Dennis Erickson—a two-time national title winner in college—and Butch Davis, another prominent college coach, had failed in the NFL. And so, of course, had Steve Spurrier, who was the example most pundits brought up as analogous to Saban's potential move. Spurrier, like Saban, had been a successful SEC coach (at the University of Florida), then had gone to the Washington Redskins, where he posted two losing seasons and quit.

Huizenga believed that Saban had two attributes that the more easygoing Spurrier lacked: He was a disciplinarian and he had coached in the NFL before. His most notable NFL experience, of course, was under Belichick, a pedigree that sealed it for Huizenga. Belichick, as the coach of the Dolphins' division rival New England Patriots, happened at the time to be coming off his third Super Bowl win in four years.

Huizenga was willing to do whatever it took to land Saban. Bertman, whom Saban kept in the loop during his discussions with Huizenga, says Saban told him: "Skip, if I don't take this offer, I'm never going to the NFL. I keep asking the guy for more, and he keeps giving it to me." What Saban wanted was what Belichick had in New England: near-total control.

On December 22, Huizenga sent a formal contract offer to Sexton. LSU fans flooded Saban's inbox with emails begging him to stay and left Little Debbie Oatmeal Cream Pies—his snack of choice—outside his house. Two days later, on Christmas Eve, Huizenga flew to Baton Rouge again. He met with Saban for ninety minutes, then with Saban and Bertman—who had remained admirably high-minded throughout the ordeal—for another two hours. The LSU athletic director made his final pitch to his football coach, reminding him that he and Terry and the kids liked Baton Rouge, and that he had recruited well and had several key players returning for the 2005 season and beyond. "I told Nick, 'You don't want someone else to coach them, do you?'" says Bertman.

As the meeting among the three men came to an end, Bertman says Huizenga turned to Saban and said, "Come see my airplane." So the men accompanied Huizenga back to the airport. "I told Nick, 'If you get on that airplane, you'll never come back,'" says Bertman.

Saban did actually walk onto Huizenga's plane, for a brief moment, then he turned around and came back out. The Dolphins' owner flew back to South Florida without a head coach. Saban issued a statement that asked for "24–48 hours" to make a decision. In actuality, it had already been made.

The next day—Christmas—Saban flew with the LSU team to Orlando to start on-site bowl preparations. When they arrived, Saban gathered his team together in a hotel room and told them the news: He was taking the Dolphins job. "It was a world-rocker," says Mike Collins. "No one knew."

Not even Huizenga, or so he claimed. Huizenga told the AP that he had no idea what Saban was going to do, and that he only found out as he watched Saban's televised announcement. "My wife and I high-fived each other," Huizenga said. During that press conference, though, Saban admitted that he had agreed to the deal in principle on Christmas Eve, but had wanted to tell his players about his decision face-to-face.

The decision hadn't been easy for Saban to make—none of them ever was for him. In the end, he finally made the move. He agreed to a five-year, $22.5 million deal and complete control over personnel, scouting, drafting, and the hiring of his assistants. Both Bertman and Gil Brandt, a well-known personnel man in the NFL who was friendly with both Saban and Huizenga, claim that one of the biggest factors in Saban's decision involved Terry. Brandt says that Huizenga, as he was leaving the Saban house, handed Terry a check and said, "Just in case y'all decide to come, here's something for you to decorate the house with." Brandt says he isn't sure how much the check was written out for, but that it included five zeroes. Bertman says it was for $500,000. Huizenga clearly knew how to close a deal.

Saban decided to coach his final game at LSU on January 1, 2005, in the Capital One Bowl against an Iowa team that was led by his former fellow assistant on the Browns, Kirk Ferentz.* His play-

---

* Keenly paranoid fans of LSU football would have been terrified the moment this game was announced. The last time a Saban-led team had gotten an invite to play a bowl game in Orlando, he'd left Michigan State, after five years there, the same length of his tenure at LSU.

.ers and coaches had mixed emotions. They knew they were losing perhaps the best coach in the game, who was just entering his
prime. Though with that excellence came a price. Some in the football program were ecstatic that he was finally leaving. Others were
left with feelings of ambivalence. "There are a ton of things I took
from Coach," says Collins, who is now the defensive coordinator
at Sam Houston State. "But I would say that one I didn't has to do
with communicating with people. Nick was stoic. He didn't let his
guard down. In the staff basketball games, it was kill or be killed. I
just feel like life's too short to live like that, and that you should say
hello to people in the hall."

Rudy Niswanger says he is constantly asked about Saban. "Who
was Nick Saban? The answer is that he is who he thinks he needs
to be at that moment. You almost didn't think he had a human side.
He ain't your daddy. He ain't your best friend. He sure as heck ain't
your momma. He's your coach."

LSU lost to Iowa, 30–25, on a fifty-six-yard touchdown pass on
the final play of the game. "That was a bad ending for Nick in the
bowl game, but he seemed happy," says Weems. "I was in the locker
room after the game, and he did a great job with his last talk. He
told his players that he would always be their coach, and that he
would always be a Tiger."

Saban did have one complication at the time, though: He had
written a book, *How Good Do You Want to Be? A Champion's
Tips on How to Lead and Succeed,* with the journalist Brian Curtis.
Within it, he laid out a bit of his backstory, offered some management tips, and recounted the national-title-winning 2003 LSU
season. At certain points he even revealed an enlightening bit of
self-awareness. "Believe it or not, some people are not wired to accept success," he wrote. "They really don't enjoy it; they are more
content going back to work than reveling in success. I guess I am
one of those people."

One section, however, would come back to haunt him. Early in
the book, he wrote: "I don't know where life will take me; perhaps
one day I will be a head coach in the NFL. Just not right now."

The book was published on December 28, 2004, just three days after he took the job with the Dolphins. Saban and his publisher had to quickly cancel book signing events in Baton Rouge and New Orleans.*

When Saban left LSU, neither Bertman nor Jacobs nor Weems bore him ill will. Jacobs remembered that in their first meeting, Saban had indicated that he someday wanted to give the NFL a try. "On more than one occasion, Nick has told me that leaving LSU was the worst decision he ever made in his life," says Weems. "I was disappointed when he left, but not surprised. But our university and the state should be thankful to him for the time he was here."

Saban had overdelivered on the promises he had made to LSU in his first interview, and he had left the football program in excellent shape. The team's academic problems had, for the most part, been resolved. When Saban was hired in late 1999, the football team had forty-seven players with grade-point averages under 2. When he left, the team had only three who fell under that mark. On the field, LSU was once again—after so many poor years—a national powerhouse. Saban also left a little good-bye present to his successor, Les Miles: Saban's recruits—led by Glenn Dorsey, Ali Highsmith, Matt Flynn, Jacob Hester, and Early Doucet—would form the backbone of the 2007 LSU team that would win a national title in Miles's third season. In fact, seventeen of the starters that year (and ten of the eleven starters on defense) were Saban recruits. (Saban left handwritten notes on all of the players for Miles.) "When Saban left, I thought, *Well, at least he's going to the NFL,*" says Weems.

The folks at LSU wouldn't be quite so magnanimous in two years' time.

---

*The book now has as its cover a picture of him holding the 2011 BCS National Championship crystal trophy while wearing an Alabama shirt—with A. J. McCarron, Alabama's quarterback, standing behind him—after the Crimson Tide beat . . . LSU. The text, however, has not been updated to include his Alabama or Dolphins years.

9

Miami Vice

THE NFL had changed in the decade Saban had been away. Free agency, in its infancy during Saban's time at the Browns, had grown into full maturity. The players were now empowered, and they weren't afraid to show it. The college game was—and remains today—about the cult of the coach. In the pros, the players now reigned. In the 2005 off-season, Saban discovered quickly—and rudely—just how different things had become.

At the Miami Dolphins' annual rookie talent show, Matt Roth and Channing Crowder—the second- and third-round draft picks, respectively, that year—decided to team up for their act. Instead of trying to sing or dance or tell jokes, they opted to go with something a bit bolder. With the coaches, players, and staff gathered in an auditorium at the Dolphins' headquarters, Crowder called the rookie head coach up to the stage, which had, as a prop, a single chair. "I looked out into the crowd and said, 'Hey, Coach, we just appreciate you giving us the chance to play in the NFL, and we want to show you some love,'" says Crowder. With that, he pointed to the chair and invited Saban to sit down.

Saban, somewhat reluctantly, obliged. He sat facing Crowder and Roth. At that moment, Kay-Jay Harris, an undrafted free agent who had been signed by the team, was supposed to start playing some loud club music over the speakers, but he couldn't figure out how to get the CD player to work. The "surprise" that Crowder and Roth had in store for Saban didn't wait for her cue, however. From behind him, a stripper—dressed in high heels, a very small bikini, and a Jason Taylor Dolphins jersey—pranced out of a door and onto the stage. She touched Saban's back. He flinched. When she walked around to face Saban, he shot straight up in his chair. Harris still couldn't get the music going. The auditorium was instead filled with shouts and catcalls coming from the seats. The stripper moved in front of Saban and began to dance provocatively. He sat completely still for one more moment, then abruptly stood up, walked off the stage, and hustled up the stairs. The room went silent. "There were like thirty stairs," says Crowder. "All you could hear was the *click*, *click*, *click* of his shoes, then the door creaking open and the *boom* when it shut behind him." The room exploded in delirious peals of laughter. "It was pretty immature on our part to include Saban in the skit," says Crowder. "But that's why we did it."

In "organized team activities" (OTAs) that spring, Saban had the entire team line up for sprints. He blew his whistle, and everyone took off . . . except for Keith Traylor, a nose tackle who weighed at least 350 pounds. According to some of his teammates, Traylor—then a fourteen-year NFL veteran and winner of three Super Bowls—had a clause in his contract that relieved him of conditioning duties. So, instead of sprinting with the rest of the team, Traylor set off on a leisurely jog. When he realized that Saban was eyeing him, Traylor began to taunt him, yelling, "Hey, Nick! Hey, Nick!" Traylor knew, as the rest of his teammates did, that Saban hated being called "Nick" by his players. He wanted them to address him as "Coach" or "Coach Saban," just as his college players always had.

Traylor kept yelling, "Hey, Nick!" Finally, Saban snapped and told him to shut the hell up and run.

Traylor responded: "Who the fuck do you think you're talking to?" and ambled over to the sideline and stood and watched as his teammates ran their sprints.

Later that off-season, during an intra-team scrimmage, Zach

Thomas, a hard-nosed and, at times, crusty nine-year NFL vet, got into a shouting match with one of the Dolphins' assistant coaches. Thomas, because of his experience and talent, was a leader on the defense. He got a kick out of occasionally switching a Saban-called play in the defensive huddle, something his coach had begun to notice. Saban's face contorted into rage when he heard Thomas yelling. He stopped practice and ran over to Thomas and told him to "shut the fuck up." Thomas told Saban to "shut the fuck up" right back, then yelled, "I'm a grown-ass man!" As the two men went at it face-to-face, Thomas's teammates sensed that the linebacker's fury was placing him on the verge of doing something he would later regret, so they grabbed him by the shoulders and dragged him away as he continued to shout and point a finger at his head coach.

When asked why he took the Dolphins job, Saban says: "I was offered several NFL jobs that I didn't take. I really liked Wayne. I thought, 'These are the right people, the right place, the right franchise, and the right time.'"

The perks that came along with it weren't too bad, either. Saban arrived in Miami like some sort of potentate. He hitched a ride to South Florida on Huizenga's private plane, then hopped on his new boss's helicopter, which landed on the Dolphins' practice field. That summer, Saban and Terry bought a $6.7 million house in the same Fort Lauderdale neighborhood in which Huizenga lived. The site of the home had apparently once been the hideout of the Al Capone lieutenant "Machine Gun" Jack McGurn, who supposedly planned the infamous 1929 St. Valentine's Day Massacre.

The Sabans also spent a vacation week with the Huizengas, cruising the Mediterranean on the billionaire's yacht. On that trip, Saban visited Croatia, the first time he had laid eyes on his family's country of origin. Huizenga later told a reporter that one morning during the trip he awoke at 6 a.m. to get in a workout and found Saban in the yacht's office watching film. Huizenga was delighted.

The Dolphins owner also lavished his coach with almost anything he wanted, football-wise. He built Saban a $10 million practice bubble, though in the end, it would be used rather sparingly. Saban was allowed to hire as many assistant coaches as he needed (he had more than twenty of them at one point) and was authorized to pay them top dollar—his offensive and defensive coordinators would make $830,000 each, and some of the position coaches would pull in as much as $400,000. Saban's own $4.5 million salary made the rookie head coach one of the highest paid in the league. (With perks, Saban's annual salary was closer to $5 million.)

Huizenga also made good on his promise to provide Saban with the final say on all hiring matters—coaching, personnel, and staff. General manager Rick Spielman was nudged out and former New Orleans Saints general manager Randy Mueller was brought in, with the foreknowledge, of course, that he would be a GM in name only. Saban even had a say in the hiring of the Dolphins broadcast team of Jimmy Cefalo and Joe Rose, two former Dolphin players.

Saban, as he had told Bertman, had everything he wanted. Now all he had to do was completely turn around an NFL franchise.

That would be more difficult than he initially realized. Wannstedt had left "a loose ship that had spun completely out of control," says one former Dolphins staffer who worked for both Wannstedt and Saban. The team had finished an ugly 4-12 in 2004. Neither of the previous two drafts had yielded an established starter, and with its salary cap nearly maxed out, the team had little financial wiggle room to improve via free agency. An upgrade through the draft didn't seem likely, either: The Dolphins had no second- or third-round picks in 2005.

Saban quickly hired Scott Linehan as his offensive coordinator. Linehan had led the explosive offense of the Minnesota Vikings for three years, and faced the challenge of trying to replicate that on a Dolphins team that had serious questions at quarterback. In college, a team could sometimes get away with a mediocre quarterback if it excelled in other areas, like the offensive line and defense. For the most part, that wasn't the case in the NFL, and the Dolphins appeared to have something less than mediocrity at its most important position. Gus Frerotte and A. J. Feeley were the only two established veterans on the roster. Feeley was merely a competent backup, though he'd been acquired from the Philadelphia Eagles the year before for the Dolphins' second-round pick in the 2005 draft. Frerotte was an eleven-year veteran whose best years—and they were never that great—were behind him.

The problems on offense were minor in comparison to the potential ones on defense. The Dolphins were old on that side of the ball. Eight of the eleven starters—including Zach Thomas, Jason Taylor, and Junior Seau, the team's three big-name linebackers—were thirty or older. Saban had decided to make a big change in the defensive scheme that year, switching from a base 4-3 defense to a hybrid 3-4, something that would require patience and focus.

The age of the defense and the scheme transition made the job of the Dolphins' defensive coordinator seem unappetizing to some. Saban's reputation for being especially hard on his defensive coordinators didn't help, either. Three men declined Saban's offer to coach the position—despite the extremely high pay—before Saban finally hired Richard Smith, with whom he'd worked at the Oilers sixteen years before.

The enormity of the task of turning around the Dolphins, coupled with the pressures of being a first-time head coach in the NFL, seemed to cause an already obsessive and uptight Saban to become even more tightly cinched. By taking on the dual roles of head coach and personnel chief, he'd perhaps bitten off more than he could chew. As a college coach, recruiting and coaching could be, at times, separated. In the NFL, figuring out the personnel puzzle was an ongoing issue. Saban first had to scout his own players to see what he had. Though he had little cap money at his disposal, he still had to look at free agents and potential trade targets on the other thirty-one teams. And, of course, he had to get up to speed on the crop of college players who had entered the 2005 draft. (The

Dolphins would recoup a few draft picks through some predraft trades.)*

Four months into his Dolphins tenure, Saban had not found the time to decorate his office. It had a desk, a video machine for watching tape, a pile of notebooks, stacked cardboard boxes that contained his handwritten journals and scouting reports going back to his assistant coaching days, and a picture of him playing golf with Tiger Woods. "He could have had forty-hour days and not been able to fix what needed to be fixed," says a former Dolphins staffer. "He didn't have time to exhale. The stress level was really building in that first year."

That stress soon became manifest. He reportedly exploded at a young staffer for getting the wrong kind of Little Debbie Oatmeal Cream Pies. (The staffer had purchased boxes of Little Debbies instead of the individually wrapped ones he preferred.) An equipment manager, after saying "good morning" to Saban one day, was instructed by a Saban lieutenant never to speak to him unless first spoken to because Saban wanted to concentrate on football.

Of course, it didn't help that Saban no longer enjoyed the counsel of the man who could have helped him navigate his first year in the NFL. Belichick was now not only a fellow NFL coach, he was a division rival. The two men had remained close since the Cleveland years. They'd gone to concerts together, seeing Bon Jovi, Elton John, and Ringo Starr. Belichick's son had attended Saban's summer football camp at Michigan State. Terry hung an oil painting by Belichick's father in their new Fort Lauderdale home. Belichick had visited Saban in Baton Rouge as recently as the week after LSU's national title—the two had pored over film and drawn up plays together. Those days and meetings were over, at least for now. The two

---

* In that draft, Saban relied on familiarity: In the first round he took Auburn running back Ronnie Brown, whom he'd coached against while at LSU. The second-round pick, Matt Roth, was a defensive end on the Iowa team that beat Saban's LSU squad in the Capital One Bowl. In the third round, he took Florida's Channing Crowder, another player against whom he'd coached. He took Travis Daniels, one of his defensive backs at LSU, in the fourth round. With his last pick, he chose Kevin Vickerson, a defensive tackle from Michigan State who'd been coached by Bobby Williams, who was now on Saban's staff at Miami.

men rarely talked during Saban's years with the Dolphins. (Belichick, when asked by the media what he thought about Saban's arrival in the NFL, rather dryly replied: "Two Croatians in the same division. You don't see that every day." He didn't elaborate much more.)

Saban battled early on to get his players to buy in to his process and focus on the details. When he spotted offensive tackle Vernon Carey wearing a baseball cap sideways on the sidelines during a preseason game, he told him to straighten it out because Carey, in his estimation, "looked like a chump and not a champ." When star receiver Chris Chambers told a newspaper that his goal was to score a touchdown in every game, Saban publicly chastised him during a press conference, describing goals like that as "clutter" and telling him instead to "focus on the next catch" and let the numbers follow. Crowder remembers one day early in his rookie season when he walked into a small bathroom set aside for the media in the Dolphins' complex. "I went in and there was Saban," he recalls. "It was just me and him. It's silent, but I feel like I have to say something because he's my coach and he's just drafted me. All I know about him at this point is that he loved Terry. He was always saying, 'Me and Terry' this and 'Me and Terry' that. So I say, 'Hey, Coach, how's your wife?' He stares at me with that stoic face and says, 'She'll be a lot better if you can cover backs on third down.' I looked at him to see if he was joking, but he still had that stoic face. He didn't laugh. I washed my hands and looked at him again. No change. And I left."

Saban's most publicized run-in with a player at the time happened in July. In the 2005 NFL Supplemental Draft, the Dolphins chose Manny Wright, a 6'5", 330-pound defensive lineman. He was a risky pick—he'd struggled with his weight, had academic problems, and had been arrested for various misdemeanors during his college career at USC. The physical potential was there, though. Saban viewed him as a project and took him under his wing, just as he had done with some of the more troubled players at LSU. "Saban gave Manny as much attention as he did anyone else on the team," says Kevin O'Neill, the Dolphins' trainer at the time. "Manny was given every opportunity to turn things around."

He didn't. Wright remained undisciplined and gained weight during training camp. Saban finally lost patience with him at one practice. Wright had walked onto the field without a helmet or pads, and he was wearing the wrong shoes. Saban exploded and yanked off his straw hat and pointed to his head. The incident lasted all of seven seconds.

To most on the team, it was no big deal. "Wright was a baby, one of those players who was lazy and overweight," says Heath Evans, a fullback for the Dolphins. "Most coaches would have made him cry." Saban himself later described the incident to the media as "C-minus butt chewing."

The problem was that there was a television camera present, which caught not only the "butt chewing," but also Wright wiping away tears as he walked back to the locker room. The footage led the sports coverage on local news shows, with smirking sports anchors referring to Saban as "the Nicktator." The glee with which they reported the incident was the first visible sign of the chasm that had begun to grow between the Miami media and the Dolphins' new head coach.

Saban had done little in his career to that point to endear himself to the media. Some of his difficulties with the press had to do with his natural shyness, but a lot of it was about control: Saban liked to exert as much of it as possible over any press conference. He couldn't control everything, however, and when he believed he had lost control, he could become a bit of a bully. When a media member asked what Saban thought was a stupid question (and he seemed to think that many of them were), he would sigh and shuffle his feet, then look around incredulously at other press folks in the room, with a cocked eyebrow and a sardonic smile, as if asking them: "Who is this buffoon?" In that way, he turned the other media members into silent conspirators. At times in the past, they seemed to be flattered by being drawn in as accomplices. Many members of the media seemed to desire the same thing Saban's players did: his respect and adulation.

At LSU, Saban lorded over the local media, to the point where, at various times, several of them stood up and clapped for him in appreciation and one even asked him to autograph a poster. The Miami media horde wasn't quite so enraptured, though. They were hardened vets in a much bigger city who had covered Super Bowl–winning coaches Don Shula and Jimmy Johnson. Saban's attitude toward them didn't help matters.

His relationship with the media in Miami had actually gotten off to a good start. The media, like the fans of the team, expressed optimism that Saban could turn around a franchise that had been stuck in a rut for years. The press had anointed him "Saint Nick" because of his Christmas Day hire. It would be the high point of their relationship with him.

After his introductory press conference in Miami, Saban didn't speak to the media again for two and a half weeks. He then clamped down on the media's access to the Dolphins facility and didn't allow them to use the media workroom except for what he deemed as special occasions. As he'd done at LSU, he also restricted media access to his assistant coaches—they needed his permission to talk. (Even Mueller, the general manager, who had worked as an analyst at ESPN before joining the Dolphins, had to run any media requests by Saban.) Saban tried to cut off the traditional Friday player interviews until the NFL intervened and told him he had to allow them. Saban once told a group of writers that if he saw an anonymous source quoted, he would root out the person and fire him, and that it would be the media's fault.

In the end, the antagonism and attempts to restrict access would backfire on Saban: No member of the local media would come to his defense when he needed them the most.

The most significant off-the-field incident for the 2005 Dolphins, however, went undiscovered by the media for many years.

Jeno James, an offensive lineman, played college football at Auburn and was drafted by the Carolina Panthers in 2000. He signed with the Dolphins in 2004 as a free agent. The 6'4", 320-pounder was soft-spoken, well liked by both his teammates and coaches, and was a key member of the Dolphins' offensive line.

Leading up to the first "two a day" practice of the Dolphins' 2005 training camp, James says that he had not been feeling well. "I didn't eat anything in the three days before we started. I shouldn't have been out there practicing, but with the pressures of the NFL, you felt like you had to be out there."

James made it through both practices in the searing South Florida summer heat. After finishing off the second practice with a set of sprints, the team headed back to the locker room. "I don't remember much after that," says James.

What happened next, say James's teammates, was one of the most frightening scenes they had ever witnessed in football. While walking in a small hallway that led to the locker room, James suddenly collapsed. "He was on the floor, this massive guy, his eyes in the back of his head, convulsing and vomiting up this gross green stuff," says Evans.* Then Saban walked in. "We all saw him," says Crowder. "Saban looked briefly down at Jeno, stutter-stepped, and then walked right over him and kept going and didn't look back."

James remained on the floor, his body shaking uncontrollably. When the medical staff eventually showed up, "they were panicking," says a former Dolphins staffer. James was dying right there on the floor. "The only thing I remember was when they put the paddles on me to bring me back," says James.

A medevac helicopter was called in and instructed to land in the back of the facility, to keep the news from the media, but a medevac helicopter turned out to be a hard thing to hide. When the media asked what had happened, they were told that James had suffered a "heat-related illness." Nothing else was said or reported at the time.

James was flown to Broward General Hospital. "When I woke up, Saban was there. He was one of the first people I saw," says James. "I don't remember if he said anything. I was still impaired,

---

* It was Evans who first told this story publicly, on a Miami radio show, in 2011.

still fighting for my life. I was happy he was there, though. But that was before I heard what happened."

On a Miami radio show in 2012, Saban was asked about the incident. His account differed somewhat from that of his players and staff. "At the time, no one really realized that Jeno was probably having as tough a time as he was. Immediately thereafter, I was with Jeno for several hours, Jason [Taylor] was too, and very, very concerned and caring. It was after practice and I was just walking upstairs, a lot of guys lying around kinda tired, you know. And I came back down as soon as I heard Jeno was having an issue and a problem," he said. "Everybody has their little, sort of, perception of how things happen and whether they look at the negative or positive side of it."

A few hours after James collapsed, Saban called a team meeting and attempted to explain his actions. "He said, 'For anyone saying anything about the way I handled the situation, I am not a doctor. It was best for the doctors to handle this,' " says Crowder. "I was like, 'I'm not a doctor, either, but I would've stopped.' The worst part about it is the old cliché. He literally and figuratively stepped over a guy."

Evans says that in his speech to the team, Saban also explained that if a leader doesn't know the answer right away, he has to go somewhere by himself and regroup. "He was trying to appear like he was in control," says Evans. "I thought, *Man, that's fine when it comes to a decision about who's going to be your quarterback, but what about natural human compassion?*" Evans says that Saban didn't lose the team that night, but that he "definitely put a dent in it. Trust is what he was selling."

As James gradually recovered in the hospital, his teammates started to call and fill him in on what had happened. "You never want to hear that another man walked over your body like that, especially after you put out so much effort and hard work. That concerned me," says James, who now works in construction in Alabama. "We never really talked about it as far as I know. My mind was all over the place. He may have asked me if I was okay, but I'm not one hundred percent sure. We never had much of a relationship after that."

The Dolphins were picked to finish last in the AFC East in the 2005 season. Their play in the preseason seemed to confirm that prognosis. They went 1-4 and averaged only a little more than thirteen points a game. The offense was booed heartily by the home crowd in the last preseason game.

The regular season started with a bang, however. On September 11, in 90-degree weather, the Dolphins beat a very good Denver Broncos team, 34–10.* Travis Daniels, the rookie from LSU, had an interception, and Jason Taylor, who had begun training camp concerned about his new roving role in Saban's 3-4 defense, returned a fumble eighty-five yards for a touchdown. The players were ecstatic, especially given what they'd been through during that off-season and the season before. Saban, channeling Rosen, immediately began warning them about "relief syndrome," telling the media that it was "poisonous" and "lethal," and that when "you have something good happen, it's harder to stay focused, to pay attention to detail. You have a tendency to want to take a break, or expect that 'I did well once, so I should take it easy now.'"

His warnings went unheeded. The Dolphins proceeded to lose four of their next five games, and they were 2-4 heading into a game against the New Orleans Saints, a game that involved a strange twist of fate for the Dolphins' rookie coach.

Because of Hurricane Katrina (which had devastated New Orleans and much of Louisiana right before the season), the Saints were playing their home game against the Dolphins in Tiger Stadium in Baton Rouge, taking Saban back to his old home. His LSU tenure was the biggest topic in the week leading up to the game.

---

*The Broncos would finish 13-3 that year and play in the AFC Championship game.

Saban admitted to the media that he still watched every LSU game on television.

The fans on that Sunday in Tiger Stadium greeted Saban warmly. His old friends Charlie Weems and Richard Gill watched the game from the Miami sideline. The Dolphins played one of their best games of the year, defeating the Saints, 21–6. When the game was over, Saban came out of his usual shell, signing autographs, kissing women on the cheek, and hugging some of his former LSU players who were on the Saints. "I'm in pro football but I still love college football and I love LSU," Saban said in his postgame press conference.

Two games later, Saban had another emotional reunion when the defending Super Bowl champion Patriots and Belichick came to Miami. Saban and Belichick chatted briefly before the game, which New England won on a late Tom Brady touchdown pass, 23–16. The loss dropped the Dolphins to 3-6, but unlike the previous year, Miami had fought hard in every one of those games.

That fight came to an abrupt end the following week. Against a weak Cleveland team, the Dolphins got trounced, 22–0. The scene in the Dolphins' locker room after the game was ugly: Jason Taylor went wild, slamming his shoulder pads against a locker. Saban went even wilder. His old friend Dennis Fryzel was in the locker room, and later told a newspaper that he froze when Saban started shouting, only managing a quick glance at the offensive line coach, Hudson Houck, who was "white as a ghost. . . . It was as close to a come-to-Jesus moment that I've ever seen with Nick. I wouldn't want anybody I know in there. I was afraid to blink."

The Dolphins' record stood at 3-7. The Cleveland loss—their sixth in seven games—was the sort that can cause a season to completely unravel. The next week, in a moment of reflection, Saban told the Miami media that he was focused on "building a team for the future," and not on the results. This was, of course, more Rosen-influenced talk, but the media interpreted it differently: They castigated Saban for giving up on the season.

Then a remarkable thing happened: The Dolphins started winning. They beat the Oakland Raiders. In a game against the Buffalo Bills, they fell behind, 23–3, in the fourth quarter but rallied to win,

24–23, on a fourth-down touchdown pass to Chambers with six seconds left in the game. (After that play, Saban screamed with joy on the sideline and punched the air with his fist.) They capped a six-game, season-ending winning streak with a win over the Patriots and Belichick. (The game didn't mean much to the Patriots, who had already qualified for the playoffs, but still . . .) The Dolphins finished at 9-7, narrowly missing out on a spot in the playoffs. The season had taken off when the players bought in to what Saban was preaching. Saban had squeezed a winning season out of what was basically the same roster that had gone 4-12 the year before. "We were the hottest team in the league at the end of the season," says Chambers.

Much of the team's success was also due to the late-season excellence of a player on whom Saban had taken a big risk in the off-season. That player was Ricky Williams.

The year before Saban arrived in Miami, after Williams had tested positive for marijuana and "retired," the running back had wandered the globe, living in a tent in Australia and spending a month at a yoga center in India. He studied holistic medicine and became a vegetarian (dropping twenty-five pounds off his sturdy frame in the process). He appeared to be done with football for good, then Saban contacted him and asked him to consider coming back to the team.

Saban, of course, had ample reason to want Williams back. Williams was a legitimate NFL star and, even though the Dolphins selected running back Ronnie Brown in the first round of the draft, Saban needed all of the offensive weapons he could get, especially because he lacked a legitimate franchise quarterback. There was more to it than that, though.

Williams, like Manny Wright, Shyrone Carey at LSU, and, later, Lane Kiffin at Alabama, became one of Saban's reclamation projects, someone whom the normally hard-edged coach opened up to and attempted to influence and help. The difference was, of course, that Saban was no longer a college coach. Williams was already a man who had earned real money (he'd received an $8 million sign-ing bonus with his first team, the Saints). In the pros, there were no scholarships that could be revoked, and Williams couldn't be kicked off the team or suspended without going through the thick tangle of bureaucracy of the NFL Players Association, who would likely fight for his rights. In other words, Williams had to genuinely *want* to be helped.

It turned out that he did. Saban convinced Williams to come back and serve out his four-game suspension for his pot bust the year before. In successfully courting Williams, Saban had also cor-rectly deduced the sentiments held by his players toward their for-mer teammate. Some fans and media pundits had branded Williams as a quitter and had held him responsible for the 4-12 record in 2004. But his teammates had never held a grudge. "Ricky was a guy who cared about others, a genuinely loving, good man," says Evans. Chambers felt the same way. "Ricky was an outstanding football player, sure," he says. "But he was also a great teammate." In fact, the move to bring Williams back actually elevated Saban's status in the eyes of his players. "We saw what he was doing for Ricky," says Crowder. "He really embraced him and took him under his wing. He gained respect for that."

Saban had seen a bit of himself in Williams. The two men were simi-lar in some fundamental ways, both shy introverts who believed they were misunderstood by the general public (Williams later ad-mitted publicly that he had been diagnosed with social anxiety dis-order). Though the manner in which they individually expressed those feelings—one became an uptight coach, the other a mystical wanderer—seemed to make for an odd pairing, the partnership was working. Then Williams found trouble again.

In early 2006, Williams failed another drug test. The punishment this time was a yearlong suspension, which left the Dolphins seri-ously hamstrung: They lost one of their best players for nothing in return—they now couldn't even trade Williams for draft picks or another player. Yet, even then, Saban stuck by him, standing up for him, both publicly and privately, after the failed test, and repeatedly telling the media that he was one of his favorite players he'd ever coached. Their relationship didn't end with Williams's suspension, either. On the eve of the 2006 NFL Draft, Saban had Williams over to his house and the two men shared a pizza. Saban even blessed Williams's temporary signing with the Canadian Football League's Toronto Argonauts, where he played one injury-marred season.

In 2013, after he retired from the NFL, Williams applied for a job as the running back coach at Incarnate Word, a small FCS school in San Antonio. He asked Saban for a letter of recommendation. Saban went one step further: He offered him a job on his Alabama staff. Though Williams declined the surprise offer, he did end up getting the job at Incarnate Word, where he coached for one year.

The Dolphins entered the 2006 off-season in search of a franchise quarterback. (They cut Gus Frerotte in March, convinced he wasn't the answer.) Saban had the option of drafting that quarterback, or to get him via a trade or free agency. Saban determined early on that there was no can't-miss quarterback in the 2006 draft class (Vince Young and Matt Leinart were the headliners that year), so the Dolphins went shopping, and Saban ultimately made the decision that would play the biggest role in his NFL fate.

Two marquee quarterbacks happened to be available that year. The problem was that both were coming off significant injuries. Drew Brees, who'd been the starter for the San Diego Chargers since 2002, was made expendable when that franchise drafted Philip Rivers in 2004. Brees had started every game for the Chargers in 2005, but he tore the labrum and the rotator cuff in his throwing shoulder in the last game of the season. The Chargers had shown only mild interest in bringing him back.

Daunte Culpepper had been the starter for the Minnesota Vikings since 2000, and had averaged more than twenty-five touchdowns a year through 2004. His 2005 season had been a disaster, though. He threw just six touchdowns against twelve interceptions, and tore ligaments in his knee in his seventh—and last—game of the season. Though Culpepper was not a free agent, he had made it clear that he wanted to leave the Vikings.

So Saban had a choice. Chambers says it was pretty clear from the way Saban talked during the off-season that he preferred Brees. (Saban and Terry had dinner with Brees and his wife one night, and Saban came away very impressed.) The most alluring thing about Brees was that, unlike Culpepper, he was a free agent, which meant the Dolphins could get him without trading draft picks or players.

The injuries to both players, however, remained concerning. Saban and Randy Mueller flew to Birmingham to visit Brees as he rehabbed with the famed orthopedic surgeon James Andrews. Andrews told Saban that though there was no precedent for a quarterback with an injury like Brees's returning to the game, he was confident that the quarterback would play again at a high level. Doctors were confident that Culpepper could return to form—there *was* positive precedent for a player with his injuries.

The Dolphins' medical staff checked out both players as well, reaching out to various injury experts for second opinions. Culpepper appeared to be further along in his recovery than Brees was. The Miami medical staff was hesitant about Brees. Saban still wanted him, though. "We actually had a deal worked out with Brees," he says. "But the medical people failed him on the physical."

Going with Culpepper was ultimately judged to be the less risky move. In the end—as with all calls pertaining to personnel—it was Saban who made the final decision. It was the prudent one at the time. History, though, wouldn't judge it so kindly.

In July of that off-season, Saban was invited to have dinner with President George W. Bush at Joe's Stone Crab, a legendary restaurant in Miami Beach. He declined. The decision, he insisted, wasn't political.* "I was also invited to play Augusta by a member right

---

* Saban has never spoken publicly about his political affiliations, though it is worth noting that Joe Manchin—one of his childhood friends, and the godfather to his son, Nicholas—is the former Democratic governor, and a current U.S. senator, from West Virginia. Saban has donated money to his campaigns in the past.

after the Masters that year. I didn't go," Saban says. "I can't change the schedules of 150 people to play golf or have dinner with the president. How does that benefit the team?"

A friend of Saban says that he believes Saban wouldn't have found it that interesting to have dinner with a president. "And, anyway, he's so focused on football that he probably thought Clinton was still president at the time."

Throughout the preseason, Saban told the media that he was "very pleased" with Culpepper's progress, and that he would be ready for the season-opening game. Privately, though, he was growing concerned about the man he'd chosen to be his starting quarterback and, by default, a leader on the team. In practices, Culpepper seemed to be playing carefully, like a man who was thinking about his injury, or worse, was still hurt.

That preseason, the Dolphins became media darlings. The narrative was not too difficult to construct: The team had finished with six straight wins the previous season, and Culpepper, presumably, would provide a significant upgrade to the quarterback position. Both *Sports Illustrated* and *ESPN the Magazine* picked the Dolphins to go to the Super Bowl. While those picks were certainly calculated ones that were made, at least in part, to help sell more magazines, they did reflect the buzz that the team and its second-year coach had generated, and the expectations that came with it.

Miami was presented with a golden opportunity to live up to those expectations in the NFL's kickoff game against the defending Super Bowl champion Steelers, who would be without their injured starting quarterback, Ben Roethlisberger. With the game in Pittsburgh—just an hour and a half from Fairmont—Saban and Terry requested seventy-eight tickets for friends and family, including Saban's mother, Mary.

What they witnessed wasn't very pretty. Culpepper was sacked three times and threw two interceptions, the last of which effectively ended the game when it was returned for a touchdown with three minutes left to play in a 28–17 loss.

The Dolphins lost two of their next three games. Culpepper's sack rate—he'd suffered twenty-one of them in the team's first four games—was alarming. He was clearly not the same player he once was, and his lack of mobility was hurting the team. The Dolphins were 1-3 heading into a game against Belichick in New England.

According to the players, up until that week Saban had the Dolphins' locker room on his side. Though Saban was still prickly and cold, his players admired his coaching abilities. He was, on the one hand, of the old school, a fiery coach who preferred a smashmouth, midwestern style of football. In other ways, he was as innovative— especially off the field—as they came. He had Rosen working on the players' mental games. The players did martial arts in the offseason, well before most other teams ever thought of that as a legitimate training method. He hired a nutritionist for the team. He also minimized hitting in practice, believing that tactic kept players healthier, an ethos the NFL would turn into a mandate for all teams a few years later.*

Most of the players also believed that Saban was making them better. Chambers remembers a pep talk he received from Saban after his slow start to the 2005 season. "He called me into his office and told me he believed in me and thought I was one of the best players on the team," says Chambers, who made the Pro Bowl that season for the first and only time in his career. "He put it all on my shoulders. He took me to another level."

Crowder says that he and the younger guys on the team "loved Saban. He maximized my ability and taught me the game. I played for Charlie Strong, Dom Capers, and Will Muschamp, and I've never

---

* On a few occasions Saban has spoken about what is inarguably the biggest issue in football today: the short- and long-term effects of head trauma on football players, which, of course, includes degenerative brain disease. Saban continues to this day to minimize hitting in practices. At Alabama, two team doctors evaluate all potential head injuries. They make the final determination about whether a player can reenter a game or practice. Saban told the *Birmingham News* in late 2014 that when it comes to potential concussions, he and his assistants "never make a decision . . . as to whether a player plays or does not play."

seen a defense like Saban's. He takes advantage of every weakness. We'd keep offenses confused, shifting from zone to man on the fly, or making it look like we were in zone when we were really in man coverage." Crowder says Saban preferred to have smart players on defense, but that he could get his points across to all players, regardless of IQ. "He could even get the dumb guys going in the right direction. He'd make it simpler for them, with some analytics. He'd tell them that, say, the Jets averaged 120 yards rushing, but that if we kept them to 80 yards, we'd win. That would give them something to hang their hats on."

Jason Taylor, in his second year as the roving linebacker in Saban's 3-4 defense, had 13.5 sacks, 9 forced fumbles, and 2 interceptions that were returned for touchdowns, and was named the 2006 AP Defensive Player of the Year. Even Heath Evans, who seems to bear little goodwill toward Saban, was impressed by his coach's thoroughness. "One thing I really respected about Nick Saban was the fact that he knew everything that was going on with the team," he says. "He knew the defense, the offense, and the special teams better than any other coach on the team. That was unusual."*

Even the earlier incidents between Saban and some of his players were taken with a grain of salt. The Jeno James episode was still viewed as pretty horrific, but it was in the past, and some chalked

---

*Evans was cut by Saban during the 2005 season and never seemed to forget it. Evans says that in early 2010, he played in a celebrity golf tournament. Saban, just coming off a national title with Alabama after the 2009 season, was one of the other featured guests. Evans, who had played college football at Auburn, says he was cajoled by the tournament hosts to say a few words at a tournament gathering. "I stood up and said that as a former Auburn Tiger, I wanted to thank Nick for being such a good judge of NFL talent. That after he cut me, I was picked up by Belichick and went to a few Super Bowls, and that I was glad that Gene Chizik [then the Auburn coach] was doing our talent evaluation at Auburn. Half the crowd booed and half of them laughed. I turned and winked at Saban. I was joking around." Saban apparently didn't like the joke. Evans says a few days later he got a call from some representatives of the tournament, who told him that Saban wanted an apology. Evans refused to offer one. He says that last year he finally did try to reach Saban. "I got his assistant on the phone and I told her to tell him that I was being a prideful, arrogant jerk back then, and that I didn't mean to hurt his feelings," he says. "I don't know if he ever got the message. But I still believe that him cutting me at the Dolphins was the best thing that ever happened to me."

it up to their coach just panicking in the heat of the moment. James was still on the team, still playing hard. Zach Thomas was an intense player, and his run-ins with his coaches were just seen as part of his mien, and they seemed to fire him up and make him a better player. When Keith Traylor and others started to call Saban "Nick" just to get his goat, their teammates saw it for what it was. "That's just what millionaire assholes do," says Crowder.

The week before the game against the Patriots, everything began to change.

Daunte Culpepper was one of the biggest off-season signings in the Dolphins' history. Because of his reputation and his excellent career to that point, he had the respect of his teammates, and he was a team leader. His new Dolphins jersey quickly became a bestseller among fans. Strangely, though, when the Dolphins had held the press conference to announce the signing of their new starting quarterback, Culpepper was nowhere to be found. Instead, Saban spoke for him, hewing to his policy of not allowing newly signed players to speak to the media. Saban spoke for half an hour and reported that Culpepper was "thrilled" to be a member of the Dolphins.

Culpepper played hard for Saban, and his coach publicly backed him during those first four games of the season. The week of the Patriots game, though, Saban had finally had enough. Culpepper's name mysteriously showed up on the Dolphins' injury report, with an unspecified shoulder ailment, though he seemed no different, physically, from how he had been at the beginning of the season.

On the Friday before the game, the Dolphins held a practice in their rarely used practice bubble. When Saban called for the first-team offense to huddle up, Culpepper made his way onto the field but found the team's second-string quarterback, Joey Harrington, already standing in the huddle. Culpepper quickly figured out what had happened—he'd been benched without any warning. "Then he started going crazy," says Crowder. Culpepper set off toward Saban, who stopped practice. As he got closer, several of Culpepper's teammates grabbed him. Then Saban started making his way toward

Culpepper, who shouted: "You better get your short motherfucking ass away from me, you lying motherfucker. Why didn't you come and tell me like a man?" He then walked off the field as the walls of the practice bubble reverberated with the sounds of a season—and, in the end, a pro coaching career—petering out.

Culpepper never played another snap for the Dolphins. Harrington, though well liked by his teammates because of his easygoing demeanor, was by no means a star quarterback. He'd been thoroughly mediocre during his four previous years with the Detroit Lions before he'd been traded to the Dolphins for a late-round draft pick to back up Culpepper. The Miami offense had to be simplified for him, which didn't inspire the confidence of his teammates.

More important, though, one of the team's leaders had been cut off. Culpepper checked out completely after that day in the bubble, and he didn't hide the fact that he now hated his coach and his team. Saban had lost the locker room for good, and likely realized at that moment that the professional game was no longer for him. "From that point on, everything got way more anal," says Crowder.

On November 4, 2006, the University of Alabama Crimson Tide football team lost a game to Mississippi State at home. At the time, this was viewed as an almost unpardonable sin for a school with the history and pride of Alabama. The next day, Saban's Dolphins beat up the previously undefeated Chicago Bears, 31–13, which improved their record to 2-6. On that Monday, a newspaper in Louisiana first floated the idea of Nick Saban becoming Alabama's next head coach. No mention was made of the uncomfortable irony that Alabama was still coached by Mike Shula, the son of the Dolphins' iconic former coach Don Shula.

The victory over the Bears was the beginning of a four-game winning streak for the Dolphins, which briefly breathed some life into an otherwise moribund season. On Thanksgiving Day, the Dolphins stood at 5-6.

A few days after Thanksgiving, Alabama fired Mike Shula, who had lost to Auburn in the Iron Bowl, his last game as the school's coach. (The Iron Bowl is the annual football showdown between the state's two large public universities.) The Saban-to-Alabama rumors started to gain some traction in the press, so much so that Saban issued a statement on the day Shula was fired, denying any interest in the job. He said he was "flattered" to be considered and asked: "Why would I have left that [the LSU job] if I was going to be interested in other college jobs?"

When asked about Saban and the rumors, Huizenga told a Miami paper: "I'm convinced he's on the right track. I like his style. I think he's our guy, I really do. I'm expecting big things."

When a reporter asked Sexton about the Alabama rumors, the agent simply replied: "It's just not true."

Charlie Weems at LSU, however, says he knew something was up. "That fall, Jimmy called me and wanted to know if there was any way Nick could come back. It was a serious question. I told Jimmy, 'No.' But I knew from that call that Nick wasn't happy, and that if Jimmy was calling us, he was going to call other folks next."

In the twelfth game of the 2006 season, the Dolphins lost to the Jacksonville Jaguars to fall to 5-7. Any hope of continuing a late-season surge and somehow making the playoffs was dashed. The following week, the 9-3 Patriots visited Miami, and Saban coached one of his finest NFL games. The Dolphins won, 21–0, and limited the Patriots' superstar quarterback, Tom Brady, to just seventy-eight yards passing. After the game, Belichick took the unusual step of walking into the Dolphins' locker room and meeting with Saban in his office. The victory evened Saban's record against his mentor at 2-2. (Total points in those four games: Saban seventy-five, Belichick sixty-nine.) It would be Saban's last win as an NFL coach. The Dolphins lost the last three games of the season to finish 6-10.

The 2006 season remains Saban's only losing season in his twenty-one years as a head coach.*

In December 2006, nearly every other day Saban denied being interested in the Alabama job. He issued flat-out denials on December 1 and 4. When he issued another one on the seventh, the saga did indeed seem to be over: Alabama appeared to have landed West Virginia coach Rich Rodriguez, but he declined the job the next day, and Saban went back to his denials. On December 10, he told the media: "I have no intentions of going anywhere." He issued more denials on the eleventh and twelfth.

Huizenga was also kept busy with questions about his coach's future. He told the *South Florida Sun-Sentinel* on December 4 that he went to Saban's office and asked him about the rumors. "I walked in and said, 'Tell me.' He said, 'No, I'm not going anywhere. I'm staying right here.' And he said, 'If I was going to go somewhere sometime, I won't go until this job is finished, and we haven't finished our job here.' That makes me feel good."

On December 11, Huizenga seemed fed up with the questions. When asked by a reporter yet again about the rumors, he replied: "I think the issue is dead." Huizenga had reason to feel confident. The self-made billionaire was accustomed to winning these battles, both in business and with the Dolphins. After all, he'd ushered Don Shula into retirement and talked Jimmy Johnson out of retirement, and he'd been the one who'd wooed Saban from a great job at LSU.

Despite the denials, Saban was indeed considering the Alabama job. He'd been, of course, talking to Chuck Moore, the nephew of Mal Moore, and telling him that he didn't much like the pro game anymore. Saban had also been in touch with others. "I talked to Nick and Terry and Jimmy on multiple occasions once they focused

---

*Technically, his first season at Alabama—in which he went 7-6—is now officially 2-6 according to the NCAA, which later vacated five wins that year because of infractions.

on Alabama, before he took the job," says Weems. "They were pumping me for information, asking me what I thought." Weems says he thinks they were genuinely interested in his view of the Alabama job, but were also trying to gauge what the reaction would be at LSU if he indeed took it.

Derek Dooley, the Dolphins' tight end coach who had been with Saban since the LSU days, says he never had any doubt about what Saban would do. "I knew the minute the rumors were coming out about Alabama," he says. "I just knew. We were walking after practice one day and he brought up that Alabama had called him and he didn't know how to handle it. He made every indication to me that he was going to stay, but I knew then that he was gone."

Saban's biggest reason for his continued denials, he says, was his commitment to the Dolphins. "I couldn't tell people what was on my mind and still coach my team without distractions."

Then, on December 21, Saban uttered what would become the most famous words to ever come out of his mouth, ones that would later haunt him. "I guess I have to say it," he told a roomful of reporters. "I'm not going to be the Alabama coach."

Saban had met with his players before the Patriots game and told them to ignore the rumors because he was staying. "We believed him," says Crowder. In retrospect, Crowder realizes there were some warning signs. "Saban hated losing, just hated it," says Crowder. "And whenever we got on the plane after a game, he would open his computer and start watching film of the game. He and Terry always sat in the front seat, with his coordinators right behind him. But after the Colts loss [in the last game of the season], he wasn't looking at film. He was on his cell phone, and he was smiling and laughing. People thought it was weird. We talked about it. And then as soon as the plane landed, he was back on his cell phone and smiling again."

On December 30, Huizenga still seemed to believe that Saban wasn't leaving. He told the *Miami Herald*: "If he didn't stay, it would be huge news to me."

Not too long after that, Saban was holed up in his house, trapped by his own anguish, with another major career decision at hand.

As a football coach—in games, on the practice field, in meetings, and on the recruiting trail—Saban is as decisive as they come. He makes difficult choices in a timely, forthright manner—without self-doubt—then moves on and lives with the consequences. That is not the case when it comes to his career. The decision about whether to stay with the Dolphins or leave and take the Alabama job was perhaps the most agonizing one in a career filled with many others like it. "When you make a coaching decision, you can be decisive because, while you don't control the outcome, you do control the processes that go into the outcome, the preparation of the team and the staff," says Muschamp, who was also an assistant at Miami under Saban. "Career decisions are different. There are a lot of unknowns that are out of your control, and you don't really know how things will change and how different they will be. I think that's what's frustrating for Nick."

Saban is also extremely loyal, to his players and staff and, in most cases, his administrators. He genuinely liked Huizenga and wanted to do well by him, just as he had liked Bertman, Emmert, and the rest of the LSU folks. Though he may not have felt terribly loyal to President McPherson at Michigan State, he did feel devoted to the team, some of the trustees, and the community. Adding to Saban's agony is his sensitivity. He knew, given his somewhat strained relationship with the Miami media—coupled with his adamant public denials—that if he took the Alabama job, he would be flayed. "I stayed up two nights in a row all night, worrying and talking on the phone," Saban says. "People don't realize that these kind of decisions aren't ninety-nine to one. They're fifty-two to forty-eight. There are personal and professional implications."

Finally, on New Year's Day, Huizenga realized that Saban was seriously considering the Alabama job. Just as he had done with Bertman at LSU, Saban kept Huizenga—who did his best to convince his coach to stay—in the loop, talking to him on the phone and meeting him in person. Saban once again had leverage: Sexton had smartly inserted a clause in his Dolphins contract that allowed him to take a college coaching job without any financial penalty.

Finally, on January 3, 2007, Saban told his boss that he was leaving. Huizenga would later tell the media: "I'm not upset. I love Nick Saban." With the media mob growing outside his house, Saban was unable to get to the Dolphins' facility to meet with his coaches, so he had a staffer gather them together in an office. Via speakerphone, Saban told them he was leaving. His players were scattered around the country, done for the season. He reached a few by cell phone, and eventually wrote them letters.

"It wasn't about the money," Saban says. This time, he could say that with a straight face: His eight-year, $32 million contract with Alabama actually worked out to about a $1 million per year pay cut. "It was just in my gut. I figured that if I was going to coach, I should be happy doing it, and that for me comes in college. I decided it was the best thing for me, my family, my future, and my well-being."

That happiness had a lot to do with control and power. Once again, by leaving one football program for another, he gained more of both, becoming the embodiment of Emerson's belief that true power "resides in the moment of transition from a past to a new state, in the shooting of a gulf, in the darting to an aim." Huizenga had given Saban about as much control as an NFL coach could have. Still, it paled in comparison to the power he would have back in the college game at Alabama. The NFL was full of external forces: a team's position in the draft, the salary cap, agents, and contracts loaded with special individual provisions. Owners in the NFL had, somewhat paradoxically, decided to run their league as a quasi-socialist enterprise to make more money for themselves. The worst teams were rewarded with the highest draft picks and the easiest schedules. The salary cap evened the playing field. It was almost as if the powers that be in the NFL were aiming for general mediocrity, which was a word—and a state of being—that Saban loathed. "In college, you are the general manager, coach, and head recruiter," he says. "You can work and develop and do more things to impact your future and control your destiny."

So Saban got on that plane with Moore, bound for Tuscaloosa, seeking happiness. It was a perfectly legitimate thing to do, and is the reason most people seek, then take, new jobs. The media—both locally and nationally—and Dolphins fans and some players didn't quite see it that way. The *Miami Herald* called him a "loser" and a "weasel." Other local outlets called him "Tricky Nicky," "Nick $aban," and a "liar." John Feinstein, writing in the *Washington Post*, said Saban was "the worst person in sports." A Cox News Service writer colorfully described him as "an impulsive scamp." Even esteemed former Dolphins coach Don Shula got in a stinger, telling a newspaper: "My reaction is that Saban in two years was 15-17. I don't think it will be any great loss. . . . He has run away from a challenge." (Of course, Saban *was* replacing his son at Alabama.) Saban would later tell a Miami newspaper that he felt "victimized" by the reaction to his departure, and that "the circumstances changed and I made a different decision. That's not lying."

Some Dolphins players were less concerned with the perceived lying than with the fact that he just left. "Looking back, he was always preaching to us about overcoming adversity," says one former player. "You'd think a guy like that wouldn't quit. Did he quit? Well, he didn't have a two-year contract, did he? He wasn't successful, so he decided to leave."

A few days later, Saban's office was almost completely cleared. The only things left were boxes of Little Debbies and Red Man chewing tobacco.

In the end, opinions vary about Saban's NFL career. For some, he was a failure, just another college coach who couldn't hack it in the pros. He had a losing record overall. His famed "Process" didn't quite work as well with professional players. His tenure was, at best, mediocre, a shade of gray that is now viewed, in retrospect, as an indelible black mark because of the impetuous and—in the eyes of many—dishonest manner in which he left.

Others argue that Saban was the victim of untenable circumstances, stuck in a franchise that was in the throes of an unavoidable death spiral, and that the job that he did in Miami—particularly in his first year—constitutes some of the finest coaching of his career. "I look back and think it's unfair to say he couldn't coach there," says Dooley. "He went 9-7 that first year with a below-average team. You don't do that if you're not a very good football coach." Indeed, the year after Saban left—with many of the same players— the Dolphins went 1-15, avoiding the ignominy of a winless season by beating the Baltimore Ravens in overtime in the third-to-last game of the season.

The answer to how Saban's NFL fling should be judged is likely found in some middle space. Perhaps, everything comes down to one single decision: choosing Culpepper over Brees. It remains one of the great "what-ifs?" of Saban's career. Brees threw for twenty-six touchdowns and led the Saints to the NFC Championship game in 2006, and is now considered a future Hall of Famer. Had he become a Dolphin, would Saban have ever made it to Alabama? Would Saban still be in the NFL? Personnel mistakes in the NFL were deadly. If a highly rated recruit in college—the equivalent of, say, Culpepper—didn't pan out, it wasn't necessarily a season-killer. If you recruited in college as well as Saban did, there was always the next guy, ready to step up.

Another question has remained ever since he left: Despite his subsequent mind-boggling success at Alabama (or, perhaps, because of it), is there still some part of him that aches to redeem himself in the NFL? All Saban has to do is look at Pete Carroll and his old friend Bill Belichick for two examples of coaches who at first failed in the NFL and succeeded in the highest way possible by becoming Super Bowl champions.

Saban himself has admitted that the Dolphins years did not go like he wanted them to, when it came to his coaching and the way he handled the situation at the end. Big Nick would not have approved: His son left some spots on the car.

10

The Battle of Mobile Bay

IN THE late afternoon of January 3, 2007, the airplane carrying Alabama's new head coach descended from a dull, gray sky and touched down at Tuscaloosa Regional Airport, sending the five hundred or so fans who had gathered there into an enraptured frenzy.* The plane taxied to a stop and Saban stepped out, hesitating for just a second at the top of the stairs. The fifty-five-year-old was wearing a purple dress shirt and a gray sports jacket. His hair was windblown, and he looked wired and pink-cheeked, as if he'd just been on a high alpine hike. He gazed out at the gathered crowd and seemed to quickly deduce that there was no way of walking around them, so he barged right in.

The mob quickly encircled him. A few folks reached out, trying to shake his hand or merely touch him, as if he possessed something— wisdom or the power to heal—that could only be obtained through direct contact. One woman on the tarmac yelled, "Thank you, Jesus! Thank you, Nick Saban!" A fan held a sign that read: "We've been Saban our hearts for you!" Another had a sign that said: "We've been Saban our money for you!" (Saban signed this one.) A blond woman in a football jersey—who appeared to have spent some serious time tailgating before the plane landed—broke free from the crowd, slung an arm around Saban, yelled something in his ear, then

---

* The number of fans likely would have been much larger, but University of Alabama students were on winter break at the time.

pulled him in close for a kiss. Just as she appeared to be maneuvering Saban into a headlock, a state trooper stepped in and hustled her away. A band of reporters stopped Terry on her way into the airport building. She broke into a broad smile. "Mr. Huizenga is the finest man you'll ever know . . . but in the end our hearts craved the college tradition. . . . Mr. Huizenga didn't want to let us go," she told them. "It took us a long time to get out of there, but we're glad to be here."

The Sabans finally made their way into a crimson-colored Chevy Tahoe. As they sped off—with a police escort leading the way to campus—the crowd chanted: "Roll Tide! Roll Tide!" Their savior had arrived.

Alabama, with the sole exception of one national championship year under Gene Stallings, had been a hot mess since its legendary coach, Paul "Bear" Bryant, had retired in 1982. NCAA sanctions had stripped the program of scholarships, bowl appearances, and much of its pride. Saban was the school's sixth coach in eight years, and not one of the previous five men had covered himself in glory. The combined record of Mike DuBose, Dennis Franchione, Mike Price, Mike Shula, and Joe Kines, after sanctions, was 51-55. The group of coaches went a collective 1-4 in bowl games.*

The coaches were only part of the problem, though. Nearly every party associated with the football program had played a role in dragging it down. The boosters had run amok: A few of them had been accused of paying recruits, which resulted in five years of probation, scholarship reductions, and a two-year ban on appearing in any bowl games. The administration had made one reckless decision after another, handing two previous coaches (DuBose and Shula) raises and extensions shortly before they were fired, which left the school on the hook for millions of dollars. The fans, too, were out of control. Various coaches—and the administrators who had hired

---

* Price was fired before ever coaching a game. Kines served as the interim coach for Alabama in the 2006 Independence Bowl after Shula was fired.

them—had allegedly received death threats. After a loss to Ole Miss one year, someone supposedly threw a brick through the window of the office of head coach Bill Curry. When Spurrier was approached about becoming Alabama's head coach before Saban came, some fans somehow got his cell phone number and deluged him with calls. They did the same to Sexton when Saban's name first surfaced as a coaching candidate.

Despite the troubles with the football program, there was still a sense of entitlement and arrogance among many fans, alumni, boosters, and administrators at Alabama. One current booster describes it as the "We are 'Bama" syndrome—a sentiment that, because of the program's storied history, it could overcome almost anything and produce national titles without actually putting in the work.

It was near the end of the Shula regime, though, when the cold, hard reality finally set in for the football program's power brokers. Shula was a personable man, devout and humble. However, according to several trustees and boosters, he ran a loose program, and by 2006 it had burst at the seams. The program needed a complete overhaul. "We were drifting," admitted Robert Witt, Alabama's president and now the Alabama university system's chancellor.

Saban stepped into a perfect storm at Alabama—a university desperate to return to national football prominence was handing the keys to a coach who was ready to fill a power vacuum and effect his own turnaround in the process. The University of Alabama—Witt, Moore, and the trustees and boosters—willingly gave Saban unprecedented power over the football program in order to save it. In the past, Alabama football coaches had been in the back pockets of the school's various power brokers. That dynamic was now flipped. They needed him more than he needed them.

Much of the power and control came from his contract. Alabama gave Saban an eight-year deal worth a total of $32 million, which was, at the time, the largest ever for a college football coach. Witt called the contract "an investment and not an expense." It just happened to be an investment with no financial downside for Saban. Once again, Sexton had worked out a deal that provided his client with all the leverage. The money was guaranteed, and the contract had no buyout clause, which was unusual for one of its size. (Tommy Tuberville, the coach at Auburn at the time, for instance, had a $6 million buyout.) Witt viewed the lack of the buyout as a personal challenge and not as a capitulation. "I don't want anyone working here who doesn't want to be here," he said at the time. "It's my job to create an atmosphere here to make Coach Saban want to be here more than any other university."

Not everyone affiliated with the school was enamored with Saban's hiring, the huge sum of money that it took to get him, and the message that his contract sent. Garry Neil Drummond, an Alabama emeritus trustee, publicly questioned the wisdom of paying a football coach $4 million a year, calling it "one of the worst things we have ever done." (The average salary of a University of Alabama professor at the time was $116,000.)

Most, though, were willing to do anything they could to please their new football coach. "When we hired him, Mark Emmert called me and told me, 'You are going to have your hands full,'" says Angus Cooper, an Alabama trustee. "He was right." In the summer of 2007, Saban invited Cooper and another trustee, John McMahon, to his house at Lake Burton. "He had this laundry list of things he wanted to change or have done, things like getting the players' graduation rates up and redoing the JumboTron at the stadium," says Cooper. "He was right about all them. It took us a few years, but we fixed most of them." Even Saban's bosses played supporting roles: Witt would eventually start to help out by hosting recruiting parties.

Saban also took on the booster organizations, which had become balkanized and thus ineffectual, and made it clear that they would all have to get on the same page if they wanted to maintain relevancy under him. Over a few months, he met with nearly two dozen influential boosters in the state, trying to find and anoint ambassadors of the program. "He interviewed me for an hour," says one of them. "What he wanted was for all of us to be reading from the same sheet of music, to help him identify recruits and line up internships. It was obvious he'd done his research. He knew a lot about me. It was like meeting the Godfather."

To the fans, and the greater University of Alabama community, Saban sought to completely wipe out any lingering sense of entitlement. "I have respect for history and tradition, but none of that impacts what we do now," he said, whenever he spoke to booster groups, to fans, and to the media. "We cannot depend on the successes of the past to help us be successful in the future. That's the kiss of death."

Of course, there was Saban's workforce—his players, coaches, and staff. They, too, were given the sheet music and were expected to follow it, to the note. Saban met with his players individually. "It was all very methodical," says Preston Dial, a freshman tight end in 2007. "He told us that there was no secret to success, that it came with hard work. He made it clear that our scholarships were one-year agreements. It was clear that he had a way of doing things and that he had done this all before at every change he'd made."

John Parker Wilson, Alabama's starting quarterback in 2007 and 2008, says: "Everybody knew his direction, from the coaches down to the cafeteria staff."

It started with creating a cultural framework that focused on the mental side of things as much as the physical. "Our goal is to help the players become more successful people, to develop thoughts, habits, and priorities to make good decisions," Saban says. "We lose games because of a lack of good judgment, both on the field and off. A player who is doing poorly in school can cost us a game. If you have the right thoughts, habits, and priorities, which in one sense is the definition of character, that determines the choices you make. We're trying to affect those things. If they can do those things here, they can do them anywhere. They can be successful as players, students, and people."

Saban reinforced that framework, stalking the meetings rooms, the weight room, and the practice field, constantly spewing a hand-

ful of maxims, updated versions of the ones once posted on the
walls of Big Nick's Idamay Black Diamonds bus:

- We want to develop thoughts, habits, and priorities.
- How you do anything is how you do everything.
- Everybody wants to win. Are you willing to do what it
  takes and what is necessary to win?
- You can't hoot with the owls late at night and get up and
  soar with the eagles in the morning.
- You never stay the same. You either get better or you get
  worse.

Saban knew that, to elite athletes, these maxims weren't the trite
clichés they appear to be to most—they meant something. As with
any motivational speaker, he also knew that saying these words
over and over not only kept his players, coaches, and staff focused;
it acted as personal reinforcement as well.

Everything was tailored to help his players achieve their potential. They were completely taken care of. Rosen continued to speak
to all the players individually, eliciting what by that time must have
felt like a familiar response. "When I first saw the Wizard, I was
like, 'Who the hell is this guy?'" says Damion Square, a defensive
lineman. "But then it started to make sense. We could see the results
in real time. You have to brainwash your players, and I don't mean
that in a bad way, to get them to all do something together." Saban
supplemented Rosen's sessions with ones from the performance and
motivational gurus Trevor Moawad and Kevin Elko, and the corporate consultants at the Pacific Institute.*

Scott Cochran, the gravelly voiced strength coach, was hired to

---

* The Pacific Institute had its own set of maxims, which reinforced Saban's. During meetings, the players were forced to chant things like: "We are a team that's
committed to excellence. It's represented in everything we do." "Our defense is
aggressive. We fly to the ball seeking always to cause big plays on every down. We
intimidate our opponents." "Our offense is consistently on top of their game, av-
eraging 38 to 48 points a game." "Our team is a family. We will look out for each
other. We love one another. Anything that attempts to tear us apart only makes us
stronger."

take on the role that Ken Mannie and Tommy Moffitt had filled before him, as the shaper of the players' physical beings.* Saban hired legions of unofficial coaches—far more than most other college programs—who were called "quality control coaches" or "analysts," to support him and his staff by organizing practices, watching and cutting film, and assisting in on-campus recruiting. One former "analyst" described his role as being part of the team's "assembly line."

Nutritionists tailored meals by different positions (linemen needed protein for strength; skill players were fed carbohydrates for fuel). Facilities were eventually upgraded—Saban's new thirty-thousand-square-foot football building features a $9 million weight room, a 212-seat theater, a waterfall, meeting rooms, a hydrotherapy room, a cooling bench and tent that stays at 65 degrees, an ice bath that players jump into after practice with their pads on, and a drying station for their pads and shoes. "You always hear that guys like Pete Carroll are players' coaches, but Saban really is, too, in a different way," says Colin Peek, a transfer from Georgia Tech who played tight end on the 2009 Alabama team. "He would do whatever it took to make sure we were taken care of. If the players complained about food, he had it changed. At Georgia Tech, they would hide the receiving gloves so we wouldn't go through them too fast. At Alabama, we could have new gloves every day if we needed them. He did everything to make us feel like we could go out and be the best in the nation."

Saban effectively put his players in a cocoon, where they could concentrate on football and all it entailed—mental and physical conditioning, academics—and remain as sheltered as possible from potential off-the-field pitfalls. "The one thing people always ask me is 'What was Saban like?' " says Damion Square, who now plays for the San Diego Chargers. "They don't ask about the national championships. And I mean it's everyone who asks me that. Teammates,

---

* Cochran is one of the few Saban assistants who has become somewhat of a celebrity, mainly because of his spazzy energy at practices and games and for his incredible voice, which sounds like a mashup of a pro wrestler's and a demented drill sergeant's. Rumor has it that at one point in his life, he had a normal-sounding voice. Cochran appears on the JumboTron at home games to pump up the crowd. Needless to say, he's effective.

NFL coaches, and even people who don't know anything about football. And I always say the same thing: He was exactly what I needed when I was eighteen years old."

Rolando McClain, a 2007 recruit, was among those who benefited most from that cocoon. McClain was a fiercely talented linebacker, but "he had his share of personal demons," as one former teammate put it. He came from a fractured family—at age fifteen he'd been forced to get a restraining order against his mother, who beat him incessantly. While at Alabama, McClain for the most part stayed out of trouble. He found it, though, after he was selected by the Oakland Raiders in the first round of the 2010 NFL Draft. McClain was arrested three different times in seventeen months, was cut by the Raiders after three seasons, and retired from the game at the age of twenty-three. In the off-season before the 2014 season, he sought out the counsel of Saban—reaching back for the cocoon, perhaps—who helped him get signed by the Dallas Cowboys. He finished second in the voting for the NFL's Comeback Player of the Year in 2014.

Others who didn't make it to the NFL still took the lessons of their playing years at Alabama with them into their lives after football. Will Lowery was a walk-on, backup defensive back from 2008 until 2011. He keeps Saban's aphorisms posted above his desk at the private investment firm where he works. Brandon Gibson, a backup wide receiver from 2007 until 2011, is now a medical sales representative in Alabama. "I played under Coach Saban. I learned his philosophies," he says. "If I'm a failure in life or in anything I do, it's my fault. There's no excuse for me to fail."

Saban tightly controlled as much of the external part of the Alabama program as he could.* He took his press conferences seri-

---

* One significant difference between football coaches at major colleges and CEOs at even the world's biggest companies is in their media availability. During the twelve or so weeks of a college football season, Saban must address the media three times a week: on Monday afternoon, Wednesday evening, and—win or lose—after every game. To be sure, CEOs—and politicians, for that matter—face their own media scrutiny, but none of them is forced to go face-to-face with the media as much as these coaches do.

ously, hyperaware that everyone—fans, administrators, his players, and even his potential recruits—was watching them. The local media gradually began to realize that his tirades—which remain big hits on YouTube—were finely calculated and never personal. "Very rarely when he dresses down a reporter is he actually talking to him," says Aaron Suttles, who covers the team for the *Tuscaloosa News*. "He's talking to someone else out there." At a press conference a few years into Saban's tenure at Alabama, Suttles asked him about the excellent depth he had on his defensive line. "Saban lit into me arguing that the opposite was true," says Suttles. "He did in fact have tremendous depth on the defensive line, but he didn't want those recruits out there to hear that."

At Alabama, Saban has continued his tradition of not allowing his assistants or players to speak to the media except on special occasions. "You'd like to have one message with multiple voices," he says. "But it sure is easier to control with only one voice." In doing so, he ensured that no one player became bigger than the team, something that has pretty much held true for all eight years he's been there. (In the early years at Alabama, he hung a sign outside the locker room that would have looked at home near the entrance of a coal mine. It read: "Out of Yourself and Into the Team.")

It didn't happen overnight, but in a sense, Saban eventually turned the Alabama football program into a corporation, with him sitting in the chief executive's chair. He had complete control over what he described as the four pillars of a program: recruiting, coaching, business administration, and media relations. He got everyone associated with the program—the administration, the boosters, the alumni, the staff, the players, and the fans—all headed in the same direction in a streamlined, highly effective manner. Even the initial naysayers eventually came around. Drummond, the doubting Thomas of the board of trustees, says now: "I was totally wrong in my evaluation of what this man could do not just for the football team, but for the university."

Saban turned the football facility into something comparable to a Silicon Valley tech company's campus: a place where you were taken care of and made so comfortable that you wouldn't want to leave. He even used corporate terminology—"R&D" meant "recruiting and development"—and other people, when talking about him, used that terminology, too. "He's an extraordinary manager from the business perspective. He understands performance from the production and manufacturing perspective. He places tremendous emphasis on recruiting. These young men are the raw materials of his program," Witt said a year after Saban had been hired, in what amounts to an unusual and extraordinary way for a university president to describe his football coach.

Saban even borrowed tactics from the corporate world. For years, Alabama had been on the defensive when it came to the NCAA and compliance, due to the program's numerous sanctions. Saban wanted that to change. He set up a compliance office that instead went on the attack, viewing the NCAA the same way that many corporate tax lawyers did the Internal Revenue Service. "You have to maximize your benefits," Saban says. He brought in trusted lieutenants, like Kevin Steele, Kirby Smart, and Lance Thompson, who had worked for him before. "I wanted folks who knew what the expectations were and who could help define them and lead by example," he says.

Saban corporatized "the Process" as well, taking Lonny Rosen's simple advice and expanding it to everything he did. When it came to the football program, it was all about doing what you could control, every minute of every day. The bigger picture wasn't the focus, but all those little steps taken that filled it out. Saban, as James and Belichick had done before him, sharply defined everyone's role within the program and worked relentlessly to eliminate what he called "clutter." His coaches didn't visualize the relief and the joy they would feel on National Signing Day, when that five-star player they'd spent a year recruiting joined the team. Instead, they did the little things every day to help further the possibility of that result. Saban constantly admonished his players not to think about lifting a trophy at the end of the season, but focus on conditioning, reps in practice, and on keeping their grades up to remain eligible to play. Control what you can control, and find fulfillment within that. Saban is the ultimate "journey" man, and not a destination one.

As Warren St. John pointed out in a 2013 *GQ* article, Saban's overhaul and modernization of the Alabama football program mimicked some of the greater changes that were taking place at the same time in the state of Alabama. Economically, the state was charging into the new century, transitioning from its roots as a steelmaking giant to become a burgeoning center of high tech, with renowned medical facilities (at the University of Alabama at Birmingham, in particular) and large, state-of-the-art aerospace and automobile plants built by Honda, Toyota, Hyundai, Mercedes-Benz, and, soon, Airbus.

One Alabama insider said it took only one game for him to realize that things would be very different for the football program under Saban. "I remember watching when Shula coached the team. After a game, the Alabama sideline was a mess, with crushed water cups and tape all over the ground. It looked like a hurricane had come through. After Saban's first game, I just happened to look at the sideline. It was pristine. There wasn't a crushed cup to be found."

Despite the clean sidelines—and the cleaned-up program—Saban's Alabama tenure would get off to a rocky start.

Just a few weeks after taking the Alabama job, Saban was in the national news again, and not for good reasons. An audiotape of what was supposed to be an off-the-record conversation with some journalists had surfaced on the Internet. On the tape, Saban had related a story that an LSU trustee had told him, and in explaining it, he referred to an LSU fan as a "coon-ass," which is considered an ethnic slur.

The LSU trustee was Charlie Weems. "Nick had called me right after he was hired at Alabama," says Weems. "He wanted to know what the reaction at LSU was. He always wanted to know what people thought of him."

Weems had told Saban that he had taken a stroll through New Orleans's French Quarter soon after he had heard that Saban was leaving the Dolphins for Alabama. He came upon a man wearing an LSU hard hat who was working in a manhole. "The guy had a serious Cajun accent," says Weems. "He said, 'Hey, man. Did you hear about Nick Saban?' I told him I hadn't. I wasn't sure if it was public knowledge yet. Then he says, 'Man, he's going to Alabama. Yeah, man, I feel like somebody is sleeping with my wife.' I never said the words 'coon-ass,' but I did tell the story in a Cajun dialect. Nick just mangled it when he retold it."

The story blew up, playing into what was then the growing public narrative about Saban, that he was surly and a mercenary, a cutthroat, a money-chaser, and, most hurtful to Saban, a quitter. Because of the manner in which Saban had left Miami, he'd found himself on the firing line, an easy target for sportswriters and editorialists. Fellow coaches played up the stereotype, too. During the 2007 off-season, Les Miles, his replacement at LSU, accused Saban of what's known as "negative recruiting," that is, bad-mouthing other football coaches when talking to recruits. The media and the general public seemed to want Saban to fail. It was the moment that he became "the devil"—the oft-used epithet thrown his way. It was a hole that Saban had dug himself into, and one from which he has only recently begun to emerge.

Alabama fans didn't care a lick, though. Sales of T-shirts that read "Sabanation" and "Got Nick?" (a play on the ubiquitous "Got Milk?" ad campaign) were brisk across the campus and the state. At a booster gathering, a man named Tim Witt, who had named his newborn son "Saban," met the coach for the first time. "Coach, I'm the crazy man who named my son after you. I've got faith in you," he told Saban. "You must have," the coach dryly replied.

That April, 92,138 fans showed up for Alabama's spring practice intrasquad game (known as the "A-Day" game), which nearly doubled the game's attendance record. Another 10,000 or so fans, unable to get into the stadium, mingled around outside it. The fans in the stadium gave Saban a standing ovation when he jogged across the field before the game. Saban shrewdly invited members of the media to be "guest coaches" for the A-Day game—to stand on the sidelines and come into the locker rooms—and afterward many of them wrote glowing reports about the experience and of the coach.

The team that took the field that year, though, didn't warrant all of that optimism. After many down years and reduced scholarships, the talent on the football team was thin, especially on the defensive side. Saban had only a month to put together his first recruiting class, which, though it produced linebacker Rolando McClain and cornerback Kareem Jackson, would turn out to be the only one during Saban's Alabama years that wasn't ranked in the top five by most recruiting agencies.

At a little after 6 p.m. on September 1, 2007, the Saban era at Alabama officially began with a home game against Western Carolina, which was, coincidentally, the first team he had played at LSU. Alabama won the game, 52–6, but afterward Saban told the media that his defense was "soft." After seven games, the Crimson Tide was a somewhat surprising 5-2. On the eve of the team's eighth game—against twentieth-ranked Tennessee—Saban and the school suspended five players who had improperly received free textbooks from the university's bookstore, a scam that had begun in 2005 under Shula but had continued into Saban's tenure. The players ended up being suspended for four games. Losing five players made an already thin roster even thinner, and two of the players—running back Glen Coffee and offensive lineman Antoine Caldwell—were among the team's best.

In the game, Alabama routed Tennessee, 41–17. Saban had started the game with a surprise onside kick, which was recovered and led to a score. "I always thought that was such a great call," says Curt Cignetti, the receivers coach and recruiting coordinator. "We were down because we'd lost those players and they had a pretty good team. That call set the tempo for the game."

After a bye week, Alabama hosted LSU in what was dubbed as "the Saban Bowl." Saban told the media before the game that LSU had some "outstanding players," which he would have known, of course—he was in the odd position of playing against a team that had more of his recruits than did the one he was coaching. (He did later credit Miles with "developing" those players.) LSU at the time was 7-1 and ranked number one in the country. Back in Baton Rouge, local sports stores sold T-shirts that read: "Nick Satan." The Baton Rouge *Advocate* ran an ad for a T-shirt that said: "Saban for Sale—Call 1-800-Sellout."

Halfway through the fourth quarter, Alabama led the game, 34–27. With 1:39 left and the score tied, Chad Jones, a freshman LSU safety—and one of the few players on LSU's defense that Saban had not recruited—sacked Alabama quarterback John Parker Wilson and forced a fumble, which LSU recovered at the Alabama three-yard line. LSU's Jacob Hester—the small running back whom Saban had recruited and affectionately nicknamed "Stubby Legs"— used those appendages to leap over the pile at the goal line and score the winning touchdown.

Alabama's season then collapsed in shocking fashion. The next week, they lost to Mississippi State, the same seemingly unpardonable sin that had initiated Shula's demise the year before. The week after that game, Alabama hosted Louisiana-Monroe, a football weakling. In a matchup that featured the highest-paid coach in the Division I football versus the lowest-paid one (ULM's Charlie Weatherbie was making $130,000 at the time), Alabama somehow lost, 21–14. In a way, the loss mirrored the one he'd had to the University of Alabama at Birmingham (UAB) in his first year at LSU: The team hit rock bottom, and everything that followed was built from there. "That was a total meltdown," says Cignetti. "But Nick just kept going. He didn't slow down. He is very compartmentalized in his thinking, and every day, no matter what happens, you get the same performance out of him. He just set his sights forward."

Saban's public portrayal of the loss, however, was far different. In a press conference, Saban invoked 9/11 and Pearl Harbor to demonstrate his program's mind-set. "Changes in history usually occur after some kind of catastrophic event," he said. "It may be 9/11, which sort of changed the spirit of America relative to a catastrophic event. Pearl Harbor got us ready for World War II . . . and that was a catastrophic event."

While Saban never explicitly compared the Alabama losses to Mississippi State and ULM to 9/11 and Pearl Harbor, that's how it was portrayed in the media. Once again, he was vilified nationally. A former coach who was on that staff at the time believes that Saban had, in fact, been calculated in those comments, and was prepared to take the slings and arrows. "He had to let the fan base know that those losses were unacceptable," says the coach. They were, after all, that serious to them.

Saban also pointedly avoided using any excuses when discussing the losses, though there were plenty to go around. During the season, he'd taken a hard line with players who had refused to acquiesce to his demands. He kicked a linebacker off the team in the middle of the season and was forced to play a walk-on in his place. He'd suspended the team's best receiver, D. J. Hall, for the first half of the ULM game. And, of course, those five players caught up in the textbook scandal had missed four games.

Things got no better for Alabama in the Iron Bowl. The 17–10 loss to Auburn was Alabama's sixth in a row to its biggest rival. (Auburn coach Tommy Tuberville walked off the field after that game holding up six fingers.) The four straight losses to end the regular season left Alabama with no guarantee of playing in a bowl game, which Saban desperately wanted, not necessarily for the game itself, but for the extra month of practice it provided. After some lobbying, Alabama got an invite to play in the Independence Bowl in Shreveport, Louisiana, the site of Saban's first-ever bowl game while at Michigan State. Alabama won the game, 30–24, over Colorado, and finished the season at 7-6.*

John Parker Wilson remembers the 2007 season as the "break-in" year. He had been recruited by Shula, who he says was a coach who relied on his players to be self-motivated. "He left it all up to

---

* The two other Saban-affected teams had wildly contrasting seasons in 2007: The Dolphins finished a woeful 1-15. LSU won the national title.

you," he says. "Saban was the complete opposite. You had to buy in completely or you were out." Josh Chapman, a defensive lineman who redshirted in the 2007 season, says: "It was like prison camp."

According to Wilson, the culture of a team is ultimately the hardest thing to change. "Coaches can be around only so much," he says. "Guys sit around and talk in the locker room and dorms. We hadn't won a lot in the last decade. We were bad, used to the mediocrity. That's what Saban was trying to change."

Cignetti agrees. "There was a lot of entitlement there when Nick came in. The program was soft," he says. "That first season was about changing the mind-set. I'll never forget the first practice. Nick uses a lot of tempo and pace in practices. Those guys weren't used to it. A quarter of the way through, they were all gassed, done. But they learned."

In 2007, Saban suffered through his second straight rough season as a coach, both on the field and off it. His recent teams hadn't been very good. He'd become a national punch line. Many were reveling in his lack of success.

Behind the scenes, though, far away from the glare of the media and public, he'd been hard at work. As the 2007 season came to a close, Saban was just putting the final touches on a recruiting class that would turn out to be transcendent.

Back when Nick Saban was growing up, and into some of his early coaching years, football's focal point was the Midwest. The game then was dominated by the hard-nosed, tough, and mostly white sons of coal miners and steelworkers, the best of whom used the game to escape those same mines and mills. Football was hugely important to the towns and communities of that region: It united them.

That focal point has changed. For the past few decades, the most talented prep-aged football players have mostly come from the states that border the Gulf of Mexico—Texas, Louisiana, Mississippi, Alabama, and Florida. The predominant industry in this area, if there is any, is also an extractive one: oil. Many of the players in the region are African American. The game is different here than it was in the Midwest—it is more explosive. Yet it retains every bit of its importance. Football—and not baseball or basketball—is the priority here, lived and breathed for 365 days a year. And it's still an avenue of escape for the best players.

One spot along the Gulf has become known as "recruiting heaven" for its high school football talent: the greater Mobile area. It is a place where Saban—very much a product of that old-school midwestern football—has come to dominate.

On February 6, 2008, in the gymnasium of Foley High School in Baldwin County, Alabama, a young man named Quintorris Lopez Jones (better known as "Julio" Jones) sat in front of ESPN cameras sporting a tie and a yellow cable-knit sweater. Foley cheerleaders smiled and fidgeted nervously behind him. Jones, a 6'4", 215-pound receiver with soft hands, powerful legs, and a sprinter's speed, was ranked by most recruiting agencies as either the best or second-best high school football player in the country. Jones had placed four hats on the table before him, representing the schools—Florida, Florida State, Oklahoma, and Alabama—that had fiercely battled one another in an effort to sign him. The stoic, soft-spoken Jones made some quick preliminary remarks, thanking all of the schools for their interest in him, and said he decided to go "where I feel most comfortable." With that he grabbed the Alabama hat and put it on his head as the cheerleaders waved their pom-poms and the gymnasium erupted in cheers.

Julio Jones remains the most important recruit of Saban's Alabama tenure, the centerpiece of the 2008 recruiting class, which is considered by many to be the best in college football history, and the one that would set the stage for a run of national titles. Along with Jones, the class included safety Mark Barron, nose tackle Terrence Cody, defensive tackle Marcell Dareus, linebacker Dont'a Hightower, running back (and eventual Heisman Trophy winner) Mark Ingram, offensive lineman Barrett Jones, and linebacker Courtney Upshaw, all of whom are playing in the NFL.*

Saban recruited all over the South and beyond for several of the stars of the class: Cody was a junior college transfer from Mississippi, Hightower and Barrett Jones were from Tennessee, and Ingram was from Michigan. The backbone of the class were the eight recruits who came from the Mobile area, headlined by Jones, Barron, and Robert Lester. Though not all of the Mobile players panned out (receiver Destin Hood decided to play baseball; two running backs, Jermaine Preyear and Ivan Matchett, eventually left the team; and highly touted receiver/defensive back B. J. Scott ended up transferring), it was Saban's utter domination of the area that was important. (Four of the Mobile-area recruits had pledged to sign with Auburn before flipping to Alabama.)

Mobile had last been a recruiting hot spot for Alabama during the Mike DuBose years in the late 1990s, but after that, Alabama's presence there had withered. Between 2001 and 2006, Alabama signed only four players from the area. The best players from Mobile had instead been routinely plucked by Auburn, LSU, Florida State, and even Oklahoma. Though Saban couldn't quite hope to seal the borders of the state as he had done at LSU (he had serious in-state competition from Auburn), he was intent on making Ala-

---

* That year, Saban also recruited a highly touted Texas quarterback named Andrew Luck, the son of Oliver Luck, a quarterback at West Virginia in the early 1980s when Saban was the secondary coach there. Landing Luck would have pushed Saban's 2008 Alabama class into a stratosphere unlikely ever to be matched. Andrew Luck liked Saban, "but he was focused on a handful of schools with a more academic side," says his father. "Not that Alabama isn't a good academic school, but he was looking at Rice, Northwestern, and Stanford." Luck, of course, ultimately chose Stanford and became the number-one overall pick in the 2012 NFL Draft and is now an NFL star.

bama the dominant school in the state again. And Mobile became the centerpiece of that plan.*

To lead the recruiting effort in Mobile, Saban turned to Lance Thompson, his outside linebackers coach. Thompson had been an excellent recruiter for Saban for a few years at LSU. It was no coincidence that he'd been on DuBose's staff the last time Alabama had been relevant in recruiting Mobile. Thompson was, in many ways, the polar opposite of Saban: a fun-loving, ever-smiling extrovert who was prone to backslapping and snapping selfies with his camera phone. "Lance is like your uncle who buys you your first six-pack," says one former Alabama coach.

Thompson's approach to recruiting was decidedly different from Saban's. He sometimes showed up at recruiting visits wearing jeans and a polo shirt and no socks. He spent serious time with the kids— in person, on the phone, via texts—getting to know them. "He talked to them about everything other than football," says Terry Curtis, the head coach of UMS-Wright Preparatory School in Mobile. "He got to know them in a way that a head coach can't. He talks to them about their girlfriends."

One of Thompson's most brilliant moves in Mobile was to get all of the area players being recruited by Alabama together as much as possible. "We'd sit around and talk and just be around each other," says Mark Barron, who is now a safety for the St. Louis Rams. "We'd all grown up in the same city, but we'd gone to different schools and we didn't really know each other. We bonded then. And once a few of us committed to Alabama, we all kind of helped recruit each other and became friends and got close in the process."

---

* Mobile has become such a hotbed for recruiting that it has become the vanguard of something akin to a recruiting industrial complex. Every year during recruiting season, Mobile becomes a hive of activity. Airplanes from different schools land and take off from the airport; cars carrying coaches show up at high schools and recruits' homes; a deluge of phone calls, texts, and emails hits recruits and their parents, coaches, and teachers. Many high schools in the area now have a person dedicated to handling requests for films, meetings, and interviews. "It's a lot of fun, but at times it gets to be a real headache," says coach Terry Curtis of UMS-Wright Preparatory School.

Thompson and Saban were a powerful one-two punch. Thompson softened up the recruit with his easygoing nature, then the businesslike Saban came in and closed the deal, talking about grades, becoming a man, and life after football.

It was Thompson who first had contact with Jones. Jones's father was pretty much out of the picture by that time. His mother, Queen Marvin, was fiercely protective of her son and didn't even allow him to play football until he was twelve. Jones was a quiet young man and was hard for some coaches to read. He seemed to retreat even further into himself as the recruiting process went on and the frenzy around him intensified. His mother liked Thompson, and she loved Saban. "Coach Saban talked to us and told us what Julio had to do to play for him," Marvin says. "He didn't tell him that he would start right away. Other coaches told him that, though. Coach Saban told him he had to work hard before he could play. I liked that."

Saban and Thompson were relentless with Jones, contacting him as much as they could and getting other parts of the Alabama football community involved. Marvin worked at a local KFC. Alabama boosters in the area ate more chicken during the months of Jones's recruitment than they ever had in their lives.

Jones was cagey until the end about which school he was going to choose. "There was lots of drama," says Cignetti. "There's always lots of drama. Nick always knows more than anyone else, so he might have known something at a certain point, but it was pretty late in the process."

When Jones announced his signing with Alabama, the other pieces fell into place. While Jones was the crown jewel of the class, there were also some hidden gems. Ingram wasn't that highly recruited nationally (his father helped convince him to go with Saban). Hightower didn't draw much interest from other schools. "And we almost didn't offer Upshaw," says Cignetti.

Just as he had done at LSU, Saban's first recruiting move at Alabama was to court the state's high school coaches. "It was unbelievable," says Curtis. "Saban took the job at Alabama one day, and he was sitting in my office the next. He asked a lot about me, where I'd been and how I coached. From that day forward, I felt like I could call him and he would call me right back. Heck, I have friends from high school who don't even do that. He's relentless. He never lets a long time go without some contact. He makes you feel important. And the funny thing is, he's known the whole time that I graduated from Auburn."

Saban relished these visits with high school coaches, away from the glare, finding with them some respite, some small protected bubbles where he could just be what he was: a football coach. "He would just come in and talk ball," says Josh Niblett, the head coach at prep powerhouse Hoover High School. "He liked to talk about things like practice schedules. We'd just sit and talk for forty-five minutes."

By the time he reached Alabama, Saban had taken his innate gift for evaluating talent and refined it into a science, with a system of checks and balances. Above all, Saban preferred to get a potential recruit on campus for one of Alabama's football camps. He wanted to see the kid play in person on his turf, to get an up-close look at not only his physical skills, but—with Rosen in mind—his overall demeanor and attitude as well. "If we could evaluate a guy in a camp, we were right about ninety percent of the time about him," says Cignetti. "If we only had tape, our hit-or-miss ratio wasn't quite that good." (Cignetti was the recruiting coordinator at Alabama from 2007 to 2010, though he says that title was only in name. "I remember one day Nick and I were talking about a receiver, and I told him that I didn't think the kid was that great. And he turned to me and said, 'Look, you're not the director of personnel. I am,'" says Cignetti.)

Sometimes, though, tape was all they had. If a player on tape was deemed worthy—after being watched by a graduate assistant or "analyst," the recruiting area coach, and the position coach—that tape went to Saban. He watched them all. If he liked the player, his name went up on a board. The player was graded by strengths and weaknesses in at least ten different categories, which included size, speed, character, toughness, academics, ankle, knee, and hip flexibility, balance and body control, and explosive power. Different-colored dots were put next to the names: Green meant the kid had character issues. Red meant potential academic problems. Eventually, all of those bits of information were processed into an overall grade—from 1 to 5, with 1 being the best. (The grading system was a mix of what Saban had learned under James and Belichick.) No player ever received a 1. Julio Jones was one of Saban's highest-rated prospects ever, and he graded out at a 1.8. Anyone who graded out around a 2 was offered a scholarship. Players with higher grades than that were evaluated by need at the position. Saban liked the scientific system, Cignetti says, because it "took the personal bias out of an individual recruiter."

Every year, Saban has twenty or so prospects who qualify for the highest category. His goal is to get at least five of those players to sign. That's where the second part of the recruiting process comes into play.

It's not too difficult to see how Saban is such a convincing recruiter these days. His résumé speaks for itself: five national titles, 133 (as of 2016) players drafted by NFL teams, and the esteem and tradition of a school like Alabama.* Back in early 2008, though, Saban was not exactly at the height of his powers. While he did have his LSU national title under his belt, he'd also suffered through three straight subpar years with his stint at the Dolphins and the 2007 season at Alabama (he had a 22-23 record since leaving LSU), and he was routinely pilloried by the media and, as it turns out, other coaches. "On the recruiting trail that year, we were getting hit with 'He lied about Miami and he'll lie about Alabama, too,'" says a

---

* One mailer sent to potential recruits in 2013 displayed the checks written out to the nine Alabama players who were drafted by NFL teams that year. The checks totaled more than $51 million. Another poster that year showed the jerseys of the 111 Saban-coached players who had become NFL draft picks at the time.

former Alabama coach. Reversing the three-year trend of mediocre-to-bad seasons was the reason the 2008 class was so important to Saban. Overcoming the negativity around him was one of the reasons it was so impressive.

By 2008, Saban had earned the moniker "the Lord of the Living Room." Saban's celebrity at the time—for both good and bad reasons—certainly helped him with recruiting. Anytime he showed up at either a high school or a recruit's house, it became an event. Most of the time he tried to arrive as inconspicuously as possible, having his driver park the car in an out-of-the-way place and entering buildings and houses though the back door. Sometimes even those precautions didn't work, however. Chris Yeager, the head coach at Mountain Brook High School in Birmingham, remembers when Saban showed up to meet Tyler Love, an offensive lineman who was part of the 2008 class. "The whole neighborhood turned out, and even some people who didn't live in the neighborhood. They just wanted to catch a glimpse of him," says Yeager. "This one little boy got his autograph on the way into Tyler's house." Niblett from Hoover High School says he was always "embarrassed" when the students—and even teachers—gathered outside the school when Saban came by for a meeting.

Saban used that fame to his advantage. In one-on-one meetings, he would turn it on its head a bit. "Everyone was sort of afraid of him. His projection preceded him a bit," says a former coach. "But he'd show these players his human side. He'd crack a joke with them and let him know he was just a guy." Ralph Potter, formerly the head coach of Brentwood Academy in Nashville, remembers when Saban was recruiting Chris Jordan, a linebacker in the 2008 class. "At one point, Chris asked him if he ever smiled," said Potter. "And Saban just deadpanned, didn't smile, didn't change his expression, and then said, 'Well, Chris, if it would help you come to the University of Alabama, I would tell a joke.' And then he smiled."

The recruits, too, felt flattered by his attention and individual focus on them. "At his office, he'd close his door with a button and it would just be the two of us and it felt like the door was closing out the outside world," says Vinnie Sunseri, a 2011 recruit.*

What Saban offered above all was a businesslike approach. Just as he was bringing a more corporate atmosphere to the administration and program, he was doing the same thing—and projecting the same image—while recruiting. He was different from other coaches. "I felt like Urban Meyer [then at Florida] and [Mark] Richt [Georgia] and [Les] Miles were more about relationships," says Yeager. "What Saban offered was a blueprint. He said, 'This is our mission and we'll do this together.' "

Todd Watson, Julio Jones's former head coach at Foley High School, says that the difference between Saban and the other coaches was that Saban was "brutally honest. He told the players that this is where he saw them, and that our train was moving forward and they could get on it or not. I think the kids like the honesty." Damion Square, who was recruited by Texas, Texas A&M, Notre Dame, and Miami but signed with Alabama in 2008, says: "A lot of guys recruit with a lot of fluff. Some of Saban's assistants did that. But he never did."

Though Saban didn't promise immediate playing time, with the thinness of his roster the opportunity to play some serious minutes and even start was implied for the members of the 2008 class, and was undoubtedly one of the reasons for the excellence of that class. Saban did make other promises. Marcell Dareus told a newspaper what Saban simply said to him: "I promise you we're going to win; I promise you you'll get your degree; I promise you you'll become a better man than when you came in."

Saban also separated himself from the other coaches with his demeanor and appearance (he kept his tailor from Miami). "The other

---

* The automatic door in Saban's Alabama office has long been an object of fascination by his recruits and journalists. "I don't know what the big deal is," says Saban. "It just saves me the time of getting up to close it." Time—even down to the second—is something Saban values. At his golf club near his lake house in Georgia, Saban procured a clicker that allowed him to get into the club through the maintenance entrance, which he calculated saved him two minutes of travel time each way.

coaches sometimes come off as used-car salesmen and Baptist ministers. He's not like that," says a former Alabama offensive coach. "A lot of these parents aren't making a lot of money, and they see this guy come in, just off the plane, wearing a suit, a guy with a plan. They don't see many people like that. What they saw with him was a man who was blunt, straightforward, and successful."

Then there was the personal touch. Saban had a secretary who updated him on each individual recruit, from all of the conversations that kid had with other coaches. All of the information was kept on what was called "Saban sheets," which were meticulously maintained. He had another secretary who updated him on his own conversations with a recruit, drilling down to details as minuscule as a certain score a recruit received on an English test. "He knew which classes I was struggling in and he always asked me if I was bringing my grades up in those classes," says Quinton Dial (no relation to Preston Dial), a defensive lineman who spent two years in junior college before playing for Saban in 2011 and 2012.

There is likely another significant reason for Saban's recruiting prowess: Perhaps, in the end, he is so good at making recruits feel wanted because he knows the feeling.

With the 2008 class, Saban delivered in spades on his airplane boast to Mal Moore, and 2008 was just the beginning.* Yes, talent evaluation and his convincing closing ability were huge factors in his recruiting success, but Cignetti says there was something else, too: "He just outhustled everybody else."

Not everyone liked being outhustled, however. By early 2008, as it was becoming clear just how superb Saban's incoming class was going to be, some of his fellow coaches banded together in an effort to stop him, or at the very least, to slow him down.

* NFL first-round picks from the 2008 class: Dareus, Julio Jones, Barron, Hightower, and Ingram. Second-round picks: Cody and Upshaw.

One of Saban's favorite times to recruit had always been during a six-week period in the spring, when high schools were going through their spring practices. One of the reasons he liked it so much was that he sometimes had the road to himself. Many of his fellow coaches didn't find the same joy in recruiting that Saban did.

The spring recruiting period had its own set of rules. A head coach was allowed to visit a high school but was not allowed to sit and talk to a recruit. According to the NCAA handbook, a head coach could say a quick hello, but then he had to take all "appropriate steps to immediately terminate the encounter." Of course, there was much gray area about what exactly constituted "appropriate steps."

In the spring of 2007, while working on the 2008 class, the hyperaggressive Saban visited a hundred high schools. The spring period, he says, "gave me an opportunity to meet coaches. I could look them in the eye and talk face-to-face. On the phone, it's easy to not tell the truth."

According to some of his fellow coaches, though, Saban frequently went too far during these visits. His presence at a high school always caused a spectacle, so in most cases running across a recruit was more likely to happen than not. There was a general sense that, on many occasions, Saban crossed the line and intentionally ran into recruits and spoke with them during the visits and didn't "immediately terminate the encounter." This is what was known as a "bump." Many college coaches walked a fine line during spring recruiting, but the *Chicago Tribune* described Saban as "the most blatant violator" of the bump rule.

Shortly after National Signing Day in 2008, the NCAA—with the support of many of Saban's contemporaries—passed a new rule that prohibited head coaches from visiting high schools in the spring. The new NCAA bylaw was immediately dubbed "the Saban Rule."

The rule's namesake was livid (which prompted the following headline in the *Huntsville Times*: "Saban Opposes 'Saban Rule' "). Saban called the new rule "ridiculous" and said: "It's just paranoia on the part of other coaches. What they didn't like is that it made them go out and have to do it."

A few months later, however, Saban had figured out a way around the new rule, following through on his pledge to "maximize" his benefits when it came to the NCAA. While at the Dolphins, Saban's players had used videoconferencing to do sessions with Rosen and other doctors. Saban wondered if he could use the same technology to talk to recruits and their coaches in the spring. "I checked with our compliance people and they checked and it wasn't illegal," he says. So he started using it. Within a few months, most other coaches at major college programs had followed suit.

In the 2008 preseason, Alabama was ranked twenty-fourth in the AP poll and was left off the *USA Today* coaches poll altogether. Major Applewhite, Saban's first offensive coordinator at Alabama, left the program for a job at Texas, the end of a rocky stint in which he and Saban never quite got over their differences, both in personality and philosophy. Saban hired Jim McElwain, who'd been the offensive coordinator at Fresno State under Saban's former assistant coaching mate Pat Hill. "McElwain handled Saban very well," says Wilson. "Saban was on the players and coaches a lot. McElwain did a great job of shielding us from a lot of that, while still getting Saban's point across."

Though it was a new season, the previous one was not forgotten. Saban had photos of the scoreboards from the Mississippi State and ULM losses posted in the locker and weight rooms. Those losses had become part of the narrative about Saban leading into the 2008 season. Rudy Niswanger, the offensive lineman for Saban at LSU, was in training camp with the Kansas City Chiefs that year when he was approached by a reporter who was working on a story about Saban. "He wanted to talk to me about Saban's losses to Mississippi State and ULM," says Niswanger. "It was pretty clear that he was looking for a negative answer. But I told him that Saban had lost to UAB in his first year at LSU, and that these things happen when you're rebuilding, and that he won a national championship two years later. I told him I was sure he'd do the same at Alabama."

Two weeks later, Niswanger received a letter in a University of Alabama envelope, a copy of the story with Niswanger's quotes, and a handwritten thank-you note from Saban, who remained as sensitive as ever to criticism and as grateful as ever to those who stood up for him.

Alabama started the 2008 season against ninth-ranked Clemson in the Chick-fil-A College Kickoff Game. Saban liked to start the season with these high-profile showdowns. They provided the team with a heightened focus in the late summer camp, and the national exposure also was a great platform for recruiting. Clemson was supposed to have an explosive offense that season, led by running back C. J. Spiller, and it was favored to beat Alabama. The Crimson Tide held Clemson to zero yards rushing and won easily, 34–10. The 2008 freshmen played significant roles in the game: Julio Jones had a touchdown reception, Ingram ran for ninety-six yards, and Hightower had a fumble recovery. "We beat the shit out of them," says Wilson. "I remember looking at their defensive line. They wanted nothing to do with us and wanted to get out of the building as soon as possible."

Three days after the game, Clemson coach Tommy Bowden—son of Florida State coach Bobby Bowden—called Saban. It was a move without precedent in the hypercompetitive world of major college football. "Saban had been studying me for months and he'd obviously done a good job of figuring me out," says Bowden. "So I wanted to know what he saw, what our tendencies were. We talked for thirty minutes or so. He's not a real talker, but he was nice and professional. He answered all of my questions. He understood my family and liked my father."

After the game, Crimson Tide fans and the media were immediately bubbling over with enthusiasm. (Alabama appeared on the cover of *Sports Illustrated* the following week.) Saban tried to tamp down expectations, telling the media: "It's one game, aiight?"* The hype became harder to dampen, though, after Alabama started the season 5-0, which included a convincing win over third-ranked Georgia.

By early November, Alabama had ascended to the number-one spot in the BCS rankings, just as Saban was headed back to Baton Rouge for his first visit to LSU as the head coach at Alabama. The welcome in the bayou was not a warm one. LSU students burned him in effigy before the game and sported T-shirts that read: "Beat $aban." The week before the game, Luther Davis, an Alabama player who had also been recruited by LSU, told a newspaper that Miles had called Saban "the devil" during recruiting. Alabama was assigned thirty-two police officers for the game. The LSU student section chanted: "Fuck you, Saban!" throughout the game. (They would employ the same chant again during the 2014 Alabama-LSU game in Baton Rouge.)

On the last play in regulation LSU blocked a short field goal attempt by Alabama that would have won the game. The Crimson Tide regrouped and eventually won, 27–21, in overtime. Alabama capped off a 12-0 regular season with a 36–0 win over Auburn in late November, breaking a six-game losing streak to the Tigers. Alabama's next game would be against Florida in the SEC Championship, putting them on the verge of a berth in the national title game, something that had seemed highly improbable at the beginning of the season.

A few days after the loss to Alabama, Auburn coach Tommy Tuberville—who had boastfully held up six fingers after the 2007

---

* "Aiight" is one of Saban's favorite verbal tics. He usually resorts to it when he's a bit perturbed or when he feels aggravated because he has to explain to the media something he believes is relatively rudimentary. One of his other verbal tics is the use of the phrase "relative to." For instance, after one practice, Saban talked to the media about a receiver who was recovering from a dislocated shoulder, saying he "wasn't able to do much relative to getting his arm up."

win over Alabama—resigned. Earlier in the year, in October—just two months after losing to Alabama—Tommy Bowden left Clemson after a 3-3 start to the season. That November, just nine days after losing to Alabama, Phillip Fulmer—the seventeen-year coach at Tennessee who had won a national title in 1998—was asked to step down. The popular notion at the time was that Saban—or the mere presence of Saban—had been the reason for the demise of these three coaches. He'd become college football's wrecking ball.

Tuberville, who is now the coach at the University of Cincinnati, is quick to point out that "I do have the best record against Nick going." (Tuberville is a lifetime 4-3 versus Saban, going back to Saban's years at LSU.) He adds, with a laugh: "I'm trying to get him on the schedule so he'll have a chance to catch up."

Tuberville says that before Saban arrived, Auburn "was getting eight or nine or ten of the recruits who were ranked in the top ten in the state. We were just dominating." Then, after Saban's first year, "things turned pretty quick." Tuberville says he knew early on that Saban was a perfect fit for Alabama. "They needed someone who would take control. I wasn't all that fired up about it. I knew things would change."

Did he think Saban was the reason he left? "Well, I ushered myself out. I didn't have any support and I couldn't get things done. It was my idea to leave, but all I had to do was look across the street. They were building something and we were just spinning our wheels."

Bowden, who'd been portrayed by Clemson fans and the media as meek for calling Saban after losing to him in the first game of the 2008 season, says that the loss and the subsequent phone call "were the beginning of my downfall, for sure."

Fulmer, like Tuberville, went through two rounds in the SEC with Saban. He says the loss to Saban's LSU team in the 2001 SEC Championship game—which, had they won, would have sent them to the national championship game—was the "toughest in my career." When Saban returned to the SEC, Fulmer's Tennessee team suffered a humiliating 41–17 smackdown to Alabama in 2007 and a 29–9 loss in 2008. By that time, Fulmer had become one of the highest-paid coaches in the country. He had Saban partly to thank for that salary. However, with the money came the added pressure to excel. "Those two losses to Alabama were certainly part of the reason I was asked to step down, I'm sure," he says.

In the 2008 SEC Championship game, top-ranked Alabama was matched up against second-ranked Florida, which was coached by Urban Meyer and quarterbacked by Tim Tebow, the 2007 Heisman Trophy winner, who had become unquestionably the most famous player in college football.*

Alabama played well for most of the game, keeping Tebow somewhat in check. Nearing the middle of the fourth quarter, the Crimson Tide led Florida, 20–17. From that point on, though, Tebow took over, leading the Gators to two touchdowns and an eventual 31–20 win. It remains Saban's only loss in a championship game. "We just weren't ready to finish," says Wilson. "We had them, and we didn't step on the gas." Florida went on to win the national title.

Alabama played a 12-0 Utah team in the Sugar Bowl a month later. Though it was favored by 10.5 points, the Crimson Tide never seemed to shake off the disappointment of losing the chance to play for the national title. In some strange way, the invitation to the Independence Bowl the year before seemed almost more important to the program, in that it needed it more, for morale and for the extra practice time to soak in Saban's process. Adding to Alabama's general malaise in the Sugar Bowl was the loss of star offensive lineman Andre Smith, who'd been suspended before the game for reportedly talking to an agent. (Saban never gave an official reason

---

* Right alongside the Drew Brees "what if?" in Saban's career is the one involving Tebow. In 2006, Mike Shula had come very close to signing Tebow at Alabama. Had Tebow chosen the Crimson Tide instead of the Gators, might he have saved Shula's job and left Saban with little choice other than to return to the Dolphins?

for the suspension.) Wilson, without his best lineman, was sacked eight times, and Alabama lost, 31–17.

That game, however, seemed to mean little to the Alabama players who would be returning in 2009. It was the Florida loss that they never let go.

11

The Dynasty

IN MID-JANUARY 2009, less than three weeks before National Signing Day, Lance Thompson abruptly left Alabama to become the linebackers coach at Tennessee, one of Alabama's biggest traditional rivals. The move was a lateral one, and he was going to work for a young, brash, and unproven coach named Lane Kiffin. Thompson told the media that the job change had nothing to do with Saban, that it was a personal and business decision. Saban tried to convince him to stay, offering him more money than Tennessee was prepared to pay him. Thompson left anyway. Saban was furious, and viewed the departure as a betrayal. It also left Saban in a possible jam.

In late 2008 and early 2009, Thompson had again helped Saban put together what appeared to be another blue-ribbon recruiting class. Thompson had been the lead recruiter for running back Trent Richardson, offensive lineman D. J. Fluker (full name: Daniel Lee Jesus Fluker), and quarterback A. J. McCarron, all of whom had verbally committed to—but not formally signed with—Alabama. With Thompson leaving so close to National Signing Day, however, those commitments were suddenly a bit less secure. Kiffin openly bragged about stealing Thompson from Saban.

In the end, of course, Saban held on to those three marquee recruits, and added other future NFL players Nico Johnson, Dre Kirkpatrick, Eddie Lacy, Kevin Norwood, and Chance Warmack in the 2009 class, which rivaled its 2008 counterpart in talent. The quality of that class provided the thirty-four-year-old Kiffin with another opportunity to take a shot at Saban. Kiffin told the media that Saban should have opened his post–Signing Day press conference by thanking Thompson "because Lance signed eight of those guys." (The shots at Saban were only part of Kiffin's boisterous entrance into the SEC that year. He also falsely accused Urban Meyer of cheating and got into a public tiff with South Carolina's Steve Spurrier. At one point, SEC commissioner Mike Slive was forced to ask Kiffin to tone it down.) The hostilities were further stoked when Thompson told a Tennessee booster club that he would "own Memphis" and that "[Saban] ain't getting any more of my [recruits]." Hours after Thompson made that proclamation, Saban signed Keiwone Malone, a four-star recruit who happened to be from Memphis. (Malone would later transfer from Alabama to the University of Memphis.)

The rift with Kiffin and Thompson was only mild turbulence compared to what was coming in that off-season. In June, the NCAA handed down its ruling on the Alabama textbook scandal. Seven football players were implicated, found to have acquired textbooks for friends and other athletes, making up to $4,000 a person in the transactions. Though the football program was not stripped of any scholarships, it was forced to vacate twenty-one wins and, more important, was put back on probation as a "repeat violator," which meant that any other major infraction in the ensuing five years would likely devastate the program. Alabama football couldn't seem to get out from under the dark cloud of NCAA sanctions, which had been its near-constant companion since the 1990s. When the university appealed the ruling, the NCAA replied with unusually stern language, calling Alabama a "serial repeat offender" with an "abysmal track record" and an "extensive recent history of infractions cases unmatched by any other member institution in the NCAA."

Saban's players also found trouble in that off-season. Linebacker Courtney Upshaw was arrested for third-degree domestic violence for allegedly shoving his girlfriend (charges were later dismissed) and Julio Jones and Ingram were implicated in a possible NCAA violation for going on an all-expenses-paid fishing trip with a man who some believed was an Alabama booster. (The NCAA found no wrongdoing and determined that the man was not a booster, and merely forced Jones and Ingram to pay him back.) Less than a week before the first game of the season, senior defensive end Brandon Deaderick was shot in the arm during a robbery attempt. (He didn't miss the game.)

Some lighthearted news, though, came from off the field. That year the program inaugurated its newly renamed visitors' locker room. In big letters, right above the locker room's entrance, were the words THE FAIL ROOM. The name came from Alabama booster James M. Fail, who told a newspaper: "When I saw the visitors' locker room as a potential naming right, I figured it was the most appropriate opportunity I would ever have to use my name." The locker room's new moniker pleased Saban greatly, fitting right into his belief in all things psychological.

Saban was entering year three in his rebuild. With the 2009 recruiting class on campus, the majority of the team's players were now his. Any Shula-era players left had either fully bought in or had been flushed out. Though experienced quarterback John Parker Wilson had graduated, Saban had Greg McElroy waiting in the wings. He was the type of quarterback whom Saban adored: a smart player (he would later become a finalist for a Rhodes Scholarship) and a leader. Saban also had depth for the first time, which created beneficial competition at some key positions. (Mark Ingram had to work hard to stay ahead of the freshman Trent Richardson, for instance.)

Saban believed that he had something special with the 2009 team. "We can be an outstanding team," he told his team in that off-season, according to multiple players. "I'm not worried about the talent on offense. I'm not worried about the talent on defense. But how bad do you want it?"

It was abundantly clear that the team's coach wanted it, badly. For two years, Saban had worked tirelessly to shape up the program, from top to bottom. He found pleasure in the entire process, and lost himself in it nearly completely. All of that work, however, came with what was now a familiar cost. Though Saban had his family with him in Tuscaloosa (both Nicholas and Kristen would eventually graduate from Alabama), he was rarely with them. "Terry only saw him once a week, really," says childhood friend Kerry Marbury. "I went down there to see a game one year and we went to his house afterwards and he told me, 'I can't remember the last time I was here.'" During the 2009 season, Saban would forget his wedding anniversary.* This is what it took.

Saban did do some Pilates with Terry, and the family had the few days they spent together in the summer at Lake Burton. Even there he had trouble getting away from football, and found only momentary respite in, of all things, gardening. "We'd be up there and Terry would tell me, 'Sit down and look at the mountains,' and I'd try, but I'd still be thinking about football," he says. "But when I was plowing sod, I wasn't." Gardening, however, rarely took precedence over watching film.

Though she didn't see her husband that much, Terry found Tuscaloosa and the University of Alabama much to her liking. She was back in her favored environment. By now she'd mastered the role of the college coach's wife, and embraced and loved it nearly as much as her husband loved coaching football. She became the smiling, human face of the machinelike program. She loved poetry—especially Emily Dickinson—and took to reciting lines of her favorite poems to Mal Moore on the bus rides to games. In the hallways of the Alabama football facility—where her husband still had trouble making eye contact with his colleagues—Terry wandered about, greeting everyone she saw with hugs. On the sidelines before games, she made it a point to greet the Crimson Tide press corps and even, on occasion, gave them hugs. Her role in the greater community had begun to grow in prominence. At Alabama's A-Day

---

* A few years later, when asked by the media how she and Saban planned to spend their anniversary, Terry quipped: "Just like a few years ago. Nick will enjoy a nice, quiet, intimate candlelight dinner . . . with Julio Jones."

games, she milled about the crowds outside the stadium, raising money for various charities, chatting with fans, and posing for pictures. She delivered speeches and organized fund-raisers for various student groups and Big Brothers Big Sisters. And she was heavily involved in the Sabans' charity, Nick's Kids Foundation, which they had started back at Michigan State.*

Terry was especially beneficial to her husband at events and dinners with high-powered trustees and boosters. Saban often came off as frosty and anxious at these events, his leg impatiently bouncing, one eye always fixed on the door. To many, his behavior was off-putting and impolite. He was, more often than not, bailed out by his wife. Terry was an endearing dinner companion, witty and chatty. "She could go toe-to-toe with the best wine drinkers," says one trustee. She could also be refreshingly honest about her husband's professional strengths and weaknesses. "She told me, flat out, that Nick wasn't that special when it came to the X's and O's, but that he could get the best kids to come play for him," says one Alabama booster. She could even have a little fun at her husband's expense. A booster once asked her: "When was the last time you saw Nick smile?" She pretended to take offense to the question, then broke out into a big smile. "About twenty to twenty-five years ago," she replied.

She could also, occasionally, take a humorous jab directly at her husband. On a 2009 trip back to West Virginia, the Sabans drove by Big Nick's old gas station, which was owned by an old boyfriend of Terry. According to a newspaper story, Saban figured he had a chance to "get" Terry. "I said, 'See, if you would have married him you would be over there helping him run the gas station,'" he said.

Terry replied: "If I married him, he'd be the head coach at Alabama."

According to one trustee, over the course of the Alabama years,

---

* Nick's Kids Foundation has reportedly doled out more than $4 million since its founding. In recent years, donors have included various Alabama boosters, CBS, Fox, Chick-fil-A, former NFL commissioner Paul Tagliabue, and singer Taylor Swift.

Terry has morphed from the queen bee of the campus to something more formidable: "an earth mother."

She also helped her husband with recruiting, mixing with the players and their parents with natural ease. While at Michigan State, she'd learned to play "bid whist," a bridge-like card game that was popular among African Americans. She has imparted enough wisdom about household furnishings and decorating to her husband so that he can speak knowledgeably and credibly about them when in a recruit's home, which charmed the mothers. And she always reminded him to send handwritten letters to those same mothers after a visit, mentioning—and praising—both the meal and the dessert.

Terry also continued her tradition of cooking home meals for some of the players. Preston Dial remembers one Thanksgiving when he and some of his teammates were invited to the Sabans' for Thanksgiving dinner. "We show up with our shirts tucked in, a little bit on edge," he says. "We get through dinner and tell a few stories. And then Terry says, 'Let's go upstairs to the game room.' Suddenly, some people are throwing darts and others are watching highlights with Coach Saban. Then the next thing I know, me and Miss Terry are singing karaoke. I looked at Coach Saban and he had this little-bitty smile on his face. Miss Terry had a way of making us feel comfortable enough to act like ourselves."

Terry, along with Sexton, has always been in the loop on all of Saban's career decisions. (The *Wall Street Journal* reported that she was copied on all of his business-related emails.) She remains fiercely protective of her husband's image and public perception. He doesn't make any big career or personal decisions without her, and she does her best to protect him from himself. She'd fueled his feeling at Michigan State that he wasn't appreciated enough. She'd been charmed by Huizenga when they went to the Dolphins. She always sat in the front row at Saban's radio/fan show in Miami. And she was the one who kept Mal Moore and Sexton after him about the Alabama job, realizing just how miserable her husband was at Miami and just how hard it would be for him to break his oath of loyalty and leave. Ultimately she convinced him that it was okay to think of his own happiness.

If anything, Terry's role in her husband's life—both professional and personal—has grown in recent years. Saban seems unable to function without her. At press conferences, as her husband talks, she stares intently at him, mouthing words, almost like a mother anxiously watching a child at a school play. Though Saban would go for long periods without spending any time with Terry in person, he calls her daily from his office. After warm-ups before each game, as Saban jogs back to the locker room, Terry is always there by the tunnel waiting for him with a kiss. And after every game, she is the first person he seeks out, greeting her with a hug and another kiss.

The 2009 season opened with fifth-ranked Alabama once again playing in the Chick-fil-A Kickoff Game, matched up against seventh-ranked Virginia Tech. The game, from Alabama's perspective, anyway, wasn't pretty—it overcame a ninety-eight-yard kickoff return for a touchdown, ten penalties, and two turnovers—but ultimately won going away, 34–24. Ingram, in a foreshadowing of what would be a special season, ran for 150 yards and scored two touchdowns.

Alabama then went on a rampage, winning its next six games by an average score of 35–10. The streak set up a home game against 3-3 Tennessee and Kiffin and Thompson. In the game, Alabama never quite got on track on offense, settling for four field goals to take a 12–3 lead late in the fourth quarter. Ingram then fumbled—his first ever as a collegian—and Tennessee scored to cut the lead to 12–10 with a little more than a minute remaining. The Volunteers recovered an onside kick, and on the game's final play, they set up a forty-four-yard field goal attempt to win it. Alabama's 350-pound nose tackle, Terrence Cody, pushed through the Tennessee line and batted down the kick with his left hand, his second blocked kick of the day. Saban told the media later that a game like that demonstrated "how fragile a season is." According to published reports, as Kiffin shook hands with Saban after the game, he grinned and said: "We'll get you next year." But Kiffin would be the head coach at USC by then, and, a few years after that, in a strange twist of fate, he'd be standing next to Saban—the coach he'd taunted in 2009—

on the Alabama sidelines in his first year as Alabama's offensive coordinator.

Alabama rolled though the rest of its schedule with the only other close call coming in a 26–21 win over Auburn. For the second straight year, the team finished the regular season with a perfect 12-0 record. Ingram, who would finish the season with 1,658 yards and twenty touchdowns, won the Heisman Trophy, the first Alabama player ever to win the award.*

Next up for Alabama was a rematch with Florida in the SEC Championship game. Though they never talked about it publicly, it was the game that every Crimson Tide player and coach had craved all season long. "You could see how much Coach wanted it in his eyes," says Josh Chapman.

The Florida Gators were the top-ranked team in the country, the defending national champions, and the winners of two titles in the previous three years. Florida quarterback Tim Tebow had won twenty-two games in a row, and remained the game's dominant personality, known as much for his demonstrative Christianity as he was for his on-the-field leadership, his unusual passing motion, and his resolute running and blocking. Tebow and his coach, Urban Meyer, had turned the Gators into the bully of the SEC.

Meyer and Saban have never been fond of each other. Their mutual dislike perhaps goes back to Saban's days as the head coach at Toledo. Meyer, then the quarterback and wide receivers coach at Illinois State, had called Saban in search of a job. He talked to Terry instead, and though she says she passed on the message, Saban never called him back.

To the Alabama players, the loss to Florida in the 2008 SEC Championship game still stung. "We definitely held that in. We carried it with us," says Barron. Florida had become Alabama's mea-

---

*Ingram played through some serious adversity in that season. In late 2008, his father was sentenced to ninety-two months in jail for money laundering and fraud. He got an additional two years tacked on when he jumped bail to watch his son play in the Sugar Bowl at the end of the 2008 season.

suring stick. It had what the Crimson Tide wanted. "We worked all year with that goal in mind, to win the SEC and, specifically, to beat Florida," says Barrett Jones.

What ensued was the single best game of Saban's tenure at Alabama to that point, the culmination of a steady, three-year transformation of the program. The Crimson Tide led the game from the beginning, and won, 32–13. Ingram ran for 113 yards and scored three touchdowns. Alabama's quarterback, Greg McElroy, did it all, scrambling, blocking, and passing for 239 yards, in what amounted to a pretty fair impersonation of Tebow. Alabama was flagged for just one penalty in the game, for five yards. "Our motto was, 'We will not be denied,'" says Brandon Gibson, the wide receiver. "Usually before a game, the locker room is filled with the sounds of music and guys yelling. Before that game, it was totally silent. It wasn't about payback or revenge. It was a mission. We were prepared, and we all knew exactly what we had to do. That game is one of the most fundamentally sound games I've ever seen played."

Barrett Jones, who would win three national titles during his time at Alabama, says the 2009 SEC Championship game was "my favorite game of my career there. And I know a lot of guys who say the same thing. It symbolized that we had made it." In fact, it was loud and clear.

The game, and its aftermath, was filled with symbolism. With 1:03 left—its outcome already long decided—television cameras caught Tebow on the sidelines with tears falling into his eye black, on which he had written in white: "John 16:33." (The Bible verse reads: "I have told you these things, so that in me you may have peace. In this world you will have trouble. But take heart! I have overcome the world.")

Jones says that he "had always been a fan of Tebow's. But we did take pride in watching him cry. It was kind of a sign. It was Alabama's time to take over."

Tebow wasn't the only Gator who appeared affected by the dominating defeat. At 4:27 the next morning, just hours after Florida returned home after the game, Meyer's wife called 911. The forty-five-year-old Meyer, who had complained of chest pains early in the night, was lying on the floor of his bedroom. He had a pulse, but he was unable to talk. "He almost sounds like he's trying to cry," his wife told the 911 dispatcher. Meyer was treated at a Gainesville hospital. He later told HBO that his doctors didn't think he'd had a heart attack, but that they weren't sure what had happened. On the day after Christmas in 2009—three weeks after the SEC Championship game—Meyer announced his resignation. The next day he reversed course and said he was merely taking a leave of absence, and he ended up coaching the Gators in 2010.

Alabama, meanwhile, was headed to Rose Bowl Stadium in Pasadena to play the 13-0 Texas Longhorns for the national title. On the quick, twenty-five-minute flight back to Tuscaloosa from the SEC Championship game, Saban watched film.

Alabama received the opening kickoff in the BCS National Championship game and promptly lost thirteen yards on its first possession. Backed up to his own twenty-yard line, Saban went for a huge gamble: He ran a fake punt. Though punter P. J. Fitzgerald had a man open downfield, he underthrew his pass and it was intercepted. Texas quarterback Colt McCoy then marched the Longhorns down the field, inside of the Alabama twenty-yard line. On Texas's fifth snap of the game, McCoy kept the ball on an option run play and was slammed at the line of scrimmage by Alabama's Marcell Dareus. McCoy stood up after the hit and shook out his right arm, which he could no longer feel. The Dareus hit had pinched a nerve in this throwing shoulder. The senior quarterback, and the Longhorns' best offensive player, didn't play another snap in the game.

Another huge play by Dareus—an intercepted shovel pass tossed by McCoy's freshman backup, Garrett Gilbert, which was returned for a touchdown—led to a 24–6 lead at halftime. Texas made a spirited run in the second half, but Alabama ultimately won, 37–21. The Crimson Tide finished the season 14-0—Saban's first and only undefeated season. He became the first coach since Pop Warner to win national titles at two different schools.

The enduring image from the game came near its end when

Saban was doused with a bucket of red Gatorade. Saban looked extremely angry as he peered down at his stained white shirt. He later told the media that he'd been clocked in the head. His stern visage played right into the national story line about a driven man who never seemed happy or satisfied, even after reaching the sport's apex. In the press conference after the game, Saban said: "This is not the end."

Early the next morning, he sent a text message to his coaches. They gathered in a room in the team's hotel. Chairs were arranged in a semicircle. "He said, 'Guys, great game,' then he quickly moved on and wrote out a list of things, and said, 'When we get back, we gotta do this and this and this,'" says Rob Sale, an assistant coach on the team. There was still no joy in triumph. Sale says that by that time the coaching staff was prepared for Saban's lack of happiness with an accomplishment, even one this significant. "You don't coach with him to have fun," he says. "You do it if you want to win and be successful."

In 2010, Lane Kiffin left Tennessee for USC, apparently finding the PAC-10—far away from Saban and the SEC—a more agreeable place to ply his trade. He was replaced by Derek Dooley, who had coached for Saban at LSU and the Dolphins. In that off-season, another former Saban assistant—Jimbo Fisher, his offensive coordinator at LSU—took over for Bobby Bowden at Florida State. Though Fisher had spent three years under Bowden, he didn't follow the iconic coach's old-school model when he took over the Seminole program. Instead he immediately clamped down on the media's access, hired psychologists and nutritionists, and even referred to his program as a "corporation." Saban's era had officially eclipsed that of Bowden and Joe Paterno.

To Saban's annoyance, the national championship game cut into his recruiting time. Nevertheless, he hit the trail hard and remained as aggressive as ever—perhaps too aggressive in one instance. On a visit to Dr. Phillips High School in Orlando, Saban ran across a highly touted recruit named Ha'Sean "Ha Ha" Clinton-Dix, who was a junior. NCAA rules specifically prohibited any contact with high school juniors during what is known as a "dead period" in recruiting, which is designed to provide coaches and recruits a bit of a break (a college coach was allowed to meet with high school coaches). Clinton-Dix told the *Orlando Sentinel* that Saban had called out his name during the visit, which, under a strict definition, could have been considered a minor rules violation.* Though nothing ever came of it, it was clear that Saban wasn't going to back off when it came to recruiting. He still felt that the NCAA was too restrictive, he was still looking to "maximize his benefits," and he sorely missed recruiting in the spring.

Saban's 2010 class was not considered one of his strongest at Alabama, even though he netted C. J. Mosley (an eventual first-round pick of the Baltimore Ravens) and Dee Milliner (an eventual first-round pick of the New York Jets). Auburn, meanwhile, was believed to have signed a solid class, which included a junior college player who, at the time, went by the name of Cameron Newton.

In the summer of 2010, one of the stars of the national title game, Marcell Dareus, was investigated by Alabama and the NCAA for supposedly attending an agent-sponsored party, which was a no-no for college football players. (He would eventually be suspended for two games in the 2010 season.) Saban believed Dareus had been the victim, and he used the incident to go off in a press conference, calling unscrupulous agents "pimps." His rant was well justified: Those self-serving agents could, in fact, ruin college players and programs. It also was a bit tone-deaf, too, for Saban himself was not immune to the benefits of various string-pullings done by his own agent.

Saban, fifty-eight years old and entering his thirty-eighth year as a coach, had not mellowed a bit. He was still exacting and prone to high-decibel, profanity-laced outbursts, and he still on occasion grabbed his butt cheek in fits of anger. "Sometimes it just seemed

---

* Of course, given Clinton-Dix's first name, Saban could have plausibly argued that he was just laughing at a joke, right?

sort of like, 'Whose day is it to get yelled at?' " says Cignetti. "We used to say it was like he just writes a name on the top of a board, and that's whose day it is." The same held true for his players. "We always joked about it. Some days he would just pick one person and just go after him," says Colin Peek, a tight end on the 2009 team. "Let's say the backup quarterback was out there trying to thread the needle in practice and throwing impossible passes. Saban would just dismantle the kid. And he wouldn't let it go. Four practice periods later, someone else would screw up and it would just ignite him, and he'd go back to his original target, the backup QB. We called that 'going in for second helpings.' Then someone else would miss a block, and Saban would go in for third helpings on that QB."

In 2010, Saban seemed to believe that the entire team needed third helpings. On paper, Alabama looked every bit as good as—if not better than—the 2009 championship team. McElroy, Ingram, Richardson, and Julio Jones were back on offense. Dareus (after the suspension), Hightower, Upshaw, Kirkpatrick, and Barron were back on defense. "I can say to this day that I think that was the best team of those years that we had athletically," says Brandon Gibson. "But there was a real sense of entitlement on the team, and a real lack of leadership." One of the leaders most missed was Javier Arenas, a defensive back and kick returner who had started his Alabama career under Shula, and never took for granted what Saban had brought to the program.

The season got off to a good start, with five straight wins, which included a 31–6 thrashing of Florida. If the SEC Championship game had been the body blow from which Meyer never recovered, the 2010 game was the mercy head shot. After the season, Meyer resigned from Florida, this time for good (though he would resurface at Ohio State in 2012 and memorably exact a bit of revenge on Saban a few years after that).

The Florida win was Alabama's twenty-ninth regular season victory in a row. Cignetti says, looking back, he and his fellow coaches should have seen the warning signs that appeared during that game. "We beat them pretty badly, but I remember in the third quarter, with the game already in hand, you could tell that on the sidelines that there was this casual attitude. I remember thinking, *Wow, this is a weird feeling.*"

The team traveled next to South Carolina to play Steve Spurrier and the Gamecocks, and got ambushed. South Carolina's quarterback, Stephen Garcia, played the game of his life. (Generally speaking, a white-hot quarterback is one of the few recipes for success against Saban's post-2007 Alabama teams.) Garcia hit on seventeen of his twenty passes, and threw for three touchdowns. Ingram and Richardson were held to sixty-four rushing yards combined. After the 35–21 loss, Saban blurted out in a press conference: "This team hasn't proved shit."

Still, three weeks later, Alabama had a 7-1 record and was in the thick of both the conference and national title races. They then headed to Baton Rouge for the fourth installment of "the Saban Bowl." Though Alabama led, 14–10, entering the fourth quarter, LSU pulled out a 24–21 win. As Saban walked into the postgame press conference, an LSU fan yelled: "How do you like that, Nick?" The last embers sometimes burn the hottest.

The loss did nothing to shake the team out of its fugue, or its coach out of his fury. Late in a blowout win over Mississippi State, Saban inserted backup quarterback A. J. McCarron. On one play, McCarron, a candidate to replace the graduating McElroy the following year, decided to throw a deep ball to a well-covered Julio Jones rather than hit an open receiver underneath. The ball was batted away, and Alabama settled for a field goal. As McCarron walked to the sidelines, Saban met him on the field and walked back with him, screaming into his ear the entire time. He punctuated the tirade with a very hard spank. "Check your ego," he told McCarron.

That year's Iron Bowl, played in Tuscaloosa, came to define the 2010 season for Alabama. Auburn was 11-0 and ranked number two in the country. Its quarterback, Cam Newton, had been a sensation, and had continued to play well even as controversy swirled around him and his father, who had allegedly solicited money from Mississippi State in return for his son signing there. In the warm-ups before the Iron Bowl, Newton was serenaded with the Steve Miller

Band's "Take the Money and Run" over the stadium's loudspeakers, and he seemed rattled as Alabama jumped out to a stunning 24–0 lead in the second quarter. The margin could have been larger. "In the 2009 game, it seemed like we got all the breaks. And then they got them all in 2010," says Will Lowery, the defensive back.

One of those breaks happened in the second quarter, with Alabama up 21–0. Ingram caught a flare pass and ran for forty-one yards before being caught at Auburn's twenty-yard line. As he struggled to gain a few extra yards, the ball was punched away from him and recovered by Auburn. Later in the same quarter, Barron tore his pectoral muscle, which effectively left him with one functioning arm for the rest of the game, an injury that would play a significant role in the game's outcome.

Alabama gained 379 yards in the first half. The second half, however, could not have gone much worse for the Crimson Tide. On a key play, Newton launched a deep pass that Barron was perfectly positioned to intercept, or at the very least knock down. Instead, because of his injury, he managed only to swat lamely at the ball, which was caught and run in for a touchdown. Alabama gained only sixty-seven yards in the second half, and Newton completed the comeback as Auburn won, 28–27, in what remains one of Saban's most devastating losses at Alabama.

A few days after the game, Saban called a meeting. Players on the team say there was a noticeable divide in the room that day. Those who were graduating or turning pro appeared unmoved by the loss, the same sort of mind-set that had plagued the team that year. "But the people who were coming back were still super upset," says Nate Carlson, a backup tight end. In his postgame meetings, Saban usually went through a list he'd compiled that he called "The Good, the Bad, and the Ugly." In that meeting, Saban breezed through that part, then set aside his notes and took off his glasses. He looked out into the room, making a point to focus on the players who would be a part of the 2011 team. "He talked for a few minutes, and told us that he knew how disappointed we were, but that he was proud of us," says Carlson. "And then he said, 'At the end of the day, all they [Auburn] want is to be us. They will always want what we have. But they will never be us.'"

That speech, according to several players, set a new tone, both for the upcoming bowl game against Michigan State and for the next year. "We all felt sort of branded by that loss to Auburn, and we didn't want to feel that way anymore," says Carlson.

Despite his at times awkward deliveries, Saban did have a way of reaching his players with his speeches. He drilled into them that football was a microcosm of life. "He said that any mistakes he'd made, in business or with his family, were from the same issues that created mistakes on the football field," says Preston Dial. "Most mistakes in blocking or on defense were caused by a lack of communication or consistency or preparation or just simply not having faith in each other."

One year he felt that the team was lackadaisical in its preparation for a game against the University of Tennessee at Chattanooga, an FCS team, so he gathered the team together. "He was all fired up," says Colin Peek. "What he said was so unexpected. It was hilarious. He told us, 'You guys don't get it. This is what's going to happen. One day, years from now, you'll be riding around in your Mercedes-Benz, and you'll see some hot girl in the car next to you. You'll roll down your window and say, 'How you doin'? And she'll look at you and say, 'Wait, aren't you the dude who lost to Tennessee-Chattanooga?'"

Saban sometimes turned to biblical stories as inspiration and could get so worked up that he'd hopelessly mix them up, causing the more ardent Christians on the team to raise their eyebrows. The stories he told were sometimes a bit hokey, and the references he used were occasionally outdated, but he told them with such surprising and genuine passion that they became endearing. On another occasion, according to a former player, after going through "The Good, the Bad, and the Ugly," Saban glanced down into the front row, where, by coincidence, a number of his players who already had children were sitting together. Saban put down his notes and started shaking his head. "You know, I don't understand you guys out there chasing pussy, having all of these kids. And then you come in here and try to play football. Ultimately it's a distraction. Ultimately, you don't want to be out there chasing after midnight. If you haven't locked it up by midnight, it's not worth it."

At this point, Saban paused, and shuffled on his feet. The color had risen in his face. His players had no idea what to expect next. "Ultimately, you never want to sleep with anybody who has less to lose than you do," he said. "So, ultimately, if I'm ever going to sleep around on Miss Terry, it's going to be with Hillary Fucking Rodham Clinton."

A few members of the team laughed so hard that they fell out of their seats. "It was funny as hell," says a former player. "And it was actually a great lesson."

At the end of the 2010 season, Alabama earned a spot in the Capital One Bowl against Saban's former school Michigan State. The Spartans, led by Mark Dantoni, who had coached the secondary at Michigan State under Saban, were 11-1 and ranked seventh in the country. Alabama, at 9-3, was ranked fifteenth. As at LSU, the old wounds Saban had caused at Michigan State had apparently never quite healed. Before the game, on Interstate 94 outside of Detroit, two graduates of Michigan State paid for a giant billboard that read: "Go State! Beat Alabama and Saban." In a press release, one of the men said the reason they paid for the billboard was that Saban had left Michigan State "under . . . let's just call it less than normal circumstances."

They would have been better off saving their money. Alabama trounced Michigan State, 49–7. "We really rededicated ourselves before that bowl game and found our identity," says Lowery. "I started in the dime package during that game because Mark [Barron] was hurt. I didn't have to do anything. Kirk Cousins [Michigan State's quarterback] never had a chance to do anything because Dareus and Upshaw were all over him. We took them to the woodshed."

Finally, the team with as much promise as any during Saban's coaching years played up to its ability, which would carry over into the following season.

By 2011, as Saban again landed the top-rated recruiting class, it had become crystal clear that he was the best recruiter in college football, and perhaps the best in the history of the game.

Even the best recruiters, though, don't get them all. One of Saban's most high-profile misses came that year, in the form of a hugely talented defensive lineman from South Carolina named Jadeveon Clowney. "We went after Clowney real hard," says Cignetti, who would leave Alabama to become the head coach of Division II Indiana University of Pennsylvania in that off-season.

According to an interview Clowney gave to Fox Sports, Saban visited him in early December 2010. They talked about Alabama's graduation rate (Saban's Alabama teams have consistently ranked near the top, both in the SEC and nationally) and the program's recent knack for sending players to the NFL. Clowney later made a visit to Tuscaloosa, where he had breakfast at the Sabans' house and met with Saban privately in his office, where he said Saban told him: "We'd love to have you. You'll help our team out. You're going to play as a freshman."

Clowney, according to the article, was not very impressed with the "Lord of the Living Room." During his meetings, Clowney said Saban "talked the whole time. . . . I was dozing off. He can talk. A lot. He talked for a whole straight hour." Clowney then added a zinger: "I don't see the big deal like everybody else. They'd say, 'He's the king of football.' That guy ain't nothing but 5'5". He's a short guy. Everybody's going crazy on Nick Saban."

Clowney said he ultimately didn't go to Alabama because Saban didn't run the type of defensive scheme that he preferred. He signed instead with South Carolina, on whose sideline he'd been standing when the Gamecocks upset the Crimson Tide in 2010.

Another miss for Saban happened the following year. Jameis Winston was a star prep quarterback at Hueytown High School in Alabama, forty-five miles or so from Tuscaloosa. During his high school years, he'd attended some of Saban's football camps, and Saban made numerous visits to Winston's home and school. "Saban wanted Jameis pretty bad," says Winston's former high school coach, Matt Scott.

Winston, who was also pursued by Florida State, LSU, Stanford, and Texas, had made it clear during his recruitment that he also wanted to play baseball in college. "Saban would often talk to Jameis about his own baseball-playing days," says Scott. "Jameis really liked him. And Saban really liked Jameis. And contrary to what people say, Saban was willing to let him play baseball at Alabama."

Scott says that many other coaches resorted to negative recruiting when it came to Saban. The main thing they harped on was the notion that Saban doesn't like—and doesn't start—black quarterbacks. (Tony Banks at Michigan State, Marcus Randall and JaMarcus Russell at LSU, and Blake Sims at Alabama would dispute that assessment.) "They were all underestimating Jameis. He knew damn good and well that Saban would play somebody if he's the best at his position. But we still got that a lot from the other coaches. They also said Saban was too businesslike, which seemed like a strange insult. I guess there weren't a whole lot of other angles they could take."

Scott says Winston's ultimate decision to go to Florida State was a difficult one because of how much he liked Saban. "He felt like he could just be himself at FSU. For instance, if he was throwing around in warm-ups before a game, and some kid called him over for a picture, he wanted to be able to do that. He just didn't see that happening in Tuscaloosa, didn't think he'd be able to do that. It may sound weird, but it made perfect sense to me."

Clowney, of course, eventually became the best defensive player in college football and was the number-one overall pick in the 2014 NFL Draft. Winston led Florida State to the national title in the 2013 season and won the Heisman Trophy. In 2014, he guided the Seminoles to a perfect regular season and a berth in the first-ever college football playoffs (where Florida State lost to Oregon in the semifinals) and was the number-one draft pick in the 2015 NFL Draft.

Saban clearly wanted both players. However, given Clowney's lack of respect for Saban, and the off-the-field issues that plagued Winston at Florida State,* it's fair to wonder if either one of them would have worked out at Alabama anyway.

The 2011 season had a little bit of everything for Saban and Alabama: the bizarre, the heartbreaking, and, ultimately, the triumphant.

In January, an Alabama fan who went by the name "Al from Dadeville" called in to the popular Paul Finebaum radio show and told the host that, after Alabama's shocking loss in the 2010 Iron Bowl, he had poisoned the oak trees in Toomer's Corner on the Auburn campus. Toomer's Corner is the traditional gathering spot for Auburn students after football victories, and the stately oaks that resided there were often rolled with toilet paper in celebration. The caller was later identified as Harvey Updyke, a fan of the Crimson Tide who had not even attended the university. The poison eventually killed the trees, and Updyke went to jail. Though the story elicited shake-your-head surprise and disgust nationally, fans of both Auburn and Alabama expressed their shock with more knowing nods. The criminal act was not seen as something totally out of the realm of possibility in a football-mad state where some fans inevitably turned rabid.[†]

A few months later, before the spring A-Day game in mid-April, a nine-foot-tall statue of Saban was unveiled on the Alabama campus. It was university tradition to honor national title–winning coaches in this manner. Saban's statue was situated alongside ones for Wallace Wade, Frank Thomas, Paul "Bear" Bryant, and Gene Stallings. Terry was deeply involved in the creation of the bronze statue. She requested a change to the nose to give it a more rounded tip. She fiddled with the earlobes. Saban, whose hair had been gradually

---

[*] While at Florida State, Winston was accused of sexual assault, was caught stealing crab legs from a supermarket, and was suspended for a game for shouting an obscenity in a university cafeteria.

[†] Two new oaks were planted in Toomer's Corner in early 2015.

thinning in his fifties, was said to be pleased with the thickness of the statue's vermicular mane. To some—Alabama's tradition notwithstanding—the statue seemed like a hasty move, an imploring gesture to get him to stay at Alabama for good. An awkward possibility was raised: What if Saban suddenly left the program? After all, he was entering his fifth season at the university, and five seasons had been his self-imposed expiration date at both Michigan State and LSU.

Eleven days after the A-Day game, on the late afternoon of April 27, a powerful tornado ripped through Tuscaloosa, producing winds of up to 190 miles per hour. Some of the Alabama players were in the weight room at the time, working out under the supervision of Scott Cochran. The skies darkened and the barometric pressure dropped, something the players could feel in their bodies. Outside, the roofs of houses on the horizon started to fly apart. Cochran, in his inimitable voice, ordered everyone into the showers. They stood there as other staff members in the football facility, including Mal Moore, began to trickle in. Saban had just left for a brief stop at home to change his clothes for a meeting. He wouldn't make it back to the office that day.

In a house not too far away from the football building, Alabama's long snapper, Carson Tinker, huddled in a closet, holding his girlfriend tight to his chest. The tornado ripped through the house and tore Tinker's girlfriend from his arms. Later at the hospital, where Tinker was taken after being found sixty-five yards from where the closet had been, he learned that his girlfriend had died. She was one of six Alabama students who were killed by the tornado. (In all, 254 people died in the state that day from tornadoes.)

The university canceled the remainder of the school year, with a week to go before final exams. Students were told to go home. Saban called the team together and encouraged them to stay and help if they could. Many of them did just that, helping to clear the rubble and rebuild houses. The Sabans donated $75,000 in tornado relief through Nick's Kids Foundation.

The Tuscaloosa tornado and its aftermath felt familiar to Saban, eerily echoing the incident that shaped his own college career: the shootings at Kent State. Many of the elements were the same—a sudden, unexpected uprising on a spring day that left students dead; the canceling of the rest of the school year; and a football team that would be tasked with the challenge of rallying a devastated campus. The tornado briefly pulled Saban out of his shell. According to Lars Anderson in his book *The Storm and the Tide,* Saban immediately pitched in on the relief efforts, making his way through the apocalyptic aftermath, handing out bottles of Gatorade. He met with relief workers, shaking their hands and thanking them. He later spoke at a memorial for the students who'd been killed.

Just two weeks after the tornado, tragedy struck again. Aaron Douglas—a 6'7", 275-pound offensive lineman who had come to Alabama from a junior college—was found dead on the balcony of a house in Florida. He'd died of "multiple drug toxicity," according to the medical examiner's report. Though he'd been with the team only a short while, Douglas had been immediately embraced by his teammates. "I think the tornado and Douglas's death really had an effect on Coach Saban," says Barrett Jones. "To that point at Alabama, he'd been grinding so hard to turn the program around. Those two things were reminders to him about what's important in life. I noticed a change. He started to focus more on the people side of the business, the players and the coaches. He definitely still had his moments, though."

On September 3, with signs of the tornado—abandoned cars, gutted houses—still present outside Bryant-Denny Stadium, Alabama opened up the 2011 season with a 48–7 win over Saban's alma mater, Kent State. The next week, the Crimson Tide traveled to State College, Pennsylvania, to play Penn State. Saban prevailed in his last meeting with Paterno, 27–11, and ended up with a 4-3 career record against the man who served him some of his toughest defeats as a young head coach.*

---

* Paterno was fired after Penn State's child sex abuse scandal later in the 2011 season. He died in early 2012.

The 2011 Alabama team was led by its defense, which would end up as the top-ranked unit in college football that year, and one of the best in recent memory. The defense was manned by the future NFL players Hightower, Barron, Upshaw, Mosley, Kirkpatrick, and Milliner. Upshaw was the only one of the group who would not become a first-round pick in the NFL Draft (he went in the second round). Alabama only gave up an average of eight points a game that year. Oddly, it was Georgia Southern, an FCS team, that scored the most points on the team that year (twenty-one), thanks in large part to its rarely seen triple-option running attack.

Talent obviously had a lot to do with Alabama's success on defense, but so did the scheme, which was put together by Saban and his defensive coordinator, Kirby Smart. Saban and Smart run a base 3-4 defense, but frequently shift to a 4-3 when playing against spread offenses. Saban requires his defenders to learn both schemes. His philosophy on defense has always been one of complexity, of coaching up his players rather than dumbing down the playbook. Saban told a newspaper that with the more complicated schemes, his players "actually developed a greater capacity to learn." It made them better at adapting to in-game situations that they may have seen before. (This, of course, runs contrary to the popular stereotype of the mental capacities of football players, especially on the defensive side.) "We had a huge range of matchups and schemes," says Barron. "I've been in three different schemes in the NFL, and Alabama's was way harder to learn and master than any of them. We just did a lot more stuff."

Opposing coaches generally knew what to expect from a Saban-led offense (at least until Lane Kiffin showed up with some new wrinkles in 2014). "One thing I always told my guys about Nick and his offense is that you weren't going to get a lot of surprises," says Tommy Tuberville. "He'll beat you just playing football."

The difficulty for opposing coaches came in preparing for his defense. "They did so many things, and always had great front guys and good corners," says the former Tennessee coach Phillip Fulmer. "It made you miserable, not just trying to figure out how to score, but how to make a first down." Defense—and especially the secondary—is still Saban's true love. At Alabama, he has continued his tradition of sitting in on all secondary meetings and coaching those players on the practice field. ("If I could make this much money as a secondary coach, that's what I'd do," he once told a newspaper.)*

Saban's defense is predicated on what's known as "pattern read" or "pattern match." Simply put, the defense lines up initially in a zone, and, once the patterns are "read" after the snap by the defenders, the defense becomes man-to-man (similar to matchup zone defenses in basketball). "Whatever your two or three favorite routes were, he took them away by reading the patterns," says Fulmer. "He always took away what you did best. And pattern-read defense is not an easy thing to learn. You have to have a great system to be able to teach it."

Smart has always commanded a lot of respect from his coaching brethren, and not just for his defensive acumen. In 2015, he will be entering his eleventh season with Saban (at LSU, the Dolphins, and Alabama), which makes him Saban's second-longest-tenured assistant after Bobby Williams. Considering Saban's trouble with holding on to defensive coordinators earlier in his career, Smart has accomplished quite a feat. "Kirby is a helluva coach, and he deserves credit for being able to hang in there as long as he has," says Mike Collins, who was the linebacker coach with Smart at LSU when Saban was there. "Kirby is a competitive dude. I think he reminds Nick of himself a little bit."

The only blip in the 2011 season for Alabama came in the fifth "Saban Bowl," when number-one-ranked LSU traveled to Tuscaloosa to face the second-ranked Crimson Tide for what was hyped

---

* Aric Morris, a safety for Saban at Michigan State, says Saban would sometimes show up at the secondary meetings and "cuss us out." The players had a tip-off to his mood, though. "If Saban came in with a chew in his cheek and a Styrofoam cup, we knew we were in trouble. It meant he'd been looking at tape that morning. If he didn't have a chew, we were usually all right."

as "the Game of the Century." Alabama's defense did its job that day, holding LSU to just nine points. The offense was another story. Alabama scored only six points in what turned out to be an overtime loss. The main problem was the kicking game.

Saban's Achilles' heel has traditionally been the quality of his placekickers (recent difficulties in the Alabama secondary notwithstanding). It's a problem that has lingered for him since his days at LSU. In the 2003 SEC Championship game, LSU had to overcome a blocked field goal attempt and two failed extra points. In the 2004 LSU season, Saban's kickers missed an astonishing eight extra point attempts. Saban once lamented to a newspaper that it was "hard to evaluate specialists [placekickers, long snappers, and punters] in high school," and that film didn't always show kicks very well. Early on as a head coach, Saban had a hard time figuring out what to do with his specialists in practice. He unsuccessfully tried running them through the drills with the rest of the team. Eventually, he let them do their own thing on the side. According to one former Alabama player, Saban is especially hard on his placekickers. "And that doesn't help. Those guys are all head cases anyway."

In that 2011 game against LSU, Alabama missed three field goal attempts and had another one blocked. Cade Foster went one-for-four in the game. Jeremy Shelley went one-for-two. Any one of those missed kicks might very well have won the game for Alabama (one of the attempts was in overtime). The problems didn't end with that game, either. In the next two games—both wins—Alabama missed three more field goal attempts. Kicking issues would continue to haunt Saban in years to come, and would come to an especially ugly head late in the 2013 season.

Saban was calm after the loss to LSU. This team, he realized, was nothing like the one from the year before. They had leaders. They were focused. The LSU game was just one of those times in football when the breaks didn't go its way, demonstrating again to Saban exactly how fragile a football season can be. "He told us after the loss that we may not play for a national championship, but we were going to be the best one-loss team that ever played," says Brandon Gibson.

Alabama rumbled through the rest of the regular season, including a 42–14 blowout win over Auburn, before which Saban had posted pictures in the locker and weight rooms that showed the final score from the 2010 game (28–27), images of Cam Newton and Nick Fairley (Auburn's defensive star in that game), and the words "Never" (in orange) and "Again" (in blue). Still, the team's fate regarding a national title was undecided in the game's aftermath.

Two previously undefeated teams, Oklahoma State and Stanford, did Alabama huge favors by losing late in the season. Oklahoma State rebounded with a 44–10 win over its rival Oklahoma, which seemed to enhance their claim to play undefeated LSU for the national title. Saban campaigned hard for Alabama and caused a minor stir by dropping Oklahoma State to number four on his ballot in the coaches' poll, a move that was hard for him to defend given Oklahoma State's season résumé.

On the evening that the BCS finals rankings were to be announced, Alabama had its year-end banquet for the players and their families. When the news came that Alabama indeed would be playing LSU in the national title game in New Orleans—they'd edged out Oklahoma State by a mere 0.086 of a percentage point in the BCS rankings—the players' families went wild, jumping out of their seats. The players, for the most part, remained seated, all business, just like their coach.

Many in the media bemoaned the rematch, saying Alabama shouldn't have been given a second chance at LSU. Saban used those slings to his advantage. At one meeting, he told his team: "Apparently, we are going to a party that apparently we weren't invited to. Let's go piss in the punch bowl."

Saban didn't change anything in his approach to the rematch with LSU, confident that he had the better team. He was right. Alabama almost dominated the game completely in a 21–0 win, allowing LSU only ninety-two total yards. LSU didn't take a snap in Alabama territory until midway through the fourth quarter. Indeed, the only time LSU got ahead of Alabama was before the game, when the Crimson Tide bus pulled over on the ramp leading to the interstate to let the LSU bus pass them, as the players on both teams stared out the window at one another, like the schoolchildren they so recently were. The only problems the Crimson Tide had in the game were, again, with the kicking game. Jeremy Shelley missed two of his seven field goal attempts, and missed the extra point attempt after the game's only touchdown.

This time Saban took the Gatorade bath in stride. The sixty-year-old had won his second national title in three years. He stayed up until 3 a.m. after the game. Three days later, he called the team together for a meeting. By then his coaches knew exactly what was coming, but some of his players hadn't yet quite caught on. "He said, 'That was a lot of fun, but it's now in the past. Last year was last year,' " says Barrett Jones. "We looked at each other and said, 'Wait, can't we enjoy this?' " They had their answer already.

A year after the national title win over LSU, *Sports Illustrated* reported that before the game, many Alabama players had used deer antler velvet, which is administered in the form of a spray. The velvet contains something known as "insulin-like growth factor 1 (IGF-1)," a growth hormone that is banned by the NCAA.

Christopher Key, the co-owner of the Alabama company S.W.A.T.S. (Sports with Alternatives to Steroids), which sold the spray, says that before the national title game against LSU he provided the spray to "easily most, if not all, twenty-two starters" from the Alabama team, and witnessed some of them ingest it. Key, who also offered holographic performance chips and light and water therapy through his company, says he first gave the spray to an Alabama player during the 2009 season, and worked with Auburn football players in 2010 and LSU players in 2011 as well. He says the NCAA (and the World Anti-Doping Agency, the NFL, Major League Baseball, and the PGA Tour) have it all wrong when it comes to banning his spray. His product, he says, is not a synthetic form of

IGF-1, but rather a natural one that helps the body produce its own growth hormones. "I didn't do this to get my players in trouble," he says. Though a few scientists have cast some doubts about the efficacy of deer antler spray, Key maintains that his products work and help enhance athletic performance in a legal manner.

In the late summer of 2013, Alabama's attorney general essentially shut down S.W.A.T.S., ordering Key and his company to cease operations. Key thinks he knows who was behind the investigation. "We believe that Coach Saban was the one who instigated the attorney general coming in and shutting us down," he says. The NCAA never formally investigated the matter.

Scandal and controversy have long been part of amateur athletics, and of college football in particular. Saban, despite his aggression when it comes to recruiting and the NCAA, has run relatively scandal-free programs as a head coach. There have been a few incidents—like the deer antler spray scandal—along the way, though:

- Perhaps the biggest potential scandal on a Saban-coached team came during his time at LSU, when two professors in the school's kinesiology department alleged that they were forced by LSU athletic officials to ignore cheating and change the grades of some football players in 2000, so that those players could remain eligible for LSU's Peach Bowl appearance that season. Mark Emmert, the chancellor of LSU, ordered an internal investigation of the matter, which produced an eighty-two-page report that concluded that a few athletes did indeed receive some improper help studying and typing. LSU recommended a self-imposed penalty of the loss of two football scholarships and four official recruiting visits. The NCAA, after reviewing the report, agreed with the school's recommended punishments, and didn't put LSU on probation. Not everyone was satisfied with the investigation, though. According to a story in *USA Today,* a person who worked in LSU's athletic department at the time called it "a whitewash."

The two kinesiology professors filed lawsuits, asking for damages related to emotional distress, mental anguish, and what they perceived to be lost career opportunities. LSU settled both lawsuits, one for $150,000 and the other for $112,000.

- Lance Thompson, Saban's ace recruiter at both LSU and Alabama, has been shadowed by some rumors of recruiting impropriety. "We were terrified when he came to LSU because of his reputation," says a trustee of the school when Saban was there. That said, no formal complaint to the NCAA about Thompson has ever been made public.

  The general consensus among many coaches—both in college and in high school—is that, despite outward appearances, recruiting is still a fairly dirty business. "The cheating is just more sophisticated these days," says one high school coach, speaking generally and not in specific about Saban, Thompson, or anyone on the Alabama coaching staff. "You don't see the kid driving around in a new car anymore. The way it happens now, it's almost invisible. They do things like make a donation to the church."

- In 2012, Ralph Cindrich, a former NFL player who is now an agent for professional football players, went on a radio show and accused Saban of paying his players, which is among the worst sins in the eyes of the NCAA. "Everybody has something on Nick Saban, for God's sake," he told Pittsburgh's NewsRadio 1020 KDKA. "And if he has a problem with anything I say, come on after me, big guy."

  Cindrich continued: "I was involved in it. I know what he tried to do. I know what he tried to cover up. If he wants to stand up and say something, I'll bring that up. If it's out of time [past the statute of limitations], I'll go to the nearest agent I know, and I'll bring up about a dozen things that are in time, because that's the way he and most big-time schools, particularly in the SEC, operate."

Cindrich never did offer any specific allegations. (He declined an interview request, writing in an email: "Should I ever have to address any part at any time, I'm prepared.") A fellow football agent says that the rant may have stemmed from a longtime beef that Cindrich has had with Saban. "Ralph's an outspoken guy, and he hates anything done to regulate agents, and Saban has often spoken out about agents. And Ralph may also have lost out on some of Saban's players over the years."

- In September 2013, a Yahoo! Sports story alleged that former Alabama football player (and Saban recruit) Luther Davis acted as a middleman between agents and some college players, including Alabama offensive lineman D. J. Fluker, who turned pro after his junior season in 2012. Davis was alleged to have given Fluker thousands of dollars and—oddly—to have arranged the heavily discounted purchase of a king-size bedroom set. Earlier in 2013, Fluker had posted the following message on his Twitter account: "Yea I took $ n college so wat. I did wat I had to do. Agents was tryin to pimp me so I pimped them. Cast da 1st stone." Fluker's own agent later claimed his client's account had been hacked.

    The allegations, if true, could have had serious implications for the Alabama football program. When Reggie Bush, a star running back at USC, was found by the NCAA to have received impermissible benefits while in college, USC was stripped of its 2004 national title (Bush also lost his Heisman Trophy). The NCAA never seriously looked into the Fluker matter. By the time the story emerged, he was already in the NFL, and the NCAA lacks the power of subpoena, which would have made a serious investigation nearly impossible to conduct.

- Much has been made of the fact that Saban's former boss at LSU, Emmert, is now the head of the NCAA. In 2004, Saban told a newspaper: "Chancellor Emmert is absolutely the best boss I've ever had. He's the most significant reason I was interested in the [LSU] job. Never once has he disappointed me."

To conspiracy theorists, those words still ring true, especially when it comes to Alabama and potential NCAA investigations. "I'm not saying Saban has done anything wrong," says David Ridpath, the president of the Drake Group, an NCAA watchdog. "But for me, it's unhealthy to think that Emmert is unbiased."

In 2013, Emmert told *USA Today*: "The president of the NCAA doesn't get involved in infractions cases. That's one of those mythologies out there." While that may be true in most cases, Emmert was deeply involved in the handling of the 2011 Penn State child sex abuse scandal. (The NCAA's director of enforcement is a man named Derrick Crawford, who graduated from the University of Alabama.) The fact that Alabama hasn't been investigated in recent years is no surprise, though. With a few notable exceptions, one of the signatures of Emmert's reign at the NCAA has been the lack of initiative when it comes to investigating its member schools.* "The NCAA for the most part won't act on something unless it's pushed by the media and becomes impossible for them to ignore," says Ridpath. "They don't want to bite the hand that feeds them."

Ultimately, when it comes to controversies and potential scandals, Saban's detractors believe they've had some ammunition to work with over the years. In the end, the gun always seems to jam.

In 2012, Saban was entering his sixth season at Alabama, his longest tenure as a coach anywhere. The itch that had nettled him

---

* In recent years, Penn State and Syracuse have been penalized by the NCAA, and North Carolina has been investigated. The NCAA also horribly botched an investigation of the University of Miami in 2013.

everywhere else seemed to be no more, at least publicly. In reality, it still simmered but never quite came to a boiling point. Saban, through Sexton, had in fact been in touch with a handful of teams, the Cleveland Browns and Notre Dame among them. While the public was kept in the dark, Sexton made sure to let the Alabama administration know that his client was still a wanted man.

In March 2012, Saban received a raise and an extension. His contract—amended for the fourth time since he'd arrived at Alabama—paid him $45 million over eight years. In a press conference after the deal was announced, Saban said that the new contract meant that he would be at Alabama "for the rest of our career." Then, to the utter surprise of many Alabama fans, he later said he "made the decision after the season when other people were interested."

Despite the championships, the accolades, and the money, Saban, as a man, has changed very little. He still has few extravagances, and no time for them anyway.* He remains a man of rigorously maintained routine. He still eats two Little Debbies every morning as he drinks coffee and flips on the Weather Channel to see if the team will be practicing indoors or out. For lunch, he has the same iceberg lettuce salad topped with turkey slices. Every Thursday evening during the season, he wolfs down a dinner of meat loaf, macaroni and cheese, and green beans. He is a regular attendee at a Catholic church in Tuscaloosa.

Saban is also still an obsessive and meticulous note taker. At practices, whenever he sees something he doesn't like, he reaches into his back pocket and pulls out a flip-top notebook, then makes a quick note, determined to never make the same mistake again. He has piles of notebooks from years past, all dated, and frequently refers to them to see what happened on that exact date on any given year. He has kept notes on nearly every game he's been involved in

---

* Saban is a big fan of movies. Some of his favorites over the years include *Gone with the Wind, Rocky, Seabiscuit, Red Tails,* and *Zero Dark Thirty.*

as a head coach, and files on the programs and individual coaches against whom he's coached, laying out the specific tendencies and strategies that those teams and coaches used against him.

Saban has also remained intensely competitive, and not just on the field or during the staff basketball games. He is a big fan of Wave Runner Jet-Skis and outguns anyone who attempts to race him on one. Every year, Saban invites the team leaders to go tubing on a nearby lake. Even then, everything becomes a game, with ultimate winners and losers. "One year, me and Cory Reamer were behind the boat doing battle tubes," says Brandon Gibson. "Cory got knocked off, but I held on. Coach Saban was flinging me around, looking back and smiling with those big white teeth. But I wasn't falling off. He looks back again and the smile goes away, and I think, *Hmm, this might be a good time to let go.* So I do. I get back on the boat and he looks at me and says, 'I knew I could get you.'"

In recent years, Saban's love of golf has deepened. It should be no surprise: There may be no other game as perfectly suited to "process thinking." Focusing on shooting a round of 72 is often dangerous and counterproductive. All concentration, instead, should be on the shot before the golfer, and on that shot alone.

In slower periods in the spring and summer, Saban heads over to the university's golf facility to hit balls and visit with Alabama's golf coach, Jay Seawell, who has won national titles of his own. Saban occasionally plays with members of his staff, like Jeff Purinton, who handles the program's media relations, and Smart. He played with Rob Sale when he was at Alabama from 2007 to 2011. "He's a grinder out there, man," says Sale. "You can joke with him a bit on the course, but he's always trying to make that par putt from fifty feet."

Saban's handicap, after the long layoff from the football season and the recruiting period, is usually around 13. But after a few days, it drops to around 7, and can get as low as 5 when he plays a lot in the summer. As if dreamed up by the Poet, the weakest part of Saban's game is his chipping, which is the golfing equivalent of the field goal attempt. He is a courteous playing partner, even though he spends much of his time on the course on his phone, still working. He rarely gets upset over a poor shot (and if he does, he moves on from it quickly, like the defensive back he used to be). He picks up the flag after his group completes a hole, and is always mindful of the clubs his playing partners have perhaps forgotten on the side of the green.

Saban has played Augusta National, and has long let it be known that he would one day like to become a member. Though he remains a guarded and private person, Saban has formed some relationships over time through golf. One of his best golfing buddies is Steve Hudson, who runs an investment firm in Birmingham. Hudson, a five-time amateur golfing champion in the state of Alabama, calls Saban "Coach" and says that the five-time national champion does indeed do some coaching on the course. "He's always reminding us to focus on the process of the game and not the end result of a round," says Hudson.

One of his golfing friends, Bob Poellnitz, a Tuscaloosa insurance executive, is among the rarefied few who are able to rib Saban without consequence. Once, when trying to get in Saban's head during a match, he mentioned that the coach had become an "old softie" and that the reason he'd lost to the Cam Newton–led Auburn team in 2010 is that he'd felt sorry for the school and "let Cam come back and kick his butt." Saban initially gave Poellnitz a stern look, but soon began to take it all in stride. Saban now introduces Poellnitz to strangers as "Cam."

In 2012, Lance Thompson, Saban's prodigal assistant, returned to the Alabama staff. Saban forgave and forgot, much like he had done years earlier with Bobby Williams. According to Cignetti, Saban didn't mind a little churn on his coaching staff each year: It was one way to combat complacency. At Alabama, though, the story hasn't been about how many assistants have left—it's about how many have returned. On Saban's 2014 staff, wide receivers coach Billy Napier, defensive line coach Bo Davis, linebacker coach Kevin

Steele, and outside linebacker coach Thompson had all left Saban at one point during the Alabama years and come back.*

The offensive side is where Saban has had the most turnover at Alabama. In 2012, Jim McElwain—Saban's offensive coordinator—left to become the head coach at Colorado State. (He's now the head coach at Florida.) He was replaced by Doug Nussmeier, the former offensive coordinator at the University of Washington.

Saban's 2012 recruiting class was—remarkably—again the top-ranked one in the nation, and included receiver Amari Cooper, running back T. J. Yeldon (who had originally committed to Auburn before flipping), and Adam Griffith, the top-rated placekicker in the country, who was believed to be perhaps the answer to the Crimson Tide's kicking woes. The most interesting incident in that year of recruiting, however, happened with safety Landon Collins, who was voted Louisiana's top prep player and was believed to be a lock for Les Miles at LSU. However, Saban convinced him to sign with Alabama. Collins's mom—a fervent LSU fan—immediately accused Saban of enticing her son by offering his girlfriend a job, a charge she later retracted. The real drama came when Collins, in front of national television cameras, announced his commitment to Alabama. His mother sat right next to him as he spoke, and she dramatically shook her head and rolled her eyes. When asked for her reaction to her son's choice, she blurted out: "I feel that LSU is a better place for him to be. LSU Tigers number one." Collins didn't listen to his mother, though.

In the 2012 season, Alabama picked up where the previous one had left off, barreling its way through its first nine games. The Crimson

---

* Indeed, Saban's 2014 defensive staff, after various comings and goings, was virtually the same one he had in 2007. In early 2015, Steele left to become the defensive coordinator at LSU and Thompson left—yet again—to become the linebacker coach at, of all places, Auburn.

Tide was again ranked number one in the country. A berth in the national title game seemed inevitable. That is, until "Johnny Football" came to town.

The Texas A&M Aggies were the fifteenth-ranked team in the country, led by a quarterback who'd been off the radar screen of most pundits and college football fans at the beginning of the season. On that early November day in Tuscaloosa, Johnny Manziel (aka "Johnny Football")—effectively won the Heisman Trophy. "I remember it seemed like the first time I looked up, we were down twenty to nothing," says Barrett Jones. "It all happened so fast. I felt like we were ready to play. Johnny was just a sight to behold that day."

Texas A&M played at a very fast tempo on offense, something that seemed to catch Alabama off guard. Eight times during the game, the Crimson Tide defense failed to get lined up before the ball was snapped. Manziel was the X-factor in the contest, though. He played the sort of chaotic, schoolyard ball that Saban hated. One play defined the afternoon. Midway through the first quarter, deep in Alabama territory, Manziel dropped back to pass. The Crimson Tide defense appeared to have the play perfectly sussed out, leaving Manziel nowhere to throw the ball. As several Alabama defenders closed in on him, Manziel scrambled to his right, ran into two of his own players, momentarily dropped the ball, then regathered it. He scrambled around a bit more—buying precious extra seconds—then threw a pass across his body to a wide-open receiver in the end zone for a touchdown. Given enough time, even a perfect defensive call will eventually break down, and Manziel stymied Alabama's defense all game long. He threw for 253 yards and two touchdowns in the game, and ran for another 92 yards.

Though Alabama eventually regrouped, made a charge, and nearly completed a comeback, Johnny Football left Bryant-Denny with a stunning 29–24 upset win. "It was a nightmare," says Jones. "It felt like our national championship hopes were gone."

Instead, just as the team had done the year before, they used the loss as a rallying point. Alabama went on to beat Auburn, 49–0, effectively ending Gene Chizik's coaching career there and winning

the SEC West. They beat Georgia in a thrilling SEC Championship game, 32–28.* Once again they made it to the BCS National
Championship game, where they faced an undefeated Notre Dame.
It seemed like a dream matchup, one that harked back to the championship battles between the two teams during Paul Bryant's coaching years.

The game was instead a nightmare for Notre Dame. After an
Alabama practice three days before the game, Quinton Dial says he
and his teammates repaired to the hotel, somewhat satisfied with
their efforts. "We thought we did okay," he says. One man didn't,
however. "After we watched the film, Coach Saban just let us have
it. It was about as pissed as I'd seen him. He told us to get our minds
right. We had two great practices after that. It got us ready."

Alabama led, 28–0, at the half, and went on to win, 41–14, in
one of the most dominating performances ever in a national title
game. Alabama became the only team in the BCS era (which started
in 1998) to win back-to-back championships, and the first to accomplish that feat since the mid-1990s Nebraska team that Saban
had so long admired.

With that title, the heralded 2008 recruiting class—the foundation of a dynasty—came to the end of its run. Overall, the class
of 2008 had gone 61-7, and helped make its coach the best of the
BCS era.

Saban, since 2007, had taken a downtrodden football program and
turned it into the best in the country. He had done it in a highly effi-
cient manner and, remarkably, had been able to get nearly an entire
university on the same page and headed in the same direction. His
effectiveness at Alabama—the utter refinement of his earlier efforts
at Michigan State and LSU and a rebuttal to his two years at the

---

* In that game, Alabama defensive lineman Quinton Dial leveled Georgia quarterback Aaron Murray after Murray threw an interception. The hit wasn't flagged
at the time, but it drew some negative attention after the game. "Coach made me
write an apology letter to Murray," says Dial. Saban was apparently worried that
Dial might be suspended for the national title game. In the end, he wasn't.

Dolphins—leaves one wondering if we'd all have been better served if Saban had taken charge of something more beneficial to society than a college football program. (William Gass once joked in his novel *The Tunnel*, "If Americans ever had a dictator, they'd call him Coach.") What if Saban had taken his process and become, say, the head of the Memorial Sloan Kettering Cancer Center? Or had been put in charge of the rebuilding of the city of Detroit? Saban's style surely wouldn't have worked for everyone. What about the results?

And yet, in the aftermath of his third national title at Alabama, and his fourth overall—a time of joy at the university—Saban fell into a deep funk. This time it had nothing to do with lost recruiting time. He told one of his best friends after the 2012 season that he was as exhausted as he'd ever been in his career. He felt immense—and to his mind, unreasonable—pressure from Alabama's administrators, trustees, and boosters to continually repeat his success. Fans of the team, he believed, had become spoiled.

Saban, for the first time in his Alabama tenure, was unhappy and restless.

PART III

PART III

12

Texas Hold 'Em

IN DECEMBER 2012, as Saban was preparing Alabama to face Notre
Dame in the BCS National Championship game, University of
Texas regent* Wallace Hall received a phone call from a friend.
"It was out of the blue. He is a UT alum, a very well thought of,
very successful guy who really isn't a huge fan of football," says
Hall. The man, whom Hall has refused to name, also happened
to be a good friend of Jimmy Sexton. "My friend told me, 'I don't
know how to put this any other way: Nick Saban wants to come to
Texas,'" says Hall.

Hall immediately sent the chairman of the board, Gene Powell,
an email, telling him that Sexton wanted to talk. Powell forwarded
it to Steve Hicks, a private equity mogul, prominent Texas regent,
and one of the board's athletic liaisons. Nothing much came of the
correspondence. After Saban won the national title, Hall contacted
Hicks directly. This time Hicks acted on it, calling on his brother
Tom, a former owner of Major League Baseball's Texas Rangers
and the National Hockey League's Dallas Stars. "I had been in pro
sports for a long time, so I volunteered to see if this was real or not,"
says Tom Hicks.

A few days after the national title game, Hall went to Tom
Hicks's house in Dallas for a scheduled conference call with Sexton.

---

* A "regent" at the University of Texas is basically the same thing as a trustee at
other universities like Alabama.

An intermediary had provided Hall with a number for him to reach Sexton, a clever move, Hall believed. "That way, from Jimmy's perspective, he could always argue that we called him," he says. Before the call, Tom Hicks told Hall that Sexton might just be playing Texas to squeeze more money out of Alabama. "And I told Tom that I didn't think that was happening here, that my friend was also friends with Jimmy, and that Jimmy wouldn't want to piss him off," says Hall. "I had called my friend and asked him if he thought he was being played. He said 'no.'"*

Hall and Tom Hicks talked to Sexton for forty-five minutes. They say that Sexton told them that Saban felt "special pressure" and a lack of appreciation at Alabama. "Sexton said that the day after the championship, Alabama boosters were pounding the table, talking about a three-peat," says Hall.

Sexton also told the men that Saban felt like he was more of a turnaround artist than a long-term CEO, and that it was easier and more fun to rebuild a program than it was to keep one at the top. Terry liked warm weather, so they wanted to stay in the South. Saban also loved lakes, something the Austin area has in abundance. Sexton floated the idea that Saban could take the Texas job—his last—bring the football program back to national prominence, then retire. "Jimmy said that winning a national championship at three different universities would be a real legacy," says Tom Hicks. Hall believed that there was serious intent behind Sexton's call, and that the agent was acting on behalf of an informed client. "No agent is going to go out and do this without consent from Saban," he says.

Hall and Tom Hicks liked the idea of Saban coming to Texas. "It all resonated," says Hall, who claims he's not much of a football fan, but was mainly intrigued by the potential financial implications of getting Saban. Texas's athletics had its own cable channel, called the Longhorn Network, a joint venture with ESPN, but it hadn't

---

* Hall, an investor, calls himself a "reformer" as a regent. In 2013, he was threatened with impeachment from the board after being accused of going too far in investigating corruption among University of Texas administrators (he was eventually merely censured). He faced the threat of a grand jury investigation for allegedly leaking sensitive documents, but, in the end, wasn't indicted.

quite yet fulfilled the potential envisioned by the university, especially when it came to getting carried by various cable companies. "If someone of Saban's caliber came to Texas, that would hugely enable ESPN to bring on other affiliates," says Hall. Yet another university viewed Saban as a vehicle of greater financial growth.

As excited as they were, Hicks and Hall realized they had one significant problem: Texas already had a football coach. Mack Brown—just two months older than Saban—had won a national title at Texas in 2005 and lost another one (to Saban) in 2009, and was entering his sixteenth season as the Longhorns' head coach. Hall believed that neither DeLoss Dodds, Texas's athletic director, nor Bill Powers, the university's president, was likely to fire Brown. The only way to get Saban to come to Texas, Hicks believed, was to get Brown's approval and even make it look like the entire thing was the Texas coach's idea. He agreed to broach the topic with Brown.

Two days after the call with Sexton, Hicks had lunch with Brown. "I was trying to give him some personal advice," he says. "I told him he should think about retiring and going out on top and becoming a TV star like he is now.* But he didn't support the idea at all. He didn't want to retire."

Hall believed that a golden opportunity had been squandered. "I am completely convinced that Saban would have come to Texas had Mack approved of the idea, or had DeLoss fired Mack," he says.

The saga didn't end there, though.

Nick Saban has had a few difficult seasons while at Alabama, at least by his standards. His first year was, record-wise, his worst by far (7-6 before sanctions wiped out five of those wins). As trying as that season was, though, it could be easily excused because it was the first in his rebuilding process. The 2010 season, with a loaded but complacent team coming off a national title, was—even with just three losses—a disappointing one, but it was partially redeemed

---

* Brown is now an analyst on ESPN.

when many of those same players rebounded with a championship season in 2011. Nothing, though, was quite like 2013 for Saban, the unquestioned annus horribilis of his Alabama tenure.

Saban and Terry entered the year contending with a civil lawsuit that had been filed against their daughter, Kristen. The suit alleged that she'd injured a former Alabama sorority sister in a fight over a Facebook post.* In late March, Mal Moore stepped down from his role as the school's athletic director after being diagnosed with idiopathic pulmonary fibrosis, a deadly disease of the lungs. Ten days later, he died. His passing was a huge loss to Saban—Moore had supported him as much as any athletic director he'd ever had—and to the Alabama community, which had remained forever grateful to him for bringing Saban to Tuscaloosa. That same year, Don James, one of the most influential men in Saban's life, also died, at the age of eighty.

Things were no better on the field for Saban. Throughout the spring practice period, he remained frustrated by his players. He used press conferences to continually call them out, saying they had become "too comfortable" and that they had "entitlement issues." That year, Saban suspended ten players, including Clinton-Dix, who was a leader on the team and perhaps Saban's best player on defense. The entire "Process"—the idea that the focus wasn't on the past or the future, but the present, and that every single action one took in life mattered—seemed to be breaking down.

Opposing coaches didn't help matters that year, either. In a span of just a few months, James Franklin, the coach at Vanderbilt (and now at Penn State), referred to Saban as "Nicky Satan," and Tim Davis, the Florida offensive line coach—and a former assistant of Saban—told a group of boosters that Saban was "the devil himself." These epithets were, of course, in some ways a testament to Saban's dominance, expressions of jealousy. They also seemed to indicate that folks outside Alabama had picked up on the dark cloud that seemed to be hovering over Saban and his program.

---

* The civil lawsuit was initially tossed out in early 2014, then was reinstated later that year. Kristen was married in 2015.

On the outside, all appeared well with the Crimson Tide football team. It started the season 8-0. In early November, it beat a solid LSU team, 38–17, and there was some hope from within the program that the team had found something and righted itself. That game turned out to be fool's gold, though. From that point on, the team's practices, already somewhat sloppy, got even worse. The players became even more content with themselves, and Saban was failing to snap them out of it. Some within the program sensed that Saban was miffed about the work ethic of his quarterback, A. J. McCarron, who had become somewhat of a celebrity, thanks in part to his girlfriend (and now wife), Katherine Webb, a comely former Miss Alabama.* The rift between the two apparently endured. After the season, McCarron told a friend that he "hadn't been done right" by Saban and the Alabama program when it came to talking him up to NFL teams for the NFL Draft. McCarron would be selected by the Cincinnati Bengals in the fifth round, much lower than he believed was deserved. Saban, conspicuously, did not show up at McCarron and Webb's 2014 wedding.

After the LSU win, Alabama won a sloppy game over Mississippi State (the Crimson Tide had four turnovers in the 20–7 victory), then blew out an overmatched Chattanooga team. Despite all the dysfunction, late in the 2013 season Alabama was the top-ranked team in the country and the presumptive favorite to win a third straight national title.

Then came the Kick Six.

It is a testament to the excellence of Nick Saban's Alabama tenure that the most memorable games of the era are the ones he's lost. In 2010, Cam Newton seemed to overcome an entire nation in his comeback win over the Crimson Tide in the Iron Bowl. In 2012, Johnny Manziel—looking like some whacked-out orchestra

---

* Some complacency for McCarron might have been understandable: At that point in his Alabama career, he had as many national titles as a starter—two—as he did losses.

director—seemingly made plays up as they unfolded to pull off an
upset over a more fundamentally sound Alabama team. The most
unforgettable game in Saban's career, though, came at the end of the
2013 regular season.

The 2013 Auburn Tigers were led by a new coach named Gus Malzahn, a professorial-looking man who favors rimless eyeglasses
and a visor. Malzahn was a former offensive coordinator at Auburn and, for one year, the head coach at Arkansas State. He was
best known for spending most of his career as a high school coach,
something he never failed to mention to high school coaches while
on the recruiting trail. "He'd tell us, 'I'm just like you, but I got a
lucky break,'" says UMS-Wright Preparatory School's Terry Curtis.

Malzahn and Saban had starkly different philosophies about
football, especially when it came to offense. Malzahn was a guru
of the hyperkinetic hurry-up, no-huddle offense, which relies on
speed of play, deception, misdirection, and a host of different options embedded in each play. Saban is no fan of this type of offense,
which has bedeviled him at various times in recent years. "He's such
a damn purist," says his former LSU assistant Pete Jenkins. Saban
believes that the hurry-up, no-huddle offense was gimmicky, and he
would, in the 2014 off-season, lobby the NCAA to slow down the
game, for what he said were safety reasons.* That style of offense
bore no resemblance to the brawny, midwestern style of football
that he loves and has mastered. Perhaps what irked him most was

---

* Saban addressed the NCAA rules committee in early 2014 about slowing down
hurry-up, no-huddle offenses. At one point, it appeared that a proposition to do
just that would be voted on, and might even pass, but then other coaches began to
let their voices be heard. Malzahn was against the proposition. Spurrier called it
yet another "Saban Rule." Bret Bielema, the head coach at Arkansas, who also opposed the fast play, clumsily brought up the death of a player at Cal in connection
with hurry-up offenses (though pace of play seemed to have nothing to do with the
player's death). The backlash against Bielema's comments most likely sealed the
fate of the proposition, which ultimately was withdrawn without a vote.

that the hurry-up, no-huddle offense had the effect of essentially reducing the impact of his favorite part of football: the defense.

The 2013 Iron Bowl kicked off in Auburn in sunny, 57-degree weather. Alabama's defense, stocked with future NFL players, was confused from the get-go. Kirby Smart, Alabama's defensive coordinator, spent nearly the entire game jumping up and down on the sidelines, alternating between looking like a tantrumic child and a restive golden retriever waiting for a ball to be thrown. Early on, Auburn receivers dropped a few passes that would have gone for huge gains; the Tigers were not as polished as Alabama, but they were athletic and fast and unafraid.

The Tigers had led a charmed life that season. They'd defeated Mississippi State with a touchdown in the dying moments of a game in September. They'd done the same at Texas A&M in October. In November, they'd beaten Georgia on a miracle seventy-three-yard touchdown pass on a fourth down with twenty-five seconds left, a pass that two Georgia defenders appeared to have a play on but instead tipped into the hands of an Auburn receiver. That good fortune continued in the Iron Bowl.

Alabama was in control of the game until its final moments, when Auburn, on what appeared to be a broken play, scored a touchdown to tie the game, 28–28, with under a minute to go. Then came the sequence of plays that ended the game and, at least for some, put a sizable dent in the Saban mystique.

Alabama got the ball back after the Auburn touchdown, and on what initially appeared to be the last play of regulation, Alabama's T. J. Yeldon ran the ball to the Auburn thirty-eight-yard line before stepping out of bounds. The stadium game clock showed "0:00." Saban, however, won an appeal to get one second put back on the clock. The game's national television announcers, Verne Lundquist and Gary Danielson, believed Saban would try a Hail Mary pass to the end zone. McCarron appeared to hold the same belief as he stood on the sidelines, ready to go back in. At the last moment,

Saban decided to attempt a fifty-seven-yard field goal. When the field goal unit took the field, starting placekicker Cade Foster was nowhere to be found. He'd been replaced by redshirt freshman Adam Griffith.

During the Iron Bowl, Saban had once again been haunted by his kicking game. During the game, Foster had missed two field goal attempts and had another kick blocked. Saban's lack of confidence in him was demonstrated in what turned out to be one of the game's most significant moments. Earlier in the fourth quarter, leading, 28–21, Alabama had faced a fourth-and-one from Auburn's thirteen-yard line. Saban eschewed a relatively short field goal attempt, and instead opted to run for the first down. But Yeldon was bear-hugged behind the line of scrimmage by an Auburn defender, and Alabama turned the ball over on downs, coming up empty after advancing deep into Auburn territory.

By the last play of the game, the field was illuminated by lights high above. After seeing Alabama's field goal unit take the field, Malzahn called a time-out. Griffith then lined up for the attempt, setting in motion the single most shocking play in Iron Bowl history. Malzahn had placed Chris Davis, his cornerback and return man, in the end zone, in the event that the kick was short. Though Saban would later say that his team was prepared for Davis, the Alabama personnel on the field for the last-second field goal attempt did not include many speedy players, if any at all.

Griffith's kick did indeed fall short. Davis caught it in the end zone and started running up the field to his right before veering to the left-hand sideline. The Alabama players were slow in reacting, lacking in any real urgency, as if a tackle was inevitable and the game would just glide into overtime. One of the Crimson Tide players even slowed his pursuit of Davis while trying to reattach a chinstrap. At Auburn's twenty-yard line, Davis dodged the outstretched arm of the last—and maybe only—Alabama player with a shot at tackling him. Davis tiptoed up the sideline in front of the Auburn bench, then veered back into the middle of the field after crossing the fifty-yard line as the Alabama players decelerated into defeated jogs well behind him. In the end zone, 109 yards from where he'd begun, Davis was engulfed by his teammates and field-crashing fans. Auburn had won, 34–28.

On the Alabama sideline, Saban threw his hands in the air and then tossed aside his headset before jogging onto the field to shake hands with the old high school coach. Saban looked shell-shocked, exhausted, and perhaps even a bit relieved. His chance at a third straight national title—unprecedented in the modern era—had come to a shocking end.

Alabama went on to a listless 45–31 loss to Oklahoma in the Sugar Bowl, which didn't seem to bother the fans all that much. Their main concern by that time was the fate of their coach.

Sexton's phone call with Hall and Tom Hicks became public in September 2013, but the details had remained a secret. Not too much was made of the call, and Saban responded to media questions about it by simply saying he was "too damn old to start all over someplace else." The Texas job, it appeared at the time, might not even open up anyway. Mack Brown, after a tough start to the 2013 season, had righted his own ship, and was in the midst of what would become a six-game winning streak.

The real hysteria began in early November when the AP obtained an email written by Tom Hicks about the Sexton call. One sentence in the email stood out: "Sexton confirmed that UT is the only job Nick would possibly consider leaving Alabama for, and that his success there created special pressure for him."

At this point, Alabama fans had reason to be worried. The signs disconcertingly echoed ones that, in the past, had led to Saban's departures: Sexton was out sniffing around, and told the Texas folks almost exactly what he'd once told Mal Moore, that the school was a place he was interested in. (Saban once told a newspaper that without his aggressive agent, "I don't think I'd ever make one change, the way I am.") Saban was again in denial mode, the inevitable precursor to all of his moves. The unnamed man whom Sexton had contacted to get to Wallace Hall played the role that Sean Tuohy had when Sexton initiated contact with LSU. The "special pressure" that Hicks said Saban felt, and the unreasonable expectations that Sexton had detailed in his phone call, harked back to his later years at LSU—the ones Skip Bertman had warned him about—when a two-loss season suddenly was viewed as a failure. As Sexton had told Hall and Tom Hicks that Saban was indeed most comfortable when he was rebuilding a program—as he had at Toledo, Michigan State, LSU, Miami, and Alabama—and not maintaining it.

Most significant, Saban was clearly displeased with both the fans (he'd lambasted them in midseason for leaving home games early) and his players in the 2013 season, and he was again feeling underappreciated. Those who knew Saban had long realized that two of the most significant aspects of his career—his "Process" and his near-constant job-hopping—were intertwined at one crucial juncture: They both, at their essence, were about the fact that Saban found it "more invigorating to want than to have," as David Foster Wallace once wrote.

The Texas football program also seemed to fit Saban's blueprint. The university, like LSU in 2000 and Alabama in 2007, was desperate to return to national football prominence. Texas had the resources—they had the biggest athletic budget in the country at $163 million—not only to provide Saban with the largest contract in college football history but also to pay for whatever facilities and other tertiary things he deemed necessary to help rebuild the program. His recruiting base would be top-notch: The state of Texas had long been hailed as among the best when it came to high school football talent.

In late November—just as Brown had begun to falter down the stretch of what was looking more and more like his last year as the Texas coach—came the public airing of what was the truest barometer of Saban's feelings. In an interview with the *Wall Street Journal,* Terry was careful to maintain that she and her husband would indeed stay at Alabama. In a moment of candor, she issued a warning shot: "You come to a crossroads and the expectations get so great, people get spoiled by success, and there starts to be a lack of appreciation," she told the paper. "We're kind of there now."

The University of Alabama's power brokers by this time knew their coach well. Like their predecessors at Michigan State and LSU, they, too, understood his restlessness and need to feel appreciated. After the 2012 national championship, they'd begun to feel jittery. In early 2013, they approached Saban. "We asked him what we could do to help him," says one trustee. The answer came that spring.

The Crimson Tide Foundation (CTF) is a nonprofit booster organization that is led by Paul Bryant Jr., the intensely private son of Alabama's legendary coach, the founder of a bank that bears his name, and perhaps the school's most powerful trustee. Bill Battle, who had replaced Mal Moore as Alabama's athletic director, is the nonprofit's president. Angus Cooper, now an emeritus trustee and perhaps Saban's most trusted confidant among the Alabama power elite, is a vice president.

In March 2013, the CTF agreed to purchase Saban's house for $3.1 million, roughly $200,000 more than he paid for it in 2007. The Sabans, of course, would be allowed to continue to live there. Buying a coach's house was nothing new at Alabama: The university had owned both of Paul Bryant's homes. Various Alabama trustees say that this purchase—as well as its timing—was a gesture of goodwill. It also, they say, helped Saban out a bit when he needed it financially, perhaps because of some real estate decisions in recent years that reportedly hadn't quite panned out as planned.

The university didn't stop with the house. Around the same time that Terry made her comments to the *Wall Street Journal*, and right before the 2013 Iron Bowl, Battle approached Saban about a revised contract, one that would provide him with a raise and an extension. As the Texas rumors burned on, Saban told Battle that he was too focused on the rest of the season to talk about his contract.

Some months later, Battle admitted to the *Tuscaloosa News* that at that point "I was worried about it, I'll tell you that."

One thing Alabama had going in its favor was that the University of Texas was in turmoil in late 2013. The school's president was under pressure to resign, and the board of regents had become an unhealthy and unproductive hive of infighting. The athletic director, DeLoss Dodds, had announced his retirement in the middle of the season. Though most assumed that Brown would resign or be fired at the end of the season, no one knew his fate for sure, or how protracted the process would be. This being the land of the independent and entrepreneurial, a few prominent Texas boosters used the uncertainty to begin the talk to, and lobby for, their own preferred head coach candidates. "To say it was dysfunctional would be about the highest-class way you could describe it," says Texas booster Red McCombs.

In November, Steve Patterson, the former president and general manager of the NBA's Portland Trail Blazers, became the school's new athletic director, replacing Dodds. Of course, he had come to Texas well after the Sexton call with Tom Hicks and Hall. It wasn't too long after Patterson had taken the job at Texas that Sexton called him, too. Patterson says he believes he knew what Sexton was up to. "I've known Jimmy for thirty years. I told him if he wanted to come here and drink bourbon and eat barbecue and talk about Saban, that'd be fine," he says. "But I told him not to come here if he just wanted to get Saban an extension and a raise at Alabama, which I thought was his intention all along. Of course, Jimmy took great affront to that, which is fine. He was just doing his job. But that was the end of the conversation. I never talked to Saban and we never made an offer." (Patterson was fired by Texas in September 2015.)

Publicly, though, the Saban-to-Texas rumors were only heating up during that time. In early December, an Oklahoma City broadcaster named Dean Blevins posted a message on Twitter that claimed Saban had been offered a ten-year deal by Texas for $100 million and a small piece of the Longhorn Network. Right around the same time, Stefan Stevenson, a sports reporter at the *Fort Worth Star-Telegram*, posted a tweet that read: "Source close to Texas executive council of regents says Nick Saban will be next Longhorns coach."

Stevenson, to this day, doesn't back down from the information in that tweet. "I had a good source, someone on the athletics staff, and I absolutely believed the source was certain," he says. "I wouldn't have tweeted it if I didn't believe the source believed it." What Stevenson wasn't prepared for was the hell storm that ensued on the Internet, which caused even those who had been dead certain that Saban would stay at Alabama to waver a bit in their conviction, and heaped much derision on its originator. "I regretted tweeting it almost immediately," he says. "But not because I didn't think it was true."

The common belief among Texas regents was that one or more "rogue" boosters were talking to Sexton behind the scenes. And given the free-for-all chaos from which the Texas leadership was just beginning to emerge, that thesis has some merit. "I think it was [the] Internet and some boosters without any authority," says Steve Hicks. Given the lack of authority that boosters had in hiring a new coach, any deal with Saban would have been hard for any of them to pull off alone, or even as a group. Saban denied having contact with anyone at Texas. A few weeks later, though, a man described as a "Longhorn lifer and big donor" told the *Austin American-Statesman*: "The funny thing is, they had Saban this time. He was coming. Only problem was, there was no formal offer from UT. Patterson was the only one who could do that."

On December 13, 2013, Alabama gave Saban a new contract, once again the largest ever in college football, that would pay him $6.9 million a year—with possible performance bonuses of up to $700,000 a year—through January 31, 2022, when he would be seventy years old.

The next afternoon, Mack Brown officially resigned as the head coach at Texas.

For the previous decade and a half—with the obvious exception of the two years with the Dolphins—Saban has been either college football's highest-paid coach, or somewhere very close to it. During his years at Alabama, his salary has risen 80 percent. In 2014, with bonuses, Saban's actual salary turned out to be $7.2 million, which made him one of the highest-paid public employees in the country. Only three NFL coaches—Sean Payton, Pete Carroll, and Bill Belichick—made more money than he did that year.

Saban's salary has long been a flash point. To various pundits, the fact that a *football coach* could make that much money in a state like Alabama is ludicrous. They point out that Saban—an employee of a public university—makes roughly seventy times more than the governor of Alabama. Much has been made about the fact that Alabama is a poor state where the median household income is $43,253, some $10,000 less than the national average, and that public funding for higher education in the state was slashed by $556 million from 2008 to 2013 (a 28 percent drop).*

Robert Witt, who was the president of the University of Alabama from 2003 until 2012, when he became the chancellor of the University of Alabama system, has always been quick to point out, as he said in 2008, that "not one penny of taxpayer money goes into Saban's salary." That contention hinges on a technicality, though.

The university indeed only pays Saban a base salary of just north of $200,000. The rest of the money, called a "talent fee," is paid by the Crimson Tide Foundation, which raises money through boosters and things like shoe and apparel contracts. Here's where the technicality comes into play: The Crimson Tide Foundation is a 501(c)3 nonprofit organization. Individual donors to 501(c)3s in Alabama get deductions on both their federal and state income taxes. So, while Witt can make the argument that no state tax dollars go into

---

* The general escalation in college football coaching salaries—seventy-two FBS coaches made more than $1 million in 2014—has also shined a harsh light on the fact that they are coaching players who have traditionally been paid exactly zero dollars. To be sure, Saban has long been a proponent of doing more for players (besides scholarships) in the form of stipends, especially for those who come from challenging socioeconomic backgrounds.

Saban's salary, the state does, at least in theory, lose out on some potential money on those donations.

Of course, there's an argument to be made that any potential lost tax revenue pales in comparison to the money that Saban—both directly and indirectly—has created for Alabama. In late 2013, Witt told *60 Minutes* that Saban was "the best financial investment this university has ever made," a sentiment that's hard to argue against.

In 2002, the university began a fund-raising campaign for athletics, in large part to upgrade many of its outdated facilities. The goal was to raise $50 million by 2007. After Saban arrived that year, donations skyrocketed to the point that the campaign exceeded its goal by $20 million, and an additional $32 million came in after the campaign was officially closed. At the utter depth of the global financial crisis, the university embarked on another campaign to expand Bryant-Denny Stadium by ten thousand seats and add high-revenue luxury boxes and club-level seats. In the same period when U.S. corporate profits plunged 27 percent and new construction in the country virtually came to a halt, the University of Alabama constructed a $65 million addition to its stadium, bringing the overall capacity to 101,821 seats, which made it one of the biggest in college football. Alabama's athletic department revenue in Mike Shula's last year was $68 million. By 2013–14, it had risen to $153 million, a gain of 125 percent. The football program accounted for $95 million of that figure, and posted a profit of $53 million of its own. (The Alabama athletic department kicked $9 million back to the university.)*

But Saban's financial impact on football and athletics tells only part of the story.

———

* One must also take into consideration Saban's impact on the Southeastern Conference. His star power and four national titles were certainly factors in the creation of the SEC Network, a joint venture with ESPN, which one analyst estimates generated revenues of more than $600 million in 2014.

When Witt came to Alabama in 2003, his grand ambition was to turn the university into a more robust academic school with better—and more—students. His plan was just getting under way when Saban arrived. While Mal Moore deserves the credit for actually nabbing Saban, Witt deserves some of his own for seeing and capitalizing on the potential positives of his new football coach. Witt viewed Saban the same way Mark Emmert once had at LSU, as a vehicle for not only growth in athletics, but also the school at large. Witt ultimately took what Emmert had done—using the football-as-the-front-porch-of-the-university metaphor—to an entirely new level.

Around the time of Saban's hiring, Witt embarked on a $500 million capital campaign for the university, and he credited Saban with helping in its success. "We have 100,000 donors in that campaign, and a major reason they support us is football," he said in 2008. By the time Witt had left the president's chair to become chancellor in 2012, Alabama's overall enrollment had increased by more than 13,000 students, to 33,602. (Enrollment has continued to grow: In 2014, it stood at 36,155.) But it wasn't just about the larger number of students—it was also about the quality of those students and where they came from. Alabama, despite the higher enrollment numbers, had actually become *more* selective. In 2003, Alabama accepted 86 percent of its applicants. The school now admits just over 50 percent of its applicants. In 2007, Alabama ranked thirtieth among all universities in the enrollment of National Merit Scholars. Five years later, the university ranked fourth. In 2007, out-of-state students—and all the incremental revenue they represent (they pay roughly $15,000 more in tuition than in-state students do)—made up 33 percent of the freshman class. By 2014, 62 percent of the incoming freshmen were from out of state, and Alabama's net tuition revenue had doubled over the same period of time to $387 million.

Saban and his football team certainly weren't the only drivers of the university's transformation. The school has ambitiously courted better students in the affluent suburbs of Atlanta, Houston, Dallas, and Nashville, and has hired recruiters in all of those areas. And, believe it or not, some of the university's biggest donors don't care a lick about football, but Saban's influence on all of this is undeniable. He and his football program have provided the school with a brand that represents winning and success. So when an Alabama recruiter knocks on the door of a National Merit Scholar in a Dallas suburb, there's a decent chance that the kid has heard of the school and generally views it in a positive light, thanks in no small part to its football team.

"I think Nick is actually way underpaid," says Angus Cooper. Given what he brings to the university, in terms of money and prestige—and the incredible pressures he faces year in and year out—Cooper is probably right.

The announcement of Saban's new deal in mid-December 2013 seemed to calm the frayed nerves of the Alabama football program's various stakeholders. Still, some drama leaked into the new year. The Texas coaching job remained vacant, and Saban's contract remained on his desk. (Saban said he was out recruiting, but the unsigned contract still left many with an uneasy feeling, perhaps something akin to how college football coaches feel when a recruit "verbally" commits to a program. Nothing is a done deal until the papers are signed and delivered.)

Finally, on January 5, 2014, Texas announced the hiring of Charlie Strong, the former coach at Louisville. Only then could Alabama put the disappointment and distraction of 2013 firmly in the rearview mirror and look ahead to a fresh new season.

Some Alabama trustees maintain that they never believed that Saban was going to Texas. "It was just Jimmy trying to squeeze more money out of us," says one. That belief, though, seems to ignore Saban's career history. There is a sense, too, at least among some trustees, that even had Saban actually left, the foundation he has laid at Alabama is so strong and secure that with a few wise choices, the good times could just keep rolling along. Those dreadful years after Bryant retired seem to have been quickly—and heedlessly—put out of mind for some.

Even with all the old familiar signs—ones that, in his younger years, had sent him off to a new job and new challenge—Saban signed that new contract with Alabama. Perhaps, as he said, it was merely age: He was sixty-two at the time, forty-two years removed from his first job as a graduate assistant at Kent State under Don James.

Or perhaps it was something else.

Saban now looked ahead to his 2014 team. With McCarron gone, he had no established starting quarterback. His secondary was young and untested, and his offensive line didn't appear to be the dominant unit it had been in years past. While he wasn't facing a rebuild—no one who recruits as well as Saban ever does—the 2014 season would, in the end, offer him something approximating one. His gigantic new contract did come with some added pressure, but it appeared that something had been lifted from his back. The Alabama community had risen up and demonstrated—financially and in other ways—its deep appreciation for him. Now when Saban said he wanted to stay at Alabama for the rest of his career, to build on his legacy there, it sounded genuine. Perhaps, somewhere, Saban heard the voice of his father, whose approval he would have undoubtedly earned by now. Yes, the process mattered. It always did, perhaps above all else, but the process has yields, and without them it is meaningless. The job, as Big Nick had always told him, needed to be finished, and it needed to be finished in the right way.

13

Epilogue

A COLLEGE FOOTBALL coach *is* his program. He is, at once, a priest, psychologist, teacher, father figure, CEO, martial leader, politician, and, at the bigger programs, a media celebrity. There is a reason that college football teams are mostly affiliated with their coaches, whereas NFL teams—with the possible exception of Belichick and the New England Patriots—are mostly affiliated with players, and mainly the quarterbacks. College coaches are the lone constant in a sea of change, annually greeting an incoming tide of fresh recruits, and annually bidding farewell to an outgoing tide of both graduating seniors and any underclassmen who have opted to leave the program early and turn pro. The success or failure of a college football team is in the coach's hands and his hands only. He is deified or demonized because of that responsibility.

At Alabama, there is one coach who is deified above all.

Paul William "Bear" Bryant coached his last football game on the evening of December 29, 1982, at the Liberty Bowl in Memphis, a tier-two (at best) postseason game. Bryant was physically and mentally a husk by then, almost a golem. Despite the fact that on that night, his once-stingy defense gave up 423 yards to a Tony Eason–led University of Illinois team, Alabama won the game, 21–15, by sheer force of will. It was Bryant's 323rd win as a head coach, which remains the fourth-highest total in major college history. Twenty-eight days later, he died of a massive heart attack at Druid City Hospital Regional Medical Center in Tuscaloosa. His funeral befitted that of a beloved head of state. An estimated 250,000 people lined the fifty-five miles of interstate highway between Tuscaloosa and Birmingham to watch the three-hundred-car procession make its way to Elmwood Cemetery, a few miles from Birmingham's Legion Field, the site of many of Bryant's triumphs.

Bryant remains a god in the state, unconditionally loved.* He was, first and foremost, a winner. During his years at Alabama, Bryant won six national titles and fourteen SEC Championships. His legacy, though, has always been about more than what he did on the field. He was something positive that Alabamans could hold on to even through some of the state's darkest and most embarrassing moments in the 1960s and beyond. "The state of Alabama had nothing to feel good about then except for Alabama football," says Cecil Hurt, the longtime sportswriter for the *Tuscaloosa News*. When the state was last in many meaningful categories—education, public funding, progress in civil rights—it was still first in football, thanks to Bryant. Even now he represents some sort of grandfatherly masculinity and ennobling genuineness, something from an era bygone.

It is impossible to escape Bryant's shadow in Tuscaloosa. The football stadium bears his name. Many of the students—and particularly the female ones—who fill that stadium on Saturdays in the fall wear replicas of his famous hound's-tooth hat. Paul W. Bryant Drive slices through campus. His statue stands tall on the Walk of Champions outside of the stadium. The Paul W. Bryant Museum is one of the biggest tourist attractions in town.

Bryant set an almost impossible standard for his successors to match. Between Bryant and Saban, Alabama had eight coaches: Ray Perkins, Bill Curry, Gene Stallings, Mike DuBose, Dennis Fran-

---

* Bryant is never called "Bear" or "the Bear" by true Alabama insiders. He is called "Coach Bryant," just as Saban is called "Coach Saban" and Mal Moore is still referred to as "Coach Moore." A respected coach at the University of Alabama is forever bestowed with that moniker.

chione, Mike Price, Mike Shula, and Joe Kines. Those eight coaches combined for an overall winning percentage of .584. (It's .672 if one doesn't include wins stripped by the NCAA.) In his twenty-five years at Alabama, Bryant's winning percentage was .824. (Saban's is .854 at Alabama.) Though Stallings did win a national title in 1992, the program in this era was best known for mediocre play on the field and ugly scandals off of it. Paul Finebaum, in Allen Barra's definitive 2005 biography of Bryant, *The Last Coach,* summed up those years thusly: "I think it's a biblical thing. Twenty-five years of glory followed by twenty-five years of plagues."

In the book, Barra continued: "If the plague era began with Bryant's death, then a golden new age should be dawning for the Crimson Tide around 2007."

Which happens to be the exact year Saban came to Tuscaloosa.

Before he arrived, Saban had no direct ties to Bryant or the University of Alabama. Though their coaching careers overlapped for ten years, Bryant and Saban never faced each other on the field. The closest link between the two comes through Ray Perkins, who played wide receiver for Bryant at Alabama in the mid-1960s, and later went on to become the head coach of the New York Giants (and after that, of course, the head coach at Alabama). Bill Belichick was Perkins's linebacker and special teams coach at the Giants from 1979 to 1982, and he considers Perkins one of his coaching mentors. It was during these years that Saban first started to hang out with Belichick, who later became his boss and a significant influence on his coaching career.

Though the link is tenuous, coaching trees have intertwined roots, and those roots—and the ideas that spring from them—are the lifeblood of the game's evolution. "Out of old fields comes all new corn," as Chaucer once wrote. It is not too far-fetched to see how something Bryant-related could have made its way to Saban.

There are some similarities between Bryant and Saban. Some of them are meaningful. Others are mere coincidences, fodder for the crowd that gets a kick out of the fact that Abraham Lincoln and John F. Kennedy were both shot on a Friday.

Both men grew up in small, unincorporated towns. Bryant was born and raised (until he was eleven) in Moro Bottom, Arkansas, a satellite town of the relative metropolis of Fordyce. Saban's hometown of Monongah, West Virginia, was one of a collection of tiny towns outside Fairmont, which he considered "the big city." Both men strived to escape those places, and both ultimately used football to do just that.

Bryant's mother was named Ida Mae. Saban played football for the Idamay Black Diamonds. Bryant's father died suddenly at age forty-six (likely from pneumonia or food poisoning, though the exact cause was never determined, according to Barra). Saban's father died at age forty-six from a heart attack.

Both Bryant and Saban got married in college to strong women who would manage their husband's lives outside of football with aplomb. Vito "Babe" Parilli, one of Bryant's former players, once described Mary Harmon Bryant as a "football den mother," somewhat similar to the "earth mother" description of Terry Saban. Both women kept up with former players and assistants and fulfilled some of the more extroverted social duties that weren't necessarily beloved by their husbands. Both the Bryants and the Sabans had two children, a son and a daughter. The sons were both given their father's names.

Both men had solid, if not spectacular, football-playing careers in college. They both suffered broken bones in their senior seasons (Bryant, a leg; Saban, an ankle), and both took coaching jobs at their alma maters under their former coaches after they graduated. (Bryant, after a brief stint at Union University, became an assistant under Frank Thomas at Alabama; Saban became a graduate assistant under Don James at Kent State.)

Bryant was long associated with a particular form of junk food: Golden Flake potato chips. Saban doesn't go a day without his Little Debbie Oatmeal Cream Pies. Bryant liked his unfiltered Chesterfield cigarettes and brown liquor. Saban used to smoke, and once had an affinity for Miller Lites (he no longer drinks alcohol). His main vice now is Red Man Golden Blend chewing tobacco. He keeps a pouch of it tucked in the door pocket of his black Mercedes-Benz, which is driven by a man named Cedric Burns, who also happened to be Bryant's driver.

Bryant and Saban were both considered nomads before taking the Alabama job. Alabama was Bryant's fourth head-coaching job in thirteen years. It was Saban's fourth team in nine years.

Both men were head coaches at four universities, and turned around the programs at each stop (Bryant: Maryland, Kentucky, Texas A&M, and Alabama; Saban: Toledo, Michigan State, LSU, and Alabama). Both stayed at their first head-coaching job for one year. Both only had one losing season as a head coach: Bryant went 1-9 in his first season at Texas A&M; Saban went 6-10 in his last season with the Dolphins. They were both known for putting their players through grueling off-season conditioning regimens. Saban has the notorious "Fourth Quarter Program" and Bryant had an infamous preseason camp at Junction, Texas, while at Texas A&M.

Each man had signature headwear. Bryant wore a hound's-tooth hat. Saban wears a straw golf hat at practices. Bryant's longtime secretary was named Linda. Saban's secretary is named Linda.

When both Bryant and Saban came to Alabama, the team was in the midst of a prolonged losing streak to Auburn. The Crimson Tide had lost four games in a row to its biggest rival when Bryant arrived, and lost five games in a row to Auburn when Saban arrived. Both men lost their first games against the Tigers.

Bryant once came very close to taking a job in the NFL. In 1969, he was offered the head-coaching job with the Miami Dolphins. After going back and forth, he decided to stay at Alabama. Don Shula got the Dolphins job instead. Saban would, of course, coach the Dolphins for two years before replacing Don Shula's son Mike at Alabama.

The two men had some striking differences. Bryant spent many of his later years at Alabama overseeing practices from a tower, one symbol of the macromanaging style he took with the program. Saban is more like the CEO of a fast-food company who still likes to teach a new employee how to best flip a burger. From day one as a head coach, Saban has been on the field for practices, working primarily with the players in the secondary.

The health of the two men differed as well. By the time Bryant won his sixth national title in the 1979 season, the sixty-six-year-old was physically deteriorated, paunchy from the heavy drinking (he'd secretly tried rehab but it didn't work), and gravelly voiced from the cigarettes. His face, as Richard Price once memorably described it, looked like "an aerial shot of a drought area."

In 2016, Saban will be entering his forty-fifth year in coaching. His waistline has slightly thickened (Merritt Norvell, the former athletic director at Michigan State, says while Saban was there he "never tolerated a weight gain of more than five pounds"), his hair has thinned, and the sun wrinkles around his eyes have become more defined but, all in all, Saban could easily pass for someone younger than his sixty-three years.

One other major difference is in their salaries. Bryant passed on his one big shot at making serious money when the Dolphins offered him $1.7 million to become their coach. He never seemed to lust for money. His personal policy at Alabama was to take a salary of exactly one dollar less than the university's president.

If Saban adhered to that same policy, his current annual salary (with bonuses) would be $654,999.

The six national titles Bryant won in his thirty-eight years as a head coach places him alone at the top for the most all-time, according to many. (Others contend that he is tied with the early-twentieth-century Michigan coach Fielding Yost, who happened to be from Fairview, West Virginia, just eleven miles from Saban's childhood home.) Bryant also won fifteen conference championships during his head-coaching career, one in the Southwest Conference and the remainder in the SEC.

In a twenty-year career as a college head coach, Saban has won five national titles and seven conference championships, one in the Mid-American Conference and the rest in the SEC.

While Saban's feats don't yet equal Bryant's, they are arguably as impressive as his were, if not more so, mostly because of scholarships. For the majority of Bryant's head-coaching career, he had no limit to the number of scholarships he could offer. In the early 1970s, the NCAA limited scholarship numbers to 105. A few years later, they lowered it to 95. Saban has had to work with the current limit of 85 scholarships—enacted in the mid-1990s—for all but his one year at Toledo. The limiting of scholarships has leveled the playing field in college football.

Like Bryant, Saban is worshipped by Alabama fans. Saving the football program, winning multiple national titles, recruiting and developing excellent players, generating enormous amounts of revenue, and doing it all, it appears, cleanly, will inspire just that. But that worship comes with a touch of wariness.* It is hard for Saban to completely shake his past, one punctuated with departures that have jolted fan bases. The Texas saga of late 2013 had Alabama fans in agony and some of the trustees on the brink of the weariness that eventually set in and hardened with the trustees at Michigan State and LSU. The Alabama trustees' hope is that his latest contract at Alabama will be enough.

Ironically, because of his constant seeking of appreciation and unconditional love, Saban himself has, in some ways, become the biggest single thing standing in the way of their ultimate attainment. Perhaps his new contract—the latest demonstration of

---

* On RollBamaRoll.com, a prominent Alabama fan website, Saban is often referred to as "Our Dark Lord," with a knowing wink.

appreciation—is it for Saban. Maybe he has found some sort of peace.*

While his natural shyness and introversion make it difficult for Saban to truly open up to many people, there has been some softening around the edges in recent years. As he's grown older, he's become far more cognizant of his own legacy. He smiles a bit more, especially when talking about his granddaughter, born in late 2013 to Nicholas Jr. and his wife. He has been warm and self-deprecating during his appearances on ESPN (where he may be laying the groundwork for his post-coaching career) and has even come to admit some culpability in his perception. "I don't want to be perceived negatively," Saban told the New Orleans *Times-Picayune* in 2012. "But I control what I do, and I guess I've created that in some kind of way through the years, whether it's the way I treated the media or whatever. And I'm responsible for that, and I've worked hard to make it better." Pete Jenkins says: "He has mellowed in recent years. But realize I said 'mellowed.' He still ain't mellow."

Somewhere down the road, perhaps long after he's retired, Saban may gain some simulacrum of the unconditional love that's been bestowed upon Bryant. That kind of love, after all, is tinged with nostalgia.

One of the most popular misconceptions about Saban is that he is not happy on the football field. "People think he's miserable,"

---

*If Saban were to leave Alabama now, the thinking is that it likely would be because of one of four reasons, or some combination thereof: (1) A few (relatively) down years resulting in him either becoming fed up with the expectations at Alabama or looking for one last shot at starting fresh somewhere else. (2) Terry. Kerry Marbury says he recently asked Saban when he was going to retire. "He said he'd give it a few more years and then get out. 'I owe it to Terry,' he said. 'She should have left me a long time ago. I need to get out sometime and give her a life outside of football.' " (3) Golf. As noted earlier, his obsession with the game—which perfectly fits his worldview—is growing. (4) The NFL: If the perfect NFL head-coaching job became available—one with stable ownership and some player talent—it's possible he could jump back into the league. A return to the NFL would more likely come in the form of a front office job with an NFL team in the South, perhaps including a piece of the franchise as a sweetener.

says Barrett Jones. "He may look like that when he's yelling on the sidelines. But he's actually a happy person. He loves what he does."

Angus Cooper remembers one of the first times he met Terry in 2007. He asked her what her husband liked to do. Cooper wanted to get to know his coach a little better, and was expecting, like most would, an answer about some hobby or enthusiasm that existed outside his job. Terry's answer: "Nick loves coaching and watching film."

Football defines Saban. It is his life. Though his father has remained one of the driving influences in that life, his drive and motivation come from more than just that now. His Process—his life in football, with all the pressures and heartbreaks and satisfaction—sustains itself now. It makes him happy to dig into the smallest details of recruiting, watch hours of film and dream up defensive schemes, to get kids to reach and maybe even exceed their potential. Barrett Jones, Curt Cignetti, Pete Jenkins, and Channing Crowder all say he appears happiest during practices. He truly loves the process. The ranting and raving on the sidelines are all part of it, just the necessary "tension relief." This happiness is perhaps the biggest difference between Saban and his father. Big Nick, though he, too, sought perfection, never seemed happy in trying to attain it. His son, provided with the years his father never had, has evolved.

In early January 2014, offensive coordinator Doug Nussmeier left Alabama to take the same position at Michigan. It was a curious move—to a team coming off a 7-6 season led by a head coach (Brady Hoke) who seemed to be hanging on by a thread and who indeed would be fired at the end of the 2014 season.* Even more surprising was Saban's choice to replace him: Lane Kiffin.

Though Kiffin had once openly taunted Saban, by 2014 they had become friends (Sexton happens to be the agent for both of them). Saban had always believed in Kiffin's talent—he'd tried to

---

* Nussmeier is now the offensive coordinator at Florida under Jim McElwain, the man he replaced as the offensive coordinator at Alabama in 2012.

hire him back in 2007. After Kiffin left Tennessee in early 2010, he and Saban started to communicate with some regularity, and Kiffin even snuck into Tuscaloosa one evening and met with Saban, talking football for three hours. Saban had invited Kiffin to observe his offense for eight days before the Sugar Bowl after the 2013 season. (In retrospect, this was not a good sign for Nussmeier.) Kiffin, given this inside glimpse of Saban's program, was blown away, mostly by how efficiently everything was handled, from the incoming freshmen, to the equipment managers and training staff, to the NCAA compliance people.

Kiffin had long idolized Saban. In fact, much of the brash talk during Kiffin's year at Tennessee—and even the poaching of Lance Thompson from Saban's staff that year—seemed to merely be Kiffin's immature way of handling that idolization. By 2014, Kiffin's reputation was in tatters. He'd been fired from the Oakland Raiders via a telephone call by team owner Al Davis, who later publicly called Kiffin "a flat-out liar." He then spent one season at Tennessee, where he raised the hackles of his fellow SEC coaches, led the team to a 7-6 record, then, to the surprise of the university and his players, abruptly left for USC. Early in his fourth season with the Trojans, Kiffin had been pulled off a team bus at Los Angeles International Airport and told he was being dismissed. Kiffin desperately needed to rebuild his career. Saban, as he had done so many times before, reached out and offered a chance at redemption to a talented person who needed the help. Because of Saban's strict rules about the media availability of his assistants, Kiffin could take that shot at redemption in relatively quiet and safe confines.

Saban seemed genuinely surprised at the reaction to his hiring of Kiffin. (One newspaper headline: "Is Saban Insane?") One writer described it as yet another example of Saban's tunnel vision. Saban's private assessment of Kiffin, however, differed greatly from the general public's perception.

Importantly, Saban felt he needed Kiffin, especially when it came to nurturing a new starting quarterback for the Crimson Tide. McCarron was gone to the NFL. None of his backups had flashed. Blake Sims, a fifth-year senior, had thrown only twenty-nine passes in 2013, and had not shown much comfort in the pocket, a trait Saban had pretty much demanded of his quarterbacks. Saban was genuinely worried about the quality of his returning quarterbacks, so much so that early in 2014, he signed a transfer named Jacob Coker, who had been the backup quarterback to Jameis Winston at Florida State. Coker had attended St. Paul's Episcopal School in Mobile—McCarron's high school—and had become the starter when McCarron left. There was a sense that the same transition would take place now at Alabama.

Before signing Coker, Saban spoke to some of his former assistants who now worked at Florida State (there were four of them, including the head coach, Jimbo Fisher) and had seen Coker up close. They gave the quarterback strong endorsements. Fisher even told the media that Coker would be the best quarterback Saban had ever had at Alabama.

That turned out to not be the case, at least in 2014. Coker missed Alabama's spring practice because he had to graduate from Florida State before enrolling, and Sims impressed Saban and Kiffin enough in the off-season to become the starter. Sims had his flaws, but he was beloved by his teammates, and Saban and Kiffin did their best to play to his strengths—mobility and leadership.

As the season began, some sense of normalcy for Alabama was restored. There was Saban—the once-peripatetic man who was now the longest-tenured Crimson Tide football coach since Bryant—on the sidelines, wearing his coaching polo, pleated khakis, and the metal-tipped belt that was popular with golfers in the 1990s. He paced up and down. He stared hard at the turf. He crossed his arms and uncrossed them and placed them on his hips. He clapped and yelled a lot. The only real discernible difference on the Alabama sidelines was that he now shared some of the camera time with Kiffin.

Alabama got off to a 4-0 start. Any dreams of a national title almost came to an end in the fifth game of the season, when the Crimson Tide lost, 23–17, to a spirited Ole Miss team. Dating back to the end of the 2013 season, the defeat left Alabama at 4-3 in its last seven games. Things got no better the following week in a 14–13 win over Arkansas that many pundits deemed "ugly." Saban didn't much care for that description. "Everybody's got such high expectations for what our team should be," he said during a press conference. "I was just happy to see our players be happy about playing a game and winning. It really sort of, if you want to know the truth about it, pisses me off when I talk to people that have this expectation like they're disappointed that we only won the game 14–13, and in the way we played."

Those expectations, as onerous as they had become to Saban, were largely of his own doing, the result of his recruiting and coaching successes. At Alabama, as is the case at other top-tier programs, the most talented juniors on the team often skipped their senior seasons to go pro. Reaching the NFL was one of the reasons they had come to Alabama to play for him, after all. For Saban, the talent would always be there at Alabama. Experience was another matter.

The 2014 season, though, turned after the Arkansas game. Alabama won eight in a row, including a tough overtime win over LSU in Baton Rouge, a win over number-one-ranked Mississippi State, a thrilling 55–44 victory over Auburn, and a 42–13 thrashing of Missouri in the SEC Championship game (which gave Saban his fifth SEC title).

In the 2014 season, Sims had played better than expected. Wide receiver Amari Cooper had finished third in the voting for the Heisman Trophy. The defense—by no means as dominant as in years past—had still held its own in most games. Saban had turned in one of the finest coaching performances of his career.

By the end of the season, Alabama had ascended to number one in the country and had become the top seed in the brand-new College Football Playoff, which had replaced the BCS system. (Saban was an early proponent of a college football playoff, pushing the idea when he started at LSU.) Alabama played Ohio State—coached by old nemesis Urban Meyer—in the national semifinal, and though at one point they led the game, 21–6, in the end, they lost by a touchdown. The win served as a sort of redemption for Meyer and payback for the crushing loss in the 2009 SEC Championship game.

Saban called his players "winners" after the game. There was a sense that they had overachieved somewhat, and not done the opposite, as Saban's 2010 and 2013 teams had. "This has been one of the most pleasurable teams we've had to coach," Saban said on his weekly radio show near the end of the season.

He'd fallen short of winning another title, but he'd stayed at Alabama and had begun to reap the benefits.

In early January 2015, Ohio State beat Oregon to win the National Championship, and Meyer joined Saban as the only coaches in the modern era to win national titles at two different universities. Combined, he and Saban had won six of the last nine national titles. With the win, Meyer—who is thirteen years younger—appeared a little closer in Saban's rearview mirror. He now had three national titles, just one behind Saban. The ground shifted quickly in college football. Suddenly Saban's lock on being considered the best coach of his generation didn't seem quite so impenetrable.

After the loss to Ohio State, Nick Saban arrived at his Tuscaloosa home in the dark and muted hours of the early morning. He was somber. He took some time to ponder the game, let it hurt a bit, and then he quickly put it out of his mind. There would be time later to dissect it, play by play.

Then his attention shifted. *I'm nothing without my players.* Soon he was out again, on the road, in the air, brushing in the final details, sealing up the commitments for a 2015 recruiting class that one prominent analyst would describe, when all was said and signed, as one of the best Saban had ever put together.

AFTERWORD

IN THE third week of the 2015 college football season, a 2-0 Alabama team lost to Ole Miss, 43–37, at home. While the loss didn't definitively end Alabama's chance for a national title in the 2015 season, it certainly made it much harder to achieve—at a minimum, the Crimson Tide had to win the rest of its games and then hope for some help.

For many, the Ole Miss loss signaled something monumental. *USA Today* was merely one of many media outlets that proclaimed, with an unmistakable hint of glee, that Nick Saban's Alabama dynasty was over.

The pundits pointed to the Crimson Tide's uninspiring performance in a 45–31 loss to Oklahoma in the Sugar Bowl at the close of the 2013 season. They derided Saban's once dominant defense, which surrendered 537 yards in a 42–35 loss to Ohio State in the College Football Playoffs semifinal game after the 2014 season. They marveled at how, in consecutive seasons, Alabama had now been defeated by a good, but certainly not great, Ole Miss team.

But inside the program, the vibe was distinctly different. After the Ole Miss loss, Saban instituted the twenty-four-hour rule: The team could pick at the wound of the loss for one day, then they would move on. This was, of course, a central tenet of the Process, that extension of Saban's worldview that was so significantly shaped by his father. Ignore the worried fans and the media. Don't worry about a championship. Focus only on the steps taken in its pursuit.

Saban's team did just that. Over the course of the next nine games, the Crimson Tide had some sublime moments (a dominating 38–10 win over undefeated—and favored—Georgia) and some rather plodding ones (a narrow 19–14 win at home over Tennessee). But they won them all.

After the 2015 season, Saban would tell the media that of all the teams he'd coached, this one was his favorite. It wasn't too difficult to see why. The team featured a smothering defense and a punishing running game that worked in concert to drain the will from its opponents. Jake Coker, the fifth-year senior quarterback in his first season as a starter, managed the crucial moments in games without making big mistakes. The team was businesslike: When 2015 Heisman Trophy–winning running back, Derrick Henry, scored a touchdown, more often than not he just handed the ball over to the referee without much of a celebration. It was a team that harked back to Saban's midwestern coaching roots.

The week after week of do-or-die wins, coupled with a dose of good fortune when Arkansas miraculously beat Ole Miss, 53–52, in overtime,* put Saban and his team back in the College Football Playoffs, this time as the number-two seed. And in the semifinal game, Alabama overwhelmed Saban's old program, Michigan State, in a 38–0 win, to earn a spot in the national title game against Clemson.

Perhaps when all is said and done, Saban's ultimate decision to sign a new contract and stay at Alabama after the tumult of the 2013

---

* In overtime in that game, Arkansas was down, 52–45, when it faced a fourth-and-25. On the ensuing play, Razorback tight end Hunter Henry caught a pass and, as he was being tackled, threw a blind lateral behind his head. The ball was recovered by one of his teammates, who advanced it for a first down. A few plays later, Arkansas scored a touchdown to get within one point of Ole Miss. The Razorbacks then elected to go for a two-point conversion to win the game. The effort failed, but a facemask penalty on Ole Miss gave Arkansas another opportunity, which it converted for the win. The defeat would end up costing Ole Miss a chance to play in the SEC Championship game, which effectively removed Alabama's biggest roadblock to making the four-team College Football Playoffs.

season will be viewed as the resolution to a career-long conflict. Just maybe, it would end up being the last time he felt underappreciated, and the last time he felt any yearning to start over and save a different program.

Saban is entering his tenth season at Alabama. Roots have taken hold. His kids and their families live in the state. He has moved his mother nearby. Terry is comfortable and happy and has made deep and lasting friendships. Saban is a partner in a Mercedes dealership outside Birmingham. He made $7.97 million in 2015. He'll turn sixty-five during the 2016 season and is now among the oldest coaches in major college football.

Near the end of the 2015 season, Saban's name popped up on the coaching rumor mill, as it always does. This time, the focus was on NFL teams. Saban was mentioned, most prominently, as a possibility for the Indianapolis Colts and the New York Giants, two organizations that had pursued him in the past. Both teams possessed something Saban had lacked during his time in the NFL with the Miami Dolphins: a good quarterback (Andrew Luck of the Colts and Eli Manning of the Giants). This time around, though, the rumors and talk seemed halfhearted at best.

Alabama trustees and boosters say they noticed something different about Saban in 2015. "His edginess remains. He's still intense. He has not mellowed in any respect," says Angus Cooper II, the emeritus trustee. "But he is more settled."

At this point, Alabama powerbrokers wouldn't want Saban to change *too* much, anyway. "Sometimes we sit around and joke and say, 'Wouldn't it be great if Nick could relax a bit? We should get him some counseling,'" says one prominent booster. "And then, inevitably, someone will say, 'No, hell no. If he became normal, we'd lose three games a year.'"

The College Football National Championship game between Alabama and Clemson was played in Glendale, Arizona, on January 11, 2016. In one regard, its outcome may have been partly determined before the ball was kicked off. On that evening in Arizona, Saban had a vastly superior number of four- and five-star recruits on his sideline—sixty-six to Clemson's thirty-seven. Indeed, Alabama had been the standard in college football since 2009, mainly because it nearly always fielded a team that simply had better players and more of them, the net result of Saban's greatest strength as a coach: recruiting.

Those highly touted recruits came through for Saban during the title game. Henry, the five-star running back, gained 158 yards and scored three touchdowns. O. J. Howard—the five-star tight end who had been underutilized during the season—exploded for 208 yards on five catches and scored two touchdowns. Four-star recruit Kenyan Drake, whose promising career at Alabama had been hindered by injuries, finally had his big moment, running a kickoff back 95 yards for a touchdown in the fourth quarter.

But even with all of that talent on the field, Saban needed something extra that night. Even with its exquisite defense, Alabama was having little success stopping Deshaun Watson, Clemson's superb quarterback. As the game entered the fourth quarter, it had begun to take on the feel of some Alabama losses in previous years, when red-hot mobile quarterbacks like Cam Newton and Johnny Manziel passed and scrambled their respective teams to victories. Alabama needed a spark.

Throughout his career, Saban had never shied away from trying a trick play, even on the biggest stage. Six years earlier, in the national title game against Texas, Saban had ordered a fake punt on Alabama's first possession. That try had failed miserably.

This time, after an Alabama field goal tied the game, 24–24, with a little more than ten minutes left in the game, Saban decided to attempt an onside kick.

Given the stakes and circumstances, the call was the boldest in Saban's twenty-two-year career as a head coach. Its ultimate outcome would make it one of the greatest in college football history.

During film study before the game, Saban and his coaches had noticed that Clemson kept its kick return unit in a tight formation, leaving the sideline areas open. Alabama had been practicing an onside-kick play designed to exploit a formation like that all season long.

Saban's attempt of an onside kick at that moment in the game made some rational sense: Clemson showed Alabama the formation needed to make it work, and Alabama needed to try to change the game's momentum. Still, it was incredibly risky: Failing to recover the ball would have given Clemson and Watson excellent field position. And in its last rehearsal of the onside kick in a practice before the game, the Alabama kickoff team had failed to pull it off.

Saban went for it anyway. To the crowd, the television announcers, and the viewing audience—and the Clemson kickoff return unit—it looked like Alabama was lined up to kick the ball deep. Instead, Alabama's Adam Griffith—one of the best kickers in the country coming out of high school—perfectly popped the ball short and skyward and over the shoulder and into the hands of his teammate Marlon Humphrey, a true freshman cornerback (and another five-star recruit).* Alabama regained possession of the ball, scored a touchdown on the ensuing drive, and went on to win a thrilling game, 45–40.

The victory gave Saban his fourth national title in the last seven years, and his fifth overall, which put him just one behind Paul Bryant's acknowledged record. With the win, every one of Saban's recruiting classes at Alabama had earned a national title.

Less than a month later, Saban signed the consensus number-one recruiting class in the country. Again.

---

*The play was quite the redemption for Griffith, the kicker who had missed the infamous "Kick Six" field goal attempt against Auburn.

ACKNOWLEDGMENTS

THIS BOOK has been in the works since the summer of 2008, when I wrote a profile of Nick Saban for *Forbes* magazine. In the intervening years, I have met with him on one other occasion, and have talked to him on the phone numerous times. All quotes from Saban—and anyone else—in this book, unless otherwise noted, were made directly to me.

I interviewed more than 250 people for this book. Not all of them made the final manuscript by name (some by choice), but each and every one of them helped.

For research, I combed through countless newspaper and magazine stories written about Saban and the games he coached. I stand on the shoulders of the men and women—feature and beat writers—who tapped out these stories.

A special thanks goes to the journalists who were generous enough to provide advice and encouragement and, on certain occasions, even sit for interviews (not always a palatable thing for a journalist to do). Brad Stone, Steve Bertoni, Randall Lane, Coates Bateman, Michael Solomon, Tom Post, Kurt Badenhausen, Dan Bigman, Jon Fahey, Nathan Vardi, Daniel Kruger, Larry Reibstein, David DiBenedetto, Tommy Tomlinson, Tom Bie, Louis Riddick, Tom Luginbill, Jeremy Crabtree, Greg Gabriel, Gil Brandt, Carl Hiaasen, Sam Sifton, Winston Groom, Warren St. John, Jack Ebling, Chris B. Brown, Dave Revsine, John U. Bacon, Paul Finebaum, Cecil Hurt, Aaron Suttles, Michael Casagrande, Duane Rankin, Jason Cole, Hal Habib, Ethan Skolnick, and Dave Hyde were all particularly helpful.

Linda Carrington, Charlie Ernst, Dana Gibson, Rammy and Courtney Harwood, Hann Livingston, Steve and Patty Huff, Dave Berman, Paul Weamer, Bob Rich, Mike Spinney, Frank Crescitelli, Joe Moglia, Tom Olivadotti, Sue Radlauer, John Peck, John D. Colombo, Shelby Gaines, and Justin and Chris Burke all provided invaluable help, in one way or another, with this project.

My agent, Richard Pine, is my lodestar. Working with him has always been one of my favorite things about this business.

My sincerest gratitude goes to everyone at Simon & Schuster, but especially to Jofie Ferrari-Adler, who made this project come to life, then made it much better. Having an editor of his talent and enthusiasm is something to be treasured.

Charles Gaines and Sid Williamson read drafts of this book and both offered very wise counsel and encouragement.

This book is also dedicated to the memory of Peter Zecher and to that of my father, Donald, whose spirit will always be with me.

My mother, Hansell, has always been my biggest cheerleader, showering me with unconditional love.

My wife, Heidi, and our three daughters are simply the loves of my life and make everything worth it.

BIBLIOGRAPHY

Anderson, Lars. *The Storm and the Tide: Tragedy, Hope, and Triumph in Tuscaloosa.* New York: Sports Illustrated Books, 2014.

Barra, Allen. *The Last Coach: A Life of Paul "Bear" Bryant.* New York: Norton, 2005.

Bly, Robert. *Iron John: A Book About Men.* Reading, PA: Addison-Wesley, 1990.

Finebaum, Paul, and Gene Wojciechowski. *My Conference Can Beat Your Conference: Why the SEC Still Rules College Football.* New York: HarperCollins, 2014.

Groom, Winston. *The Crimson Tide: An Illustrated History of Football at the University of Alabama, National Championship Edition.* Tuscaloosa: University of Alabama Press, 2010.

Halberstam, David. *The Education of a Coach.* New York: Hyperion, 2005.

McAteer, Davitt. *Monongah: The Tragic Story of the Worst Industrial Accident in U.S. History.* Morgantown: West Virginia University Press, 2007.

Moore, Mal M., with Steve Townsend. *Crimson Heart: Let Me Tell You My Story.* Birmingham, AL: Mal and Charlotte Moore Crimson Heart Foundation, 2014.

Saban, Nick, with Brian Curtis. *How Good Do You Want to Be? A Champion's Tips on How to Lead and Succeed at Work and in Life.* New York: Ballantine Books, 2005.

Saban, Nick, with Sam King. *Tiger Turnaround: LSU's Return to Glory.* Chicago: Triumph Books, 2002.

INDEX

Audas, Rick, 120–22, 136
Augusta National Golf Club, 207–8, 286
Austin, Tex., 294
Australia, 204
Avery, Bob, 50–51

Baglio Charles, 152
Baker, Merrily Dean, 112, 113, 117
Baldwin County, Ala., 237
Ball State, 89
Baltimore Ravens, 88, 102, 219, 264
Banks, Carl, 104
Banks, Tony, 115, 123, 271
Barnett, Harlon, 73, 98–99
Barra, Allen, 313, 314
Barron, Mark, 238, 239, 245n, 260, 265, 267, 269, 275
Baton Rouge, La., 138, 139, 140, 152, 154, 156, 158, 168–69, 170, 177, 181, 185, 187, 190, 196, 202, 234, 249, 266, 322
Baton Rouge *Advocate*, 234
Battle, Bill, 303–4
BCS (Bowl Championship Series), 134, 170, 174, 175, 249, 278, 289, 322
BCS National Championship game, 161, 170, 174, 175, 278–79, 289, 293, 323
  of 2003, 175–77, 178–79
  of 2009, 262–63
  of 2011, 190n, 278–29
  of 2012, 289
Beck, Aaron, 131
Belichick, Bill, 82, 187, 203, 204, 209, 210n, 219, 230, 242, 306, 311
  clash between Saban and, 97, 104
  as Cleveland Browns head coach, 93–107
  game film as obsession of, 96
  Saban as defensive coordinator of, 93–107
  as Saban's mentor and friend, 66–67, 77, 90–91, 93, 94–95, 103, 196, 313
  as Saban's NFL division rival, 196–97, 213
Belichick, Steve, 66, 67, 97n, 196
Berlin, Brock, 152
Bertman, Skip, 151, 158, 172–73, 174, 180–81, 184–85, 187, 188, 190, 194, 216, 302
Bethlehem No. 44 mine, 17, 24, 32
Big 12 Championship, 175, 176
Big Brothers Big Sisters, 257
Big Ten Championship, 59
Big Ten conference, 56, 58, 70, 72, 75, 78, 96, 114, 117, 118, 125, 127, 134
Birmingham, Ala., 31, 207, 243, 286, 312
Bledsoe, Drew, 106
Blevins, Dean, 304
Blind Side, The (film), 153n
Blind Side, The (Lewis), 143n, 153n
"Bluegrass Miracle," 170
Bly, Robert, 45–46
Bohl, Al, 85–86, 90–92

Booty, Josh, 157
Bostic, Keith, 78, 79
Boston, David, 186
Boston College, 55, 151
Bowden, Bobby, 19, 31, 45, 52, 112, 140, 142, 248, 263
Bowe, Dwayne, 171
Bowersox, Ted, 38
Bowling Green State University, 91
Brady, Tom, 134, 203, 213
Brandt, Gil, 188
Brees, Drew, 134, 206, 207, 219, 251n
Brentwood Academy, 243
Bresnahan, Chuck, 66, 100, 101, 102, 103
Broderick, Steve, 38–39, 40, 43
Brodowicz, Mark, 64, 65
Broussard, Alley, 173
Broward General Hospital, 200
Brown, Alberta, 72
Brown, Chris B., 82–83
Brown, James, 80, 176
Brown, Mack, 161, 295, 301, 302, 304, 305
Brown, Paul, 30, 95
Brown, Ronnie, 196n, 204
Bruce, Earle, 41, 55, 56, 57, 58, 59, 60, 61, 62, 75, 96, 131
Bryant, Ida Mae, 314
Bryant, Mary Harmon, 314
Bryant, Paul "Bear," 2, 57n, 87, 162, 222, 272, 289, 303, 321
  as Alabama head coach, 311–13, 315–17
  funeral of, 312
  Saban compared to, 313–18
Bryant, Paul, Jr., 4, 303
Bryant-Denny Stadium, 274, 288, 307
Buffalo Bills, 81, 90, 203–4
Burke, Bill, 132, 134, 137, 139
Burnett, Rob, 95, 97, 98, 104
Burns, Cedric, 315
Burress, Plaxico, 122, 128–29, 134
Bush, George W., 207–8
Bush, Reggie, 282
Byrd, Robert, 33

Caldwell, Antoine, 233
California, University of, at Los Angeles (UCLA), 58, 122
California Bowl, 89n
California State University, Fresno, 101, 247
Cambodia, 35
Campbell, Amp, 128, 134, 139
Campbell, Scott, 59
Capers, Dom, 47n, 61n, 209
Capital One Bowl, 184, 188–89, 196n, 269
Carey, Shyrone, 164, 169, 204
Carey, Vernon, 197
Carlson, Nate, 267–68
Carolina, W.Va., 11, 13, 19, 25, 31
Carolina Panthers, 161, 199